FINDING THE WILD WEST: THE SOUTHWEST

ARIZONA, NEW MEXICO, AND TEXAS

MIKE COX

TWODOT®

ESSEX, CONNECTICUT
HELENA, MONTANA

A · TWODOT® · BOOK
An imprint and registered trademark of Globe Pequot, the trade division of
The Rowman & Littlefield Publishing Group, Inc.
4501 Forbes Blvd., Ste. 200
Lanham, MD 20706
www.rowman.com

Distributed by NATIONAL BOOK NETWORK

British Library Cataloguing in Publication Information available

Library of Congress Cataloging-in-Publication Data

Names: Cox, Mike, 1948- author.
Title: Finding the Wild West : The Southwest. Arizona, New Mexico, and Texas / Mike Cox.
Description: Essex, Connecticut : TwoDot, [2022] | Series: Finding the Wild West | Includes index.
Identifiers: LCCN 2022010530 (print) | LCCN 2022010531 (ebook) | ISBN 9781493064137 (paperback) | ISBN 9781493064144 (epub)
Subjects: LCSH: Historic sites—Southwest, New—Guidebooks—19th century. | Southwest, New—History—1848- | Arizona—History—Guidebooks—19th century. | New Mexico—History—Guidebooks—19th century. | Texas—History—Guidebooks—19th century.
Classification: LCC F786 .C85 2022 (print) | LCC F786 (ebook) | DDC 979—dc23
LC record available at https://lccn.loc.gov/2022010530
LC ebook record available at https://lccn.loc.gov/2022010531

∞™ The paper used in this publication meets the minimum requirements of American National Standard for Information Sciences—Permanence of Paper for Printed Library Materials, ANSI/NISO Z39.48-1992.

CONTENTS

PREFACE: FINDING THE WILD WEST

Ain't nothing better than riding a fine horse in a new country.
—Gus McCrea in *Lonesome Dove*

Like most Baby Boomers, I learned about the Old West in the mid-1950s and early 1960s watching black-and-white television westerns and John Wayne movies in color. But that was Hollywood's Old West.

Thanks largely to my late granddad, L.A. Wilke, I began to learn about the real Old West. He was born in Central Texas in the fading days of that era, just long enough ago to have learned how to ride a horse well before he ever got behind the wheel of an automobile. Too, as a youngster and later as a newspaperman, he met some notable Wild West figures, from Buffalo Bill Cody to old Texas Rangers who had fought Comanches. A fine storyteller, he shared his experiences with me. Also, he passed his copies of *True West* and *Frontier Times* on to me. At the time, his friend Joe Small published both magazines in Austin, where I grew up.

Even before I started reading nonfiction Western magazines and books, again thanks to Granddad, I got to visit some Old West historic sites when they were still just abandoned ruins. With him, as a first grader I prowled around old Fort Davis in West Texas well before the federal government stabilized it as a National Historic Site. Later, Granddad took me to several southwest New Mexico ghost towns, including Shakespeare, Hillsboro, and Kingston. This was in 1964, when many of that state's roadways were not yet paved. In that desert high country, I experienced for the first time the still-vast openness of the West and the sense of adventure in exploring an old place new to me.

So why was the West wild?

I think you will come to understand the "why" when you experience the "where" of the Wild West. Though many of the sites described in these books are in populated areas, some are as remote or more remote than they were back in the Wild West's heyday. In visiting these sites, say a ghost town well off the beaten path, you should be able to feel the reason why the West was wild. When I stand in the middle of nowhere, distant from nothing, I feel the sense of freedom that must have driven so much of human behavior in frontier times. In such emptiness, usually scenic, it's easy to believe you can do anything you, by God, want to, be it bad or good.

Some see the West as being all the states west of the Mississippi, which includes twenty-three states. Others maintain that the West begins at the ninety-eighth meridian. My belief is that the Mississippi River is what separates the East from the West in the US.

Accordingly, moving from east to west, this series of travel guides divides the West into five regions: along the Mississippi (Louisiana, Arkansas, Iowa, Minnesota, and Missouri); the Great Plains (Oklahoma, Kansas, Nebraska, South Dakota, and North Dakota); the Southwest (Arizona, New Mexico, and Texas); the Mountain West (Colorado, Montana, Nevada, Utah, and Wyoming); and the Pacific West (Alaska, California, Idaho, Oregon, and Washington).

Having described what I consider the West, what constitutes "wild?"

Former Wild West History Association president Robert G. (Bob) McCubbin, a history buff who acquired one of the world's most inclusive collections of Western photographs, ephemera, books, and artifacts, a few years back offered his take on the matter.

"The Wild West was a time and place unique in the history of the world," he wrote. "It took place on the plains, prairies, mountains, and deserts of the American West, from the Mississippi River to the

Pacific Ocean. It began about the time of the California gold rush and was at its height in the 1870s through the 1890s, fading away in the decade after the turn of the twentieth century—as the automobile replaced the horse."

He went on to explain that Wild West does not mean wilderness wild. It means lawless wild. While untamed grandeur was certainly a part of the Wild West, it was the untamed men and women who made the West wild.

"Of course," McCubbin continued, "during the Wild West period there were many good and substantial citizens who went about their business in a law abiding and constructive way. Most of those are forgotten. It's the excitement of the Wild West's bad men, desperadoes, outlaws, gunfighters, and lawmen—many of whom were also, at times, cowboys, scouts, and buffalo hunters—and the dance hall girls and 'shady ladies,' who capture our interest and imagination."

While mostly adhering to McCubbin's definition of the Wild West, I could not stick to it entirely. Some things that happened prior to the California gold rush—Spanish and French colonial efforts, the Louisiana Purchase, the Lewis and Clark Expedition, the exploits of mountain men, the development of the great western trails, and the Mexican War of 1846 to 1848—were critical in shaping the later history of the West. That explains why some of the sites associated with these aspects of history needed to be included in this book.

For the most part, 1900 is the cut-off date for events related in this series of books. But the Wild West did not end at 11:59 p.m. on December 31, 1899. Some places, particularly Arizona, Oklahoma, New Mexico, and far west Texas stayed wild until World War I. Sometimes, events that occurred in the nineteenth century continued to have ramifications in the early twentieth century. An example would be the life and times of Pat Garrett, who killed Billy the Kid in 1881. Garrett himself was shot to death in 1909, so his death site is listed.

The Finding the Wild West series is not intended as a guide to every single historic site in a given city, state, or region. Some towns and cities had to be left out. It would take an encyclopedic, multivolume work to cover *all* the historical places throughout the western states. I have tried to include the major sites with a Wild West connection, along with some places with great stories you've probably never heard.

These books focus primarily on locations where there is still something to see today. Those sites range from period buildings and ruins to battlefields, historical markers, tombstones, and public art. In addition to historic sites, I have included museums and libraries with collections centered on "those thrilling days of yesteryear." Again, I have *not* listed every museum or every attraction.

A note on directions: Since almost everyone has access to GPS applications or devices, locations are limited to specific addresses with "turn here" or "until you come to" used only when necessary, with the exception of block-row-plot numbers of graves (when available). GPS coordinates are given for more difficult to find locations.

The Wild West has long since been tamed, with nationally franchised fast-food places and big-box stores standing where the buffalo roamed and the deer and the antelope played. Considered another way, however, the Wild West hasn't gone anywhere. It still exists in our collective imagination—a mixture of truth and legend set against the backdrop of one of the world's most spectacular landscapes.

Wild Bill Hickok, Jesse James, George Armstrong Custer, Billy the Kid, Wyatt Earp, and others received a lot of press and rose from the dead as Western icons, but there were many more characters—from outlaws to lawmen, drovers to cattle barons, harlots to preachers—whose stories are yet to be brought to life. Indeed, every tombstone, every historical marker, every monument, every ghost town, every historic site, every place name, every structure, every person has a story to tell. Like a modern-day prospector, all you need to do is pack these books in your saddlebag, mount up, and ride out in search of the Wild West.

—Mike Cox
Wimberley, Texas

INTRODUCTION: THE SOUTHWEST

European settlement of the Southwest began in the sixteenth and seventeenth centuries as Spain expanded its New World empire northward from what is now Mexico. While it never established missions, presidios, and towns any farther north than Santa Fe or midway up the California coast, by 1770 Spain had claimed most of the land west of the Mississippi.

Overextended, Spain ceded the distant territory it had earlier acquired from the French back to them, creating the area France would sell to the young US in 1803. But Spain continued its presence in what became the states of Texas, New Mexico, Arizona, and California until Mexico won its independence in 1821.

A year before, a Missourian named Moses Austin struck a deal with Spain to colonize a portion of future Texas. Following Mexican independence, that new republic allowed Austin's son (Moses had died) to develop a colony between the Brazos and Colorado Rivers in Mexico's new province of Coahuila y Tejas. While that seemed like a good idea to Mexico at the time, the land grant to Stephen F. Austin began a chain of events that would cost the Mexican republic nearly half its land.

The northern boundary of the Mexican province was the Red River. Above it, and immediately west of Arkansas, the US created the Indian Territory in 1830 and proceeded to uproot five Southern American Indian tribes and move them to the new territory.

Austin's colony brought the first Anglos to the Southwest, and within a decade enough settlers had arrived to become interested in

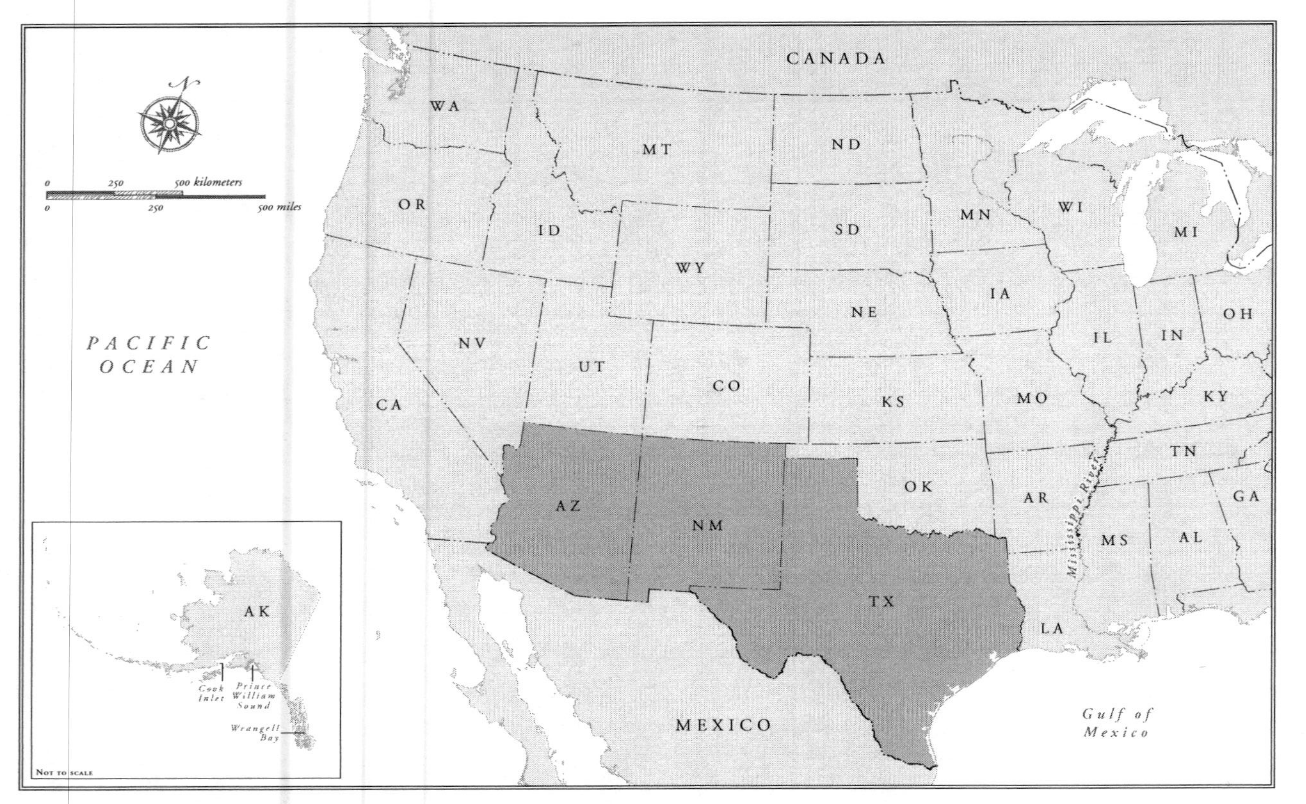
CANADA
0 250 500 kilometers
0 250 500 miles
PACIFIC OCEAN
WA
OR
CA
ID
NV
MT
WY
UT
AZ
CO
NM
ND
SD
NE
KS
OK
TX
MN
IA
MO
AR
LA
WI
IL
MI
IN
OH
KY
TN
MS
AL
GA
Mississippi River
MEXICO
Gulf of Mexico
AK
Cook Inlet
Prince William Sound
Wrangell Bay
Not to scale

forming their own country. Grievances with an authoritarian Mexican government and the simple, if less noble, desire to acquire more land triggered a revolution in 1835. The fight was costly to both sides, but Sam Houston's defeat of Gen. Antonio Lopez de Santa Anna in the Battle of San Jacinto in the spring of 1836 succeeded in wresting Texas from Mexico.

As a republic, Texas boldly claimed land in portions of New Mexico, Oklahoma, Kansas, Colorado, and Wyoming, though it only had control of the eastern third of Texas. Recognized by the major European powers, the shaky nation held for nearly a decade before becoming the twenty-eighth state of the Union in 1845. The following year, a dispute over whether the Rio Grande or the Nueces River should be the border between the new state and Mexico resulted in war between Mexico and the US. Defeated within two years, in 1848 Mexico ceded 42 percent of its land to the US by the Treaty of Guadalupe Hidalgo. That territory included the future Southwestern states of New Mexico, Arizona, and California.

In 1850, following the purchase of the far western land claimed by Texas, the US Congress created the New Mexico Territory. In addition to the future state of New Mexico, the territory included two-thirds of the land that would become Arizona. The southern third of future Arizona and the Mesilla Valley of New Mexico were acquired from Mexico in the 1853 Gadsden Purchase. With the consummation of that deal, the US owned all the land that would become the future states of New Mexico and Arizona.

During the Civil War, the Confederate States of America tried to gain control of the New Mexico Territory but did not succeed. In 1863 President Abraham Lincoln signed off on a measure that created the Arizona Territory, cutting the original territory roughly in half. Both territories finally became states in 1912, New Mexico effective January 6, followed by Arizona on February 14.

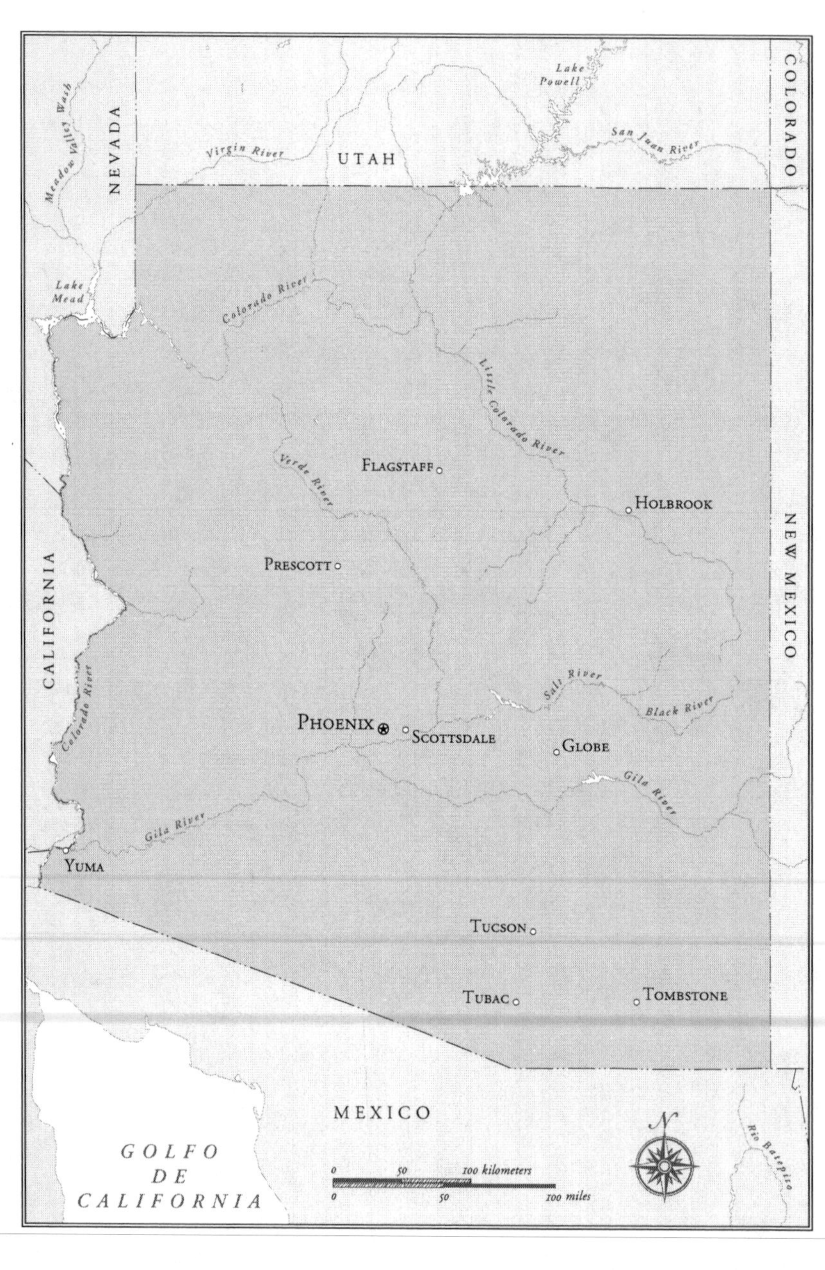

NEVADA
UTAH
COLORADO
CALIFORNIA
NEW MEXICO
MEXICO
GOLFO
DE
CALIFORNIA
Meadow Valley Wash
Virgin River
Lake Powell
San Juan River
Lake Mead
Colorado River
Little Colorado River
Verde River
Flagstaff
Holbrook
Prescott
Salt River
Black River
Phoenix
Scottsdale
Globe
Gila River
Colorado River
Gila River
Yuma
Tucson
Tubac
Tombstone
Rio Batepito
N
0
50
100 kilometers
0
50
100 miles

ARIZONA

Bisbee (Cochise County)

The Bisbee story began in 1877 when a US Army lieutenant in command of a troop of calvary found what he believed to be copper ore. He later told a prospector about his discovery, hoping to eventually partner with him in staking mining claims in the area. But his confidant cut the officer out of the deal and the lieutenant gained nothing from his discovery of what turned out to be one of the world's richest copper mining districts. The **Copper Queen Mine** opened in 1880, which marked the beginning of Bisbee. Known as the "Queen of the Copper Camps," for a time the mining boomtown ranked as the largest city between St. Louis and Denver. Tombstone surpassed it in violence, but Bisbee made a notable showing. Known as Brewery Gulch, the roughest part of Bisbee had more than two score saloons, gambling joints, and houses of negotiable female affection. By the time the mines closed in 1975, the area had yielded more than $6 billion in gold, silver, copper, lead, and zinc.

With twenty-five historically significant buildings dating back more than a century, once-booming Bisbee showcases its Wild West roots in a way few Southwestern towns can. Most of the historic structures are within the Bisbee Historical District, listed on the National Register of Historic Places.

The Bisbee Massacre

As with all mining towns, Bisbee was about making money. That could be done honestly through hard work, easily with good luck, or even more easily by simply appropriating someone else's money by illegal means.

When John Heath heard the $7,000 payroll for the Copper Queen Mining Company would be stored in the safe at Goldwater-Castenada Mercantile (which also served as a bank), he conspired with others to rob the store. Unfortunately for the robbers, the payroll had not yet arrived, and they netted very little from the safe. More unfortunately for all concerned, five innocent bystanders, including a pregnant woman and her near-term child, died in the shooting that broke out as the robbers fled town that cold night of December 8, 1883.

Among those who breathlessly showed up to join a posse in pursuit of the outlaws was Heath. The posse failed to find the robbers that evening, but within weeks all the suspects had been captured. From them, the authorities learned of Heath's role in planning the robbery.

The five direct participants in the robbery—William (Billy) Delaney, Daniel (Big Dan) Dowd, James (Tex) Howard, Daniel (York) Kelly, and Comer W. (Red) Sample—were taken to the county seat in Tombstone for trial. Soon convicted, they were sentenced to hang. Heath, who was tried separately, received a sentence of life in prison, one he would never serve (see Tombstone).

The holdup and subsequent shoot-out took place in and outside of the store located at 26 Main Street and opened earlier that year by Prussia native Joseph Goldwater, grandfather of former US senator and presidential candidate Barry Goldwater. Now known as the "Letson Block," the buildings were constructed between 1883 and 1888. After a fire destroyed most of Main Street in 1888, the buildings were rebuilt. One was occupied by the Turf Saloon, which flourished until the Arizona Territorial legislature outlawed gambling in 1907. Still, the establishment survived another eight years until the state began enforcing the prohibition of alcohol in 1915.

Irish immigrant James Letson, a Cochise County lawman and Bisbee city councilman, and his wife Maggie opened the Mansion House Hotel on Main Street in 1890. In 1902, the hotel was renamed the **Letson Loft Hotel** (26 Main St.; 520-432-3210) and is still in business today.

The **Bisbee Mining and Historical Museum** (5 Copper Queen Plaza; 520-432-7071) is Arizona's largest mining museum, the first in the Southwest to become a Smithsonian affiliate. The museum occupies the 1896-vintage Phelps Dodge headquarters, which the company used until 1961. Ten years later, it was listed on the National Register of Historic Places.

The **Queen Mine** (478 North Dart Rd.; 520-432-2071), once Arizona's mother lode of copper ore, is no longer being worked but visitors can take a tour 1,500 feet down into the mine. Retired Phelps Dodge miners serve as guides. Those taking the tour will be fitted with a miner's hard hat, head lamp, and yellow slicker.

Built in 1902, the **Copper Queen Hotel** (11 Howell St.; 520-432-2216) is Arizona's oldest continuously operated hotel. Famous guests over the years range from President Theodore Roosevelt to John Wayne to Julia Roberts.

During the Great Depression, artist R. Phillips Sanderson earned $180 from the federal Emergency Relief Administration to create a monument to Bisbee's miners. Cast in concrete and covered with a thin layer of copper, the **Miner's Monument** (100 Quality Hill Rd.) was completed in 1935 and is located across from the Cochise County courthouse. Bisbee native Lee Petrovitch posed for the sculpture.

Canyon de Chelly National Monument

Of the 574 federally recognized American Indian tribes, the Navajo Nation is the largest, their reservation covering northeast Arizona and parts of Utah and New Mexico. In the heart of Navajo land is the **Canyon de Chelly National Monument**, long a home for two score Navajo clans.

Established in 1931, the monument takes in some 84,000 acres and includes numerous archeological sites representing 4,000 years of human occupation.

To reach the park, take US 191 from Chinle and then turn east on Route 7. The park's visitor center (928-674-5500) is three miles off US 191. Cell and GPS service is spotty throughout the Navajo Nation, and the National Park Service urges visitors to take only the recommended route to the park.

Clifton (Greenlee County)

Clifton developed as a copper mining town in 1870 at the confluence of the San Francisco River and Chase Creek. With forty-one vintage buildings, its thirty-seven-acre historic district went on the National Register of Historic Places in 1990.

During its first decade, Clifton's miscreants and felons were sentenced to work in the mines. But mines did not make good clinks, so in 1881 the town built a jail by hollowing out part of a solid granite cliff. Using picks, drills, and blasting powder, stonemason Margarito Varela built the unusual lockup. Iron bars two inches wide and three quarters of an inch thick separated a small room intended for the most dangerous inmates, while less violent prisoners went into a room twenty feet long and eight feet wide. The jail's windows were ten feet above the floor and the only way to get in or out of the jail was to climb up the side of the cliff. Legend has it that Varela had the distinction of being the first prisoner in the jail he built when he supposedly celebrated completion of the job a bit too heartily, shooting up a dance hall that just happened to be owned by a deputy sheriff. The jail's most notorious occupant was Augustine Chacon, who spent time there in 1895 following a shoot-out at nearby Morenci. A flood in 1906 filled the jail with sediment and debris and law enforcement abandoned the unique structure in favor of a more conventional lockup. Restored in 1929, the **Cliff Jail** (171 Coronado Blvd.) is marked by a historical plaque placed in 1962.

Begun in 1880, Arizona's first steam-powered railroad hauled ore five miles from the Longfellow Mine to a smelter on Chase Creek in Clifton. Shipped by rail to La Junta, Colorado, and transported to Arizona in ox-drawn freight wagons, ten so-called baby-gauge locomotives soon stayed busy feeding the smelter. The trains were called baby-gauge because they ran along trackage only twenty inches wide, as opposed to thirty-six-inch-wide narrow-gauge or fifty-eight-inch standard-gauge tracks. The only survivor is locomotive Number 8, better known as the **Copper Head**. Built in 1897, it continued in operation until 1922. The old locomotive was rescued from a junk dealer, refurbished, and put on display in 1937. The railroad relic stands near the Cliff Jail.

Douglas (Cochise County)

John Horton Slaughter's long, storied life amounts to a history of the Wild West. Though born in Louisiana (October 2, 1841) he grew up in Texas, and as Civil War soldier, Texas ranger, trail driver, and cattleman he built his reputation and earned his lasting nickname, Texas John Slaughter. He moved to southeastern Arizona in 1877 and in 1884 purchased sixty thousand acres and began ranching fifteen miles west of present Douglas, a town he later helped found. Elected sheriff of Cochise County in 1886, Slaughter served two terms. During his lifetime he is said to have dispatched a dozen men, but none who didn't need killing, as the Old West expression had it. Tough as he was, he and his wife adopted several American Indian children over the years, including Apache May, an Apache girl he found while chasing the Apache Kid in 1896. Slaughter died in his sleep February 16, 1922. In 1958, Walt Disney produced the first of seventeen episodes of a television series called *Texas John Slaughter*.

A registered National Historic Landmark, the now 140-acre **Slaughter Ranch** (6153 Geronimo Trail; 520-678-7935) is located fifteen miles due west of Douglas. Originally known as the San Bernadino Ranch, it includes a collection of structures built by Slaughter in 1893 and restored in the 1980s. The ranch also has a museum.

Slaughter was buried in what was then known as the Douglas City Cemetery, now **Calvary Cemetery** (1501 5th St.; plot number F-082-7). He had asked his wife not to bury him in Tombstone's Boot Hill Cemetery because he believed the town would not survive.

Eagar (Apache County)

Originally a Mormon settlement, Eagar developed less than two miles away from the much wilder town of Springerville. Still, Eagar had one notable Wild West episode that showed there was no honor among thieves.

Relentless law enforcement pressure did not bring the **Bill Cavanaugh gang** down, the outlaws did themselves in, literally. In 1878 an argument developed among the members of the gang on a hill near the Eagar Cemetery over how to split the proceeds from a recent robbery. The outlaws resorted to six-gun mediation and when the shooting stopped, anywhere from three to nine of them lay dead. Some accounts say only three outlaws died in the shoot-out but that the gang soon got into two additional shooting scraps that further reduced their number. A stone marker (off South River Road, a tenth of a mile south of West Central Avenue in Douglas), placed in 2002, stands at the approximate site of the shoot-out and the graves.

Fairbank (Cochise County)

Fairbank, named for mine owner Nathaniel Kellogg Fairbank, reached its peak population of four hundred in 1890—only eight years after its founding—but in its early years it was a lively town. Nine miles from Tombstone, Fairbank is where residents of that more famous Cochise County town had to go to catch a train or pick up supplies. The rail connection also was vital to local mining operations and cattle shipment.

On February 15, 1900, the Burt Alvord gang tried to rob the Benson-to-Nogales train. What the outlaws had not figured on was the man guarding the Wells Fargo express car, former Texas Ranger Jeff Milton. When the train pulled into the station and Milton opened the express car door to find an assemblage of masked men pointing guns at him, he thought it was a joke. But when an outlaw's bullet knocked his hat off, Milton's smile vanished as he went for his shotgun. By the time the shooting stopped, Three-Fingered Jack Dunlop lay badly wounded, and Milton's shattered left arm hung uselessly from his shoulder. Milton's arm got better. Three-Fingered Jack did not.

The Fairbank post office remained open until the early 1970s, but by that time only the postmaster and two others lived there. In 1986 the federal Bureau of Land Management acquired the ghost town and ranch land around it and folded it into the **San Pedro Riparian National Conservation Area**.

An original adobe building that had been a general store, saloon, and post office still stands. Also dating from the town's heyday are the foundations of the old Montezuma Hotel, built in 1889. The depot where the shooting took place continued as a Southern Pacific freight station until the company discontinued it in 1966. A short time later, the structure was cannibalized for its lumber. The legend persists that the depot had been moved to Tombstone in 1961 and turned into a library, but that is not correct. The only evidence of Fairbank's one-time importance as a rail stop is an old loading platform just west of the townsite.

Flagstaff (Coconino County)

An emigrant party headed to California felt the need to observe the nation's centennial, so they stripped a tall pine tree and on July 4, 1876, affixed a then-thirty-seven-star US flag atop the bare tree. The makeshift flag staff became a waymark and the namesake of the town that developed in its vicinity. The arrival of the Atlantic and Pacific Railroad in 1881 assured the community's permanence. The San Francisco Peaks, Arizona's highest mountains, loom behind the downtown historic district.

Known world-wide, the privately owned, nonprofit **Museum of Northern Arizona** (3101 North Fort Valley Rd.; 928-774-5213) has a huge collection of natural and cultural material focused on the story of the Colorado Plateau. Harold S. Colton and Mary-Russell Ferrell Colton founded the museum in 1928.

Operated by the Arizona Historical Society and housed in a 1908 rock building that served as Flagstaff's first hospital, the **Pioneer Museum** (2340 North Fort Valley Rd.; 928-774-6272) focuses on the city's medical and cultural history.

Former **Sheriff Commodore Perry Owens** (1852–1919), the man who dispatched three outlaws and wounded a fourth during a shoot-out (see Holbrook), died of natural causes on May 10, 1919, at the age of sixty-six and is buried in **Citizens Cemetery** (1300 South San Francisco St.; tract J, block A, lot 12, space 2).

Also buried in Citizens Cemetery is **Gladwell Grady Richardson** (1903–1980), a man who transformed an evocative place name into a rip-snorting Wild West town that never was. A Texan, Richardson came to Arizona after service in the navy. Under the pen name of Maurice Kildare, he wrote more than two hundred pulp Western stories and one nonfiction book, *Two Guns, Arizona*. The book has a chapter on the ghost town of Canyon Diablo (the latter word Spanish for "devil") but Arizona historians have found no evidence to substantiate the action-packed story in Richardson's book.

Florence (Pinal County)

Founded by Levi Ruggles in 1866 where the trail from Tucson to Phoenix forded the Gila River, Florence has more than 150 structures or sites listed on the National Register of Historic Places. It is one of Arizona's oldest and best-preserved towns.

In 1878 Levi Ruggles designed and built the **first Pinal County Courthouse** (715 South Main St.; 520-868-4382) a two-story adobe building that, on its ground level, included a courtroom, a judge's chamber, the sheriff's office, and jail. Upstairs was a jury room and accommodations for visiting peace officers. Despite all the trappings of jurisprudence and law enforcement, on one occasion the good people of Pinal County sought speedier justice. Vigilantes stormed the sheriff's office in this building in 1888, dragged two accused stagecoach robbers from their cells, and hanged them in the corridor of the jail. Members of the mob were never prosecuted. The building, which also served as the town's social center, continued as a courthouse until 1891. Since then, it has functioned as a hospital, health center, World War II German POW camp, home for the elderly, and a museum. Listed on the National Register of Historic Places in 1974, the site was a state park until 2008 when it was closed for renovation. Budget issues kept it shuttered until 2011 when the City of Florence began operating it.

Designed by Arizona architect James M. Creighton, the **current Pinal County Courthouse** (135 Pinal St.) is a three-story American-Victorian building completed in 1891. Lady stagecoach robber Pearl Hart was tried here in October 1899. The building was listed on the National Register of Historic Places in 1978.

An 1878-vintage adobe house (180 North Granite St.) was built for Indian agent and newspaper publisher John P. Clum. He started Florence's first newspaper, the *Arizona Citizen* and went on to publish one of the most famous newspapers in the West, the *Tombstone Epitaph*. A historical marker was placed outside the structure in 1988.

William Clark, an engineer with the Silver King Mine, had a two-story adobe and wood American-Victorian house built in 1883 through 1884 for his fiancé, Ella. Clark supposedly designed the house so that in the event of an Indian attack, he and his family could escape to the top via a ladder and trapdoor. While that may be just a legend, not until 1886 was the Apache threat to this part of Arizona a thing of the past. Once a social center as well as a home, the house was occupied until 1956. From then it stood vacant until the early 1990s when the city received a grant to stabilize it. Later the structure was more thoroughly renovated by the owner of the local newspaper. A historical marker was placed outside the **Clark House** (190 North Main St.) in 1988.

Pinal County Sheriff W. C. Truman built an adobe house in the late 1880s. During the same time, he became nationally famous as the lawman who captured Pearl Hart. Now known as the **Truman-Randall House** (550 South Main St.), it is listed on the National Register of Historic Places.

Tunnel Saloon Shoot-out

Sheriff J. P. (Pete) Gabriel hired thirty-nine-year-old Josephus (Joe) Phy (1844–1888) as his deputy in 1883. Nearing the end of his third term, Gabriel opted not to seek reelection in 1886 and supported Deputy Phy for the job. Then they had a falling out and Gabriel withdrew his support. Once friends, the two became bitter enemies. Their mutual ill will climaxed at 8:00 p.m. on May 31, 1888, with a gunfight in John Keating's **Tunnel Saloon** that spilled onto the street. Phy caught three bullets and died at 2:00 a.m. on June 1. Doctors thought Gabriel, shot once in the chest and once in the groin, would die, but he lived another decade.

The shooting took place in what is now the **Charles Rapp Building** (361 Main St.). Rapp put up the building in 1875 and promoted it as an "Elegant Club and Reading Room in Connection with the Bar."

Phy was buried in the **Florence Cemetery** (425 East Ruggles St.; block 7, lot 3, grave 2), one mile south of Florence via State Highway 79.

In 1908, Arizona closed the Arizona Territorial Prison at Yuma and used convict labor to build the new **Arizona State Prison at Florence**. During the construction, inmates and their guards lived in tents. The new prison featured a death chamber with built-in gallows. Hanging remained the mode of execution at the prison until 1933. Expanded and remodeled over the years, the prison continues in operation.

The **Pinal County Historic Society and Museum** (715 South Main St.; 520-868-4382) focuses on the history of Florence and Pinal County. Its holdings include a collection of used hangman's nooses from the Arizona State Prison, some dating back to 1910 during the latter days of the Wild West, and an exhibit on Pearl Hart.

Tom Mix Monument

Having been in 291 movies in a career dating back to 1909, cowboy silent screen star **Tom Mix** knew how to get what he wanted out of a horse, but on the night of October 12, 1940, he proved somewhat less skillful in the operation of his 1937 eight-cylinder, 125-horsepower, yellow Cord 812 Phaeton. Of course, as the sixty-year-old Western actor sped toward Florence after a night of gambling and drinking in Tucson, how could he have known that high water had washed out the bridge ahead of him? Going so fast he had no time to stop, his car became airborne. When it landed on the other side, an aluminum suitcase loaded with cash, traveler's checks, and jewelry flew from the rear seat into the back of his head, breaking his neck. The inscription on the 1947 monument standing near his death site notes: "In memory of Tom Mix whose spirit left his body on this spot and whose characterization and portrayals in life served to better fix memories of the old West in the minds of living men."

The accident occurred twenty miles south-southeast of Florence on what is now State Highway 79. The monument marking the site features a metal silhouette of the actor's famous horse Tony. In the movies Mix mixed it up with horse thieves. Ironically enough, the original metal Tony was rustled in 1980. By the time the original turned up again, a new metal Tony, fashioned by Arizona State Prison inmates, had been placed on the monument. Now the original Tony stands outside the Pinal County Historic Society and Museum in Florence. The draw spanned by the bridge that washed out later became known as Tom Mix Wash.

Fort Apache (Navajo County)

One of the Wild West's best-known forts dates to the 1870 establishment of Camp Ord. Renamed Camp Mogollon that August, a month later it received yet another name, Camp Thomas. By 1879 the post was important enough to be designated a fort. This time the military chose a more evocative name, one that would endure in popular culture: **Fort Apache**.

American Indians rarely attacked US military posts, but that's what happened on September 1, 1881, in what became known as the

Battle at Fort Apache. Mounted Apache warriors carefully stayed out of rifle range but made several forays against the post. Three soldiers suffered wounds along with an unknown number of Indians. The fort held, even though (unlike cavalry posts depicted in most twentieth-century Westerns) it had no stockade.

Throughout the Geronimo campaign, Fort Apache remained tactically important. After the notorious Apache's capture in 1886, the post remained active until 1922 as the home base of the US Cavalry's famed Apache Scouts. A year after the army left, the government transferred the property to the Bureau of Indians Affairs, which used it as a school for reservation children.

Even with its memorable name, Fort Apache might have been just another old army post had it not been for noted movie director John Ford. In 1948 he assured Fort Apache's lasting place in Wild West lore when he filmed one of his classic Westerns, *Fort Apache*. Hollywood being Hollywood, he shot the movie in Monument Valley and built his own Fort Apache, but with John Wayne as its star, the RKO film proved popular and profitable. Fort Apache had been saved from historical obscurity but received another boost in the 1950s with the production of a tin and plastic toy set marketed as "Fort Apache."

Fort Apache State Historic Park is seven miles south of Whiteriver on State Highway 73 on the Fort Apache Indian Reservation. Many of the fort's buildings still stand, including a log cabin occupied by Gen. George Crook, who organized the famed Apache Scouts here. Interpretive exhibits with American Indian and military artifacts focusing on the history of the White Mountain Apaches can be viewed at the **White Mountain Apache Cultural Center** (928-338-4625). A recreation of an 1880s Apache village stands nearby.

Fort Bowie (Cochise County)

America's longest conflict, the Apache Wars in the Southwest, began with a brash if unwise move on the part of a twenty-four-year-old second lieutenant. On January 27, 1861, Apaches raided the John Ward

Ranch near present Patagonia in Santa Cruz County and kidnapped Ward's stepson, Felix Martinez. The family notified the military, and troops soon began searching for the raiders and the captured youth.

Farther east, Second Lt. George Bascom took troops to Apache Pass. There he met with Chiricahua Chief Cochise who said White Mountain Apaches, not any of his people, had taken the boy. He offered to have the youth returned within ten days, but Bascom seized the chief and six family members, saying he would hold them until the boy's return. Infuriated, Cochise drew his knife and slashed his way out of the tent where he and the lieutenant had been talking. Amid a hail of bullets, the chief escaped, leaving his family behind. That ignited a figurative gunpowder trail of alternating, ever-escalating reprisals that within three months claimed scores of lives. Any real possibility of peaceful relations between the Apaches and whites was dead.

The captured Felix never saw his family again. He grew up among the Apaches, who called him Mickey Free, and went on to serve as a scout for the army. After hostilities ended, Free spent the rest of his life on the White Mountain Apache Reservation, where he died in 1914.

The so-called Cochise War, which later expanded into hostilities with all Apaches in Arizona, New Mexico, and far west Texas, brought the establishment of **Fort Bowie** at the east opening of Apache Pass in 1862. The location of a robust spring used by American Indians and later Euro-American travelers, the four-mile-long Apache Pass was the only way through the Chiricahua Mountains from the Dos Cabeza Mountains. For more than a quarter century, Fort Bowie was the command-and-control center of the US Army's campaigns against the Apaches. Two of the army's most noted Indian fighters, Gen. George Crook, followed by Gen. Nelson Miles, directed operations from here that subjugated four storied Apache leaders who fought long and hard to hold their homelands, Cochise, Mangas Colorado, Natchez, and Geronimo. The army abandoned the fort in 1894.

Fort Bowie National Historic Site (3500 Apache Pass Rd.; 520-847-2500) is 13.1 miles southeast of Bowie. Only adobe and stone ruins remain, but they are extensive and haunting in what is still an isolated desert landscape. A visitor center has interpretive exhibits and artifacts. A moderate-level, three-mile, round-trip hiking trail with numerous interpretive markers takes visitors through the fort's ruins and to other sites in Apache Pass.

Fort Huachuca (Cochise County)

Established in 1877 only fifteen miles north of the Mexican border, Fort Huachuca is still an active army post. The garrison was of strategic importance during the Apache Wars and was home for the famed Tenth Cavalry Regiment until 1933.

The **Fort Huachuca Museum** (340 South Grierson Ave.; 520-533-3638) covers the history of the post, the African-American Buffalo Soldiers, and the long conflict with the Apaches. Of the seventy-thousand-acre military reservation, what's known as the Old Post covers 150 acres and includes many of the early post buildings, including the adobe post headquarters built in 1884. Visitors must enter through the Van Deman Gate Visitor Control Center and pass a background check. The fort is four miles west of Sierra Vista on State Highway 90.

Fort Verde (Yavapai County)

Established in 1866 as Camp Verde, the post protected Verde Valley settlers during the central Arizona Indian Wars. In 1872 and 1873, Gen. George Crook headquartered here during the Yavapai Campaign. Following the post's abandonment in 1891, its buildings were sold by the government in 1899. Four of the fort's original twenty-two structures still stand, including the post headquarters and quarters for the commander, post surgeon, and bachelor officers. A nonprofit group began working with the state in the 1960s to acquire the property and preserve the remnants of the old fort (which also includes two sets of ruins). In 1970 it opened as **Fort Verde State Historic Park** (125 East Holloman St.; 928-567-3275). The post headquarters houses a museum with interpretive exhibits and numerous artifacts.

Globe (Gila County)

Old West mining towns tended to go from wild and woolly to deserted and desolate within only a few years. But Globe, founded in 1876 as a silver mining town, enjoyed a second act in the late 1880s when copper mining began. Another thing that sets Globe apart is that its remoteness contributed to a longer-than-average era of violence and crime, from Apache depredations to stagecoach robberies and murder. Gambling and prostitution also flourished.

Not that Globe's more law-abiding folks did not want to clean up the town. Local ordinance prohibited a bawdy house from being within four hundred feet of a school. Unfortunately, when the new central school opened, someone noticed that a house of assignation stood within the buffer zone and the call arose to close the bordello. Demonstrating Solomon-like wisdom, the sheriff stretched a long rope between the new educational facility and the business in question. Finding that four hundred feet extended only three feet inside the structure into its front parlor, he decreed that all customers had to be accommodated in a back room. Still, Globe did not settle down until World War I.

The **Gila County Historical Museum** (1330 North Broad St.; 928-425-7385) has exhibits on the history of Globe and Gila County.

Apache Kid

Before Gila County Sheriff **Glenn Reynolds** (1853–1889) left to take the outlaw Apache Kid and seven other renegades (plus one Hispanic prisoner) to the territorial penitentiary at Yuma, he was offered an escort of seasoned Apache Scouts. "I don't need your scouts," he declared. "I can take those Indians alone with a corncob and a lightning bug."

The thirty-five-year-old lawman had indeed outsmarted or outgunned his share of outlaws and bad Indians. But this time, he should have accepted help. On November 1, 1889, Reynolds and Deputy **William (Hunkydory) Holmes** left Globe on horseback with the prisoners shackled inside the stagecoach that would take them to the railhead at Casa Grande. From there they would complete the trip to Yuma by train. Not considering him an escape risk, Reynolds allowed the Hispanic prisoner—convicted of embezzlement—to ride alongside the coach.

On the second day out, at a point called Kevin Grade near Florence, the prisoners had to be taken off the stage so it could lumber up a steep incline. Suddenly, two of the prisoners attacked the sheriff, trying to wrest away his shotgun. As Reynolds struggled with them, two other men overpowered Holmes and seized his rifle. With that weapon, one of them shot and killed the deputy and the sheriff. The driver of the stage urged his team into a run, but the man with the rifle shot him before the coach made it very far. The Hispanic prisoner, meanwhile, hid in the brush until the rest of the prisoners fled. Returning to the stagecoach, he found the driver seriously wounded but still alive. Then he took a horse from the team and rode hard to Florence to get help.

The Apache Kid was never seen again, at least by Arizona law enforcement or the military. Reynolds and Holmes were buried in the Globe Cemetery. The prisoner who forsook an opportunity to escape to notify authorities of the double murder received a pardon.

Dating from 1871, the city-operated **Globe Cemetery** (328 Hackney Ave.) sits on a hill overlooking the town just west of the business district and extends over thirty-two acres. In addition to its more famous occupants, the cemetery became the final resting place for European immigrants who worked in the mines, Chinese laborers, African-American Buffalo Soldiers, and several hundred unknowns whose graves are no longer marked.

The ornate stone marking the grave of **Albert Sieber** (1844–1907), one of the Wild West's most famous Indian scouts, is both a memorial to a colorful life and the nature of irony. Or perhaps, revenge. A German native who emigrated to Pennsylvania with his mother, Sieber fought in some of the Civil War's bloodiest battles. After the war, he prospected in California and Nevada before moving to Prescott, Arizona Territory. Ranching in one of the wildest, most dangerous regions of the nation, Sieber honed his survival skills by trailing and fighting Apache raiders. Gen. George Crook made him his chief of scouts in 1871 and for the next twenty-five years, climaxing with the 1886 surrender of Geronimo, he distinguished himself in the Apache Wars. But in managing the Apaches who rode for the army as scouts, Sieber would readily hang or shoot those who disobeyed orders.

Having dodged a violent death in the Civil War and at the hands of hostile Apaches, Sieber died on February 19, 1907, when a boulder fell on him as he supervised a work detail during the construction of Roosevelt Dam. The Wild West History Association's website notes that there has been speculation over the years that Apaches still holding a grudge had dislodged the boulder that killed him. While that is unsubstantiated, it is well documented that Apaches were employed on the project as well as whites, Mexicans, and blacks. In the 1953 movie *Arrowhead*, Charlton Heston played a character inspired by Sieber's exploits; a year later, John McIntyre portrayed him in *Apache* and Robert Duvall played him in *Geronimo* in 1993.

Another of the many transplanted Texans who played a role in Arizona's Wild West history was **John Henry (Rimrock) Thompson** (1861–1934), who for years served as Gila County sheriff. Thompson hit Arizona Territory in the early 1880s and homesteaded 160 acres just beneath the rugged limestone and sandstone cliffs of the Mogollon Rim and that's how he came by his nickname. After marrying, Thompson and his wife moved to Payson, where he became postmaster. But in 1890, when the man who had been appointed to fill the unexpired term of the late Sheriff Glenn Reynolds drowned while trying to save a life, Thompson succeeded in getting the endorsement of an influential citizen and became the second man named to figuratively fill Reynolds's boots. Though not consecutively, Thompson went on to serve eight terms as sheriff, traveling farther, making more arrests, and getting more convictions than anyone else in Arizona's territorial history. He apprehended several notorious killers, saved others from lynching, and never had an escaped prisoner stay escaped. It was a murder that ended Thompson's law enforcement career—one in which he was the suspect. In December 1911, while the sheriff and a friend were having drinks in the Globe Saloon, a gunshot sounded, and bartender Mike Juraskovich fell dead. Thompson and his friend, Harry Temple, were indicted for murder and on January 8, 1912, the fifty-one-year-old sheriff resigned at the request of county officials. At their trial, both men were found not guilty, but the episode marked the end of Thompson's career.

"An Orderly Lynching"

In August 1882, Lafayette V. Grimes and C.B. Hawley held up the Florence-to-Globe stage and in the process killed Wells Fargo guard Andrew Hall and Dr. T.S. Vail. The bandits made off with some $5,000 in gold. Soon captured by a posse, they were jailed in Florence. But Hall, who had been with John Wesley Powell during his famous 1869 exploration of the Colorado River, was a well-liked local and no one in town wanted to wait for a formal trial of his accused killers. Accordingly, the men were summarily lynched. The sycamore that made possible their public demise stood for many years before dying of old age. In 1997 a granite historical marker (strangely dedicated to "Gila County Law Enforcement") was placed on the site (North Broad St., just south of Hackney; GPS coordinates: N33° 23.95', W110° 47.33'). The marker notes that the two accused robbers were duly "tried" before a justice of the peace (who had no legal authority to preside over a capital case) and "sentenced" to hang. Local saloons closed for the occasion, which the marker assures was "an orderly lynching." Not mentioned on the marker is that before their deaths, the two robbers led authorities to the place they had hidden their loot. Also not mentioned is that when his turn came, Grimes supposedly sat down and removed his footwear. "I'll be damned if I'll die with my boots on," he declared.

The Female Bandit

In a bit of a financial squeeze, twenty-eight-year-old **Pearl Hart**, a soiled dove from a good family, prevailed upon her paramour of the moment, Joe Boot, to join her in robbing the stage between Globe and Florence. Dressed as a man, she, along with Boot, stopped the stage on May 30, 1899, and relieved its passengers of $450 give or take. Graciously, Hart redistributed a dollar to each passenger to cover food and lodging at their next stop. Though the robbery went well considering the perpetrators' lack of experience, their getaway did not go as smoothly. A posse led by Pinal County Sheriff W.C. Thurman easily tracked them down, recovered their take, and jailed them in Florence. The holdup the couple pulled off has been labeled the last Wild West stagecoach robbery, but *one* of the last is more accurate. Even so, at the peak of the yellow journalism era, newspapers had a field day with the story.

Tried jointly for robbing the stage, the couple did not experience equal justice. Boot was convicted and sentenced to thirty years in the territorial prison at Yuma, but Pearl, a pretty young woman with a come-hither smile, was acquitted by the all-male jury. That did not please the prosecution, which then charged her with another count of robbery for having relieved the stagecoach driver of his revolver.

Transferred to the Pima County Jail in Tucson, she soon escaped. Deciding she'd spent enough time in Arizona, she left the territory and headed east. But she was captured in New Mexico and returned for trial. In that proceeding, a jury less taken by her charms found her guilty and sentenced her to five years at Yuma. As it turned out, she only served eighteen months before being released.

Pearl Hart either died around 1925 or thirty years later, depending on which story one believes. But the basis of both tales is shaky, so neither may be correct. If Hart died in 1925, no one knows where she's buried. If she died in 1955, it was as the wife of Gila County rancher George Calvin Bywater and she is buried in Pinal Cemetery in Central Heights (GPS coordinates: N33° 24.77', W110° 48.93') under the name Pearl Bywater.

Grand Canyon National Park

The enormous expanse of land now included in Grand Canyon National Park has cultural ties to eleven American Indian tribes dating back ten thousand years. In the second half of the nineteenth century, the area was explored by John Wesley Powell and later explored by prospectors. But the difficulty of getting ore out of the canyon prevented any extensive mining.

Buckey O'Neill gained a reputation as a determined Arizona lawman, newspaper editor, lawyer, and politician before dying a hero in the Spanish-American War. Less known is that in addition to everything else he did in his thirty-eight years, he played a significant part in the development of the Grand Canyon as a world-class attraction.

His first connection with the canyon came in the 1890s as a would-be miner. In prospecting the canyon, he found a substantial copper deposit but soon realized that getting the ore out of the canyon would cost too much to be profitable. O'Neill built two cabins on the canyon's South Rim, one as an office, the other as a bunkhouse. What the canyon needed, he realized, was a railroad.

By 1897 he had raised enough capital to charter the Santa Fe and Grand Canyon Railroad Company. With O'Neill as president, the company would build a line connecting the South Rim with the Santa Fe's mainline at Williams, Arizona. A year later, having been elected mayor of Prescott, he volunteered for military service when war broke out with Spain. He was shot and killed at San Juan Hill in Cuba.

Two years after his death, the company he founded finally started laying tracks from Williams to the canyon. Just ten miles shy of the South Rim, the company went broke. The Santa Fe bought the failed company, rebranded it the Grand Canyon Railway, and resumed work on the tracks. With completion of the line in 1901, for the first time the future national park was easily accessible to any who wanted to see it.

O'Neill's cabin, the oldest structure on the rim, was refurbished in 1935 when the Fred Harvey Co. built Bright Angel

Lodge at what is now known as **Grand Canyon Historic Village** (888-297-2757). The cabin, listed on the National Register of Historic Places, is still available to overnight guests. The lodge has interpretive exhibits on O'Neill and the history of the South Rim. The Grand Canyon Railway, though no longer owned by the corporate successor of the Santa Fe, is a heritage railroad still carrying visitors to the park. In addition to the cabin that bears his name, the canyon's **O'Neill Butte** (GPS coordinates: N36° 03.44', W112° 08.47') is named for the entrepreneurial pioneer.

The **Grand Canyon National Park South Rim Visitor Center** (South Entrance Rd., Grand Canyon Village) has interpretive exhibits on the park's American Indian heritage, the explorations of Powell, and other aspects of the park's natural and cultural history.

Holbrook (Navajo County)

A combination store, restaurant, and saloon catering to westbound travelers on the Beale Wagon Road opened in 1878 at the juncture of the Rio Puerco and Little Colorado River and a small community called Horsehead Crossing developed around it. When the Atlantic and Pacific Railroad came through the area in 1881, soon followed by the Santa Fe Railroad, a new town named for Atlantic and Pacific engineer H.R. Holbrook arose west of Horsehead Crossing. A railroad crossroads, Holbrook flowered like a cactus in spring, but all desert cacti have thorns. Good folks and bad arrived to take advantage of opportunities afforded by any new western town.

What the railroad didn't do for Holbrook, the Hashknife soon did. One of the Atlantic and Pacific's stockholders, Edward Kinsley, came to Holbrook in the spring of 1884 to inspect the new railroad. An abnormally wet winter had left the Little Colorado River Valley looking deceivingly lush. Seeing the area as incredible cattle-raising country, Kingsley returned to New York and convinced investors they needed to get in the ranching business. When the railroad offered more than three thousand sections of land for sale cheap the following year, the newly created Aztec Land and Cattle Company bought a million acres and imported a large herd of cattle from Texas along with Texas cowboys to run them. That was the beginning of the **Hashknife Ranch**, a giant spread second in size only to Texas's famed XIT Ranch and in the lore of the Old West, roughly a tie with the Lone Star State's legendary King Ranch. The Hashknife continued in operation until the early 1900s, and while the famous Hashknife brand is no longer registered in Arizona, much of the old Hashknife land is still leased for grazing.

Commodore Perry Owens

The late writer-historian Joseph G. Rosa, an Englishman who specialized in the violent history of the Old West, said what happened in Holbrook on September 4, 1887, "is unequaled in the annals of the west."

When long-haired Commodore Perry Owens took over as sheriff, one of his first official acts was serving more than a dozen arrest warrants on hard cases his predecessor had been unable—or unwilling—to find. One of those warrants was for Andy Blevins, a cattle thief. Armed with the court document and a Winchester, Owens went to Blevins's house to take him into custody. The warrant he held was for cattle theft. The sheriff did not know that only two days before Blevins had been involved in the murder of two men. Nor did Owens know that other members of Blevins's gang, also armed, were with him that Sunday. As it turned out, Blevins was not inclined to go to jail. When the wanted man wouldn't come out after the sheriff told him he carried a warrant for his arrest, the situation quickly deteriorated into gunfire. One against several, the lawman started working the lever on his rifle. When the black powder smoke drifted off, Owens was still standing. Five other men were not, and four of them would never be getting up.

"Too much credit cannot be given Sheriff Owens in this lamentable affair," declared the *Arizona Herald* four days later.

"It required more than ordinary courage for a man to go single-handed and alone to a house where it was known there were four or five desperate men inside and demand the surrender of one of them. And when one takes into consideration that the combatants were separated by only a few feet at the commencement of the difficulty, it seems miraculous that Mr. Owens should come out of it uninjured."

The wood-frame **Blevins House** where the gun battle occurred still stands just west of the intersection of 2nd Street and Northwest Central Avenue. It is now used as a senior center.

The **Navajo County Historical Society and Museum** (100 East Arizona St.; 928-524-6558) is located in the old county courthouse. Built at a cost of $15,000, the three-story brick structure opened in 1899 and served until 1976. The museum has an exhibit on the Blevins House fight, including a model of the house. Also displayed is an old chuck wagon once used on the Hashknife Ranch and a Hashknife branding iron.

Jerome (Yavapai County)

Spanish explorers in the sixteenth century found silver ore in the vicinity of what would come to be called Cleopatra Hill, but the discovery of rich copper deposits in 1876 is what led to mining in the area. The original claim owner and his two partners could not raise enough money to open a mine and sold their interests. The new owners still needed capital to begin production and in 1882 induced New York financier Eugene Jerome to invest $200,000. Jerome had one stipulation before any money changed hands: The town that developed when mining began had to be named after him. The young attorney with the deep pockets must have been satisfied enough that the new mining community bore his name because he never visited it.

Clinging at a thirty-degree angle to Cleopatra Hill, Jerome boomed, reaching a population of fifteen thousand and for a time ranked as Arizona's third-largest city. Mine workers and tradesmen from all over the world, including Chinese, Italians, Irish, Mexicans, Slavs, and Russians, enhanced Jerome's cultural heritage. But when the mines played out, so did Jerome. The ghost town was named a National Historic Landmark in 1967.

Twenty-three historic structures or properties dating from Jerome's prime have historical markers. Three extensive fires destroyed most of the town's earliest buildings, but eight marked structures predate 1900. The oldest was built in 1885 as a mine manager's office.

The **Jerome Historical Society** (407 Clark St.; 928-634-1066) has an extensive archival collection relating to the ghost town's story.

Opened in 1953 and operated by the Jerome Historical Society, the **Mine Museum** (200 Main St.; 928-634-5477) tells the story of Jerome's development and its rich ethnic heritage. Much early mining equipment is on display, along with the Colt revolver Marshal Johnny Hudgens (1880–1946) used quite effectively to bring law and order to the once rowdy mining town. Sworn into office in 1910 following the line-of-duty killing of his predecessor, Hudgens had to shoot and kill three men in three different incidents during his career as Jerome marshal.

Jerome State Park (100 Douglas Rd. off US 89A; 928-634-5381) is only a single structure, the 1916 mansion of mining king Dr. James (Rawhide Jimmy) Douglas, Jr. (1868–1949). The Canadian-born industrialist, whose father had been a key figure in Arizona copper mining, continued in the family business. His nickname does not have as romantic an origin as it sounds—it came from his adaptive use of cattle hides to protect rollers in the ore-crushing process.

Jerome's Sliding Jail

It's usually prisoners who try to make a run for it, but in Jerome, the old jail itself went on the lam. An underground dynamite blast in the 1930s caused the entire building to slide 225 feet downhill from its original location. While the ruins of the 1905 poured-concrete jail survive, they are one of the few. From the 1930s to 1950s, many of the ghost town's vintage buildings had to be razed because they posed a danger in their downhill migration.

Jerome's sliding jail, now owned by the Jerome Historical Society, is protected from further escape attempts by bars and concrete barriers. It is located on Hull Street just before it intersects Main Street. A nearby historical marker tells the jail's story.

Like practically all boomtowns, Jerome had a flourishing red-light district. Indeed, one out-of-state journalist assured readers in 1903 that Jerome was the "Wickedest city in America." Passed in 1913, a city ordinance restricted houses of ill fame from operating downtown, but that was largely ignored. Still, proprietors and customers engaged in some discretion. An alley from Main Street to Hull Avenue, where the bordellos stood, came to be called "**Husband's Alley**." Further to public decency, the town for a time had a women-only jail. Jerome's **ladies' jail** was on the first floor of the 1917-vintage New State Motor Building (110 Main St.).

Kingman (Mohave County)

Kingman, a mining and ranching town, developed in 1883 when the Atlantic and Pacific Railroad arrived. The engineer who determined the route the tracks would take, Lewis Kingman, thought Kingman would make a regal name for the new town. The general route the newly laid trackage followed, however, owed its existence to the endurance of camels.

Lieutenant Beale's Noble Brutes

The orders a US Navy lieutenant received to investigate whether African camels would make suitable replacements for horses in the desert Southwest was not some admiral's idea of a joke. Lt. Edward F. Beale was instructed to survey a wagon road from Texas to California, following the thirty-fifth parallel to the extent possible. Along with mule-drawn wagons, Beale's expedition would be relying on thirty-three camels as an experimental mode of transportation for the military. Beale endorsed their future use by the military, calling them "noble brutes."

Established in 1857, his route came to be called **Beale's Wagon Road**. The road later evolved into a segment of US Route 66, the nation's most famous twentieth-century highway. A monument to Lieutenant Beale and his camels stands in Locomotive Park across the street from the Mohave Museum of History and Art.

A tour of Kingman is best begun at the **Powerhouse Visitor Center** (120 West Andy Devine Ave.; 928-753-6106). Built in 1907, the stone powerhouse generated electricity for Kingman and the mines around it until the Hoover Dam went online in 1938. The center has information on local historic sites and Route 66–related exhibits.

The **Mohave Museum of History and Art** (400 West Beale St.; 928-753-3195) focuses on the history of northwestern Arizona. Founded in 1961, it is operated by the Mohave County Historical Society. A self-guided walking tour of historic downtown buildings is available at the museum or visitor center.

Oatman (Mohave County)

When prospector John Moss found gold in the Black Mountains in the 1860s, he staked two mining claims, the Moss and the Oatman. The latter honored Olive Oatman, a young woman captured in Arizona by American Indians in 1851 and held for more than five years. Despite the early discovery of precious metal, mining activity in the area did not take off until the Vivian Mining Company began production in 1904. Over the next three years, their mine yielded more than $3 million in gold. Just as the Vivian began to peter out, a major discovery in 1908 led to the opening of the Tom Reed Mine. The following year, the mining community first known as Vivian was renamed Oatman. Yet another big strike in 1913 brought Oatman to its peak population of ten thousand. Area mines produced an estimated $36 million in gold, and even in the twenty-first century small-scale mining continues in Mohave County. But decreased production and the relocation of Route 66, which once passed through town, reduced Oatman to near ghost town status. Despite several major fires during its heyday, many of Oatman's old buildings have survived. Some scenes from the 1962 classic *How the West Was Won* were filmed in Oatman and buildings constructed for the set add to the town's Old West look.

Built of adobe in 1902, the two-story Hotel Drulin (181 Main St.; 928-768-4408) later was renamed **Hotel Oatman**. Listed on the National Register of Historic Places, the eight-room hotel accommodated all the various types drawn to boomtowns. Though no longer hosting overnight guests, the old hotel has a restaurant and a private museum upstairs. The legend that Clark Gable and Carol Lombard honeymooned there in 1939 has added to the building's appeal to visitors.

Four-legged Tourist Attractions

Laden with supplies, equipment, or ore, long-eared burros were as important to early-day prospectors and miners as pickaxes and shovels. Spanish missionaries brought the first burros (derived from the Spanish word "borrico," meaning donkey) to Arizona in the 1600s and the smart, smallish, and hardy critters have been doing just fine ever since. Over time, escaped or abandoned burros propagated and became feral across the Southwest, but particularly in mining country. In Oatman, burros—federally protected as "living symbols of the historic and pioneer spirit of the West"—wander into town from the mountains and have become a major tourist draw.

Payson (Gila County)

Roughly midway along the rugged Mogollon Rim, a two-hundred-mile-long escarpment cutting across northern Arizona, Payson started in 1882 as Green Valley. But when the community warranted a post office two years later thanks to help from Illinois Congressman Levi Joseph Payson the community was renamed in his honor. The same year Payson received a post office and a new name, the community staged a rodeo that continues to be held annually. Promoters say the event is the world's oldest "continuously operating" rodeo, though at least two other towns west of the Mississippi (Pecos, Texas, and Pendleton, Oregon) claim to have staged the first rodeo.

The last major battle in the long Apache Wars took place on July 17, 1882, between some 350 troopers of the Third and Sixth Cavalry Regiments and a band of sixty White River Apache warriors under Na-tio-tish. Twenty Apaches, including Na-tio-tish, died in the fight. Only two cavalrymen were killed, with six wounded. During the Great Depression, the US Forest Service and Civilian Conservation Corps placed a granite marker at the site. The engagement became known as the **Battle of Big Dry Wash**.

The battle site is northeast of Payson, just beyond the Mogollon Rim, but it is a circuitous if scenic two-plus-hour drive. From Payson take State Highway 87 north through the small communities of Pine and Strawberry to Forest Road 300. Follow that road to its intersection with Forest Service Road 705 and turn north. The monument is just a short distance from the intersection (GPS coordinates: N34° 27.24', W111° 15.04').

"Bear-ing" A Grudge

Ohio dentist turned Western novelist Zane Grey, one of the writers who helped mythologize the Wild West, visited Payson in 1918. He soon bought land along Tonto Creek and in 1921 built a cabin where he would write numerous books. (Of Grey's fifty-seven novels, twenty-eight have Arizona themes.) An avid outdoorsman, Grey also hunted in the area each fall. When he came to Payson in 1929 with a film crew to shoot a movie on bear hunting, he found that the season had already closed. He tried to get a special permit allowing him to take a bear for the film, but officials would not bend the rules. In a fit of pique, he abandoned his cabin, vowing never to return to Arizona. And he never did. The cabin fell into ruin but was restored in 1962 and 1963, used as a private residence, and later turned into a museum. After a disastrous wildfire destroyed the structure in 1990, a nonprofit foundation acquired the site and reconstructed the cabin. In 2005 it opened as the **Rim Country Museum and Zane Grey Cabin** (700 South Green Valley Pkwy.; 928-474-3483).

Phoenix (Maricopa County)

All but two of Arizona's rivers flow into the Salt River Valley in the center of the state, a sprawling alluvial plain extending from the Superstition Mountains to the Sierra Estrella. Around 700 AD an advanced culture came to the valley and by 1100 AD they had developed a network of communities where as many as a hundred thousand people lived. No one knows what they called themselves, but they came to be known as the **Hohokam**. That is a Pima word for "vanished ones," which describes what the culture did more than six centuries ago—disappear. They left behind a sophisticated series of irrigation canals, the ancient infrastructure that one day would lead to another megalopolis existing where their civilization once thrived.

No Euro-Americans settled in the valley until 1865. That followed the Army's establishment of Camp McDowell on the Verde

River about twenty miles to the northwest. With nearly five hundred troops stationed in the middle of nowhere, a ready market existed for hay and vegetables that could be grown in the valley. Realizing the potential, in 1867 one Jack Swilling talked a group of miners from Wickenburg into joining him in forming the **Swilling Irrigation and Canal Company**. The miners dug out one of the old Hohokam canals, the Swilling Ditch as it was called, and by 1871 it flowed with enough water to irrigate four thousand acres.

Jack Swilling was not without a few character flaws. A Confederate deserter, morphine addict, and mean drunk, he ended up in the Yuma prison on a stagecoach robbery conviction (historians say he was probably innocent) and died there in 1878. By that time, more extensive irrigation canals watered a much-expanded agricultural area and a townsite had been laid out along the Salt River. By all rights, the promoters should have named their new town Swilling, but given that the settlement would be developed on the site of an ancient metropolis, someone with a knowledge of the classics suggested Phoenix as an ode to the mythical bird that rose from its own ashes. Phoenix indeed rose from the figurative ashes, in 1889 becoming Arizona's capital and growing into its largest city.

Located in the old Carnegie Library, the **Arizona Hall of Fame** (1101 West Washington St.; 602-255-2110) focuses on notable men and women who shaped Arizona.

Founded by Dwight and Maie Heard in 1929, the **Heard Museum** (2301 North Central Ave.; 602-252-8840) is internationally known for its extensive collection of more than forty thousand examples of art produced by American Indians in the West and Southwest from centuries ago to the present day. Major collections include Hopi kachina dolls, Navajo and Zuni jewelry, Navajo textiles, and Southwestern ceramics and baskets.

Located in the copper-domed 1901 territorial capitol, the **Arizona Capitol Museum** (1700 West Washington St.; 602-926-3620) covers all aspects of the state's history, from its government to cultural heritage. The museum is operated by the Arizona State Library and Archives.

Heritage Square is home to restored buildings dating to the late nineteenth century and is the only remaining group of residential structures from the original Phoenix townsite. A visitor center at the square offers a self-guided tour of this sole surviving part of early Phoenix. Some of the structures—including the **Rosson House** (113 North 6th St.; 602-261-8063), a ten-room, 2,800-square-foot Victorian mansion built by Dr. Roland Rosson in 1895—have been restored and are open for tours.

Established in 1884 and used until 1914, **Pioneer and Military Memorial Park** (1317 West Jefferson St.) is the collective name of seven old cemeteries covering a full city block in downtown Phoenix. The Pioneers' Cemetery Association works with the City of Phoenix to maintain the property. Of an estimated 3,700 burials, fewer than six hundred graves have headstones. Among the cemetery's notable burials is **Jacob Waltz** (1810–1891), the central figure of the Wild West's classic treasure tales, the so-called Lost Dutchman Mine of the Superstition Mountains. Also buried here is the last victim of the Pleasant Valley War, Tom Graham (see Young, Arizona). The Pioneers' Cemetery Association, which has offices in the restored 1897 Smurthwaite House (1313 Jefferson St.; 602-534-1262) offers a self-guided walking tour of the park.

The Phoenix Police Department dates to 1881 when Henry Garfias (1851–1896) served as the then small but unruly town's first marshal. On the first floor of the old Phoenix City Hall, the **Phoenix Police Museum** (17 South 2nd Ave.; 602-534-7278) has exhibits, artifacts, photographs, and archival records reflecting on all aspects of the department's history. Amazingly, no Phoenix officer died in the line of duty prior to 1925. Garfias is buried in Pioneer and Military Memorial Park.

Prescott (Yavapai County)

A gold discovery in 1860 led to the development of Prescott, but compared with other Wild West mining booms, the rush for riches that came three years later transpired in a downright orderly manner.

In 1863, after staking a claim in Central Arizona along the upper Hassayampa River, noted fur trapper, trader, and explorer Joseph R. Walker and two dozen others in his Walker Prospecting and Mining Company drafted a set of "Laws and Resolutions" for what they called the Walker Mining District. As the Prescott chapter of the Westerners would put it generations later, the document "can be considered Prescott's birth certificate."

Five miles south of the gold discovery site, the military established Fort Whipple in late 1863. The following year, Arizona having gained territorial status, the army moved the fort to a better location a few miles south. With soldiers to protect its settlers from American Indians incensed by the growing Anglo incursion on their homeland, a nearby town named for historian William Prescott became the first territorial capital. During the Civil War, many of those settling in Prescott came from the northern states and brought their pro-Union views and northeastern culture, including their taste in architecture, with them. Enough of the structures built during that time remain to support the tongue-in-cheek claim that Prescott is the most eastern town in the West. In 1867, the capital was moved to Tucson. (Tucson remained the seat of government for a decade, but Prescott regained the title in 1877 and continued as the capital city until 1889, when Phoenix was selected.)

More than eight hundred Prescott buildings are listed on the National Register of Historic Places. Located in the old city hall and jail, the **Prescott Chamber of Commerce** (117 West Goodwin St.; 928-445-2000) provides a self-guided tour of historic downtown structures.

When Prescott became the territorial capital, work soon began on a residence for the governor that would also serve as his office. Built at a cost of $6,000 the mansion was used until Prescott lost its status as capital city to Phoenix. In 1928 writer-historian Sharlot Hall, a longtime collector of Arizona-related artifacts, opened a museum in the old mansion. Over the years, the **Sharlot Hall Museum** (415 West Gurley St.; 928-445-3122) has grown into a four-acre complex of restored historic buildings and more modern structures. Other than the mansion, the two most noted buildings are Fort Misery, a trading post built in Prescott in 1864 and now Arizona's oldest surviving log cabin, and the John C. Fremont House. Fremont, a soldier and explorer, lived in the house while he was territorial governor.

A Man Named Pauline

Long before Johnny Cash sang of a boy named Sue, **Pauline Weaver**'s (1798–1867) parents saddled him with a feminine first name. Born in Tennessee to a Cherokee mother and white father, Weaver came to Arizona in the 1820s and never left, at least not while he was alive. He trapped, served as an army scout, and successfully prospected for gold without ever enriching himself. He got along with most of Arizona's American Indian tribes, but in the mid-1860s was wounded when attacked by a Yavapai war party. Figuring he was about to die Weaver began intoning a Plains Indian death song. Not knowing what he was singing, the Yavapai thought the old man must be crazy and rode off. Weaver walked home, recovered, and lived until the summer of 1867. He had been to every corner of Arizona and in death continued his travels. First, he was buried at Camp Verde. When the army abandoned the post, his remains were shipped to California for reburial. In 1929 school children raised enough money for his remains to be returned to Arizona for burial in Prescott. Today, Weaver is buried on the grounds of the Sharlot Hall Museum. Two historical markers nearby summarize his life.

Fort Whipple

Established in 1864 at its present location on Granite Creek just east of Prescott, **Fort Whipple** was one of the Southwest's few forts originally surrounded by a timber stockade. The post served as the military headquarters for Arizona Territory and was home to Gen. George Crook from 1871 to 1875. Troops from Fort Whipple took part in the Battle of Big Dry Wash on July 17, 1882, the last major Indian fight in Arizona. At the beginning of the Spanish-American War in 1898, the famed Rough Riders, a volunteer cavalry unit, was mobilized at the post. When the last soldiers marched away in 1913, the military repurposed the post as an army tuberculosis hospital. Later the Veteran's Administration (now Veterans Affairs) took over the facility (one mile east of Prescott on State Highway 89 at State Highway 69).

The **Fort Whipple Museum** (500 State Highway 89 North; 928-445-3122) is just north of the intersection on the grounds of the Veterans Affairs Medical Center.

Whiskey Row

Catering to off-duty soldiers, miners, freighters, cowboys, politicians, and all other frontier types, several dozen saloons in Prescott ran wide open around the clock. The establishments lined a several-block stretch of Montezuma Street that came to be called **Whiskey Row**. By 1900, the high point of low life along the row, anyone hankering for a drink could choose among forty different emporiums. But on July 14 that year, fire destroyed most of the saloons and a couple of hotels. As flames moved from building to building toward the Palace Saloon, patrons worked frantically to move the large, ornate bar from the building before it, too, went up in smoke. Most of the burned bars, including the Palace, were quickly rebuilt, though almost all of them were gone by World War I. But **The Palace** (120 South Montezuma St.; 928-541-1996) still stands, is still a watering hole, and customers can still belly up to the original bar. Two plaques near the entrance to the bar offer details on the history of The Palace and Whiskey Row. Another historical marker tells the story of **Hotel St. Michael** (106 Montezuma St.; 928-776-1999), a three-story brick hostelry that opened in 1901.

Citizen's Cemetery

Founded in 1864 on open land east of newly founded Prescott, **Citizen's Cemetery** (815 East Sheldon St.) went through several property owners and names before the county acquired it in 1884. Used until 1933, the six-and-a-half-acre cemetery has more than three thousand graves but fewer than a third are marked. Though many of the graves are without headstones, Yavapai County maintains a list of burials, cause of death, and grave locations. A section in the cemetery known as "Murderer's Row" has the graves of several Wild West bad men, including train robber James Fleming Parker (1865–1898). Parker's partner in the robbery was killed by a posse but Parker was captured. He later broke out of jail and gunned down the district attorney on the courthouse square. Captured again, he was convicted of murder and hanged—also on the courthouse square.

Rough Rider

On July 3, 1907, less than a decade after the end of the Spanish-American War, a larger-than-life bronze statue called ***The Rough Rider*** was dedicated on the courthouse plaza (120 South Cortez St.) in downtown Prescott. Despite its formal name, the impressive piece of public art by Solon Borglum (1868–1922), considered one of the finest equestrian statues ever cast, is more commonly known as the Buckey O'Neill statue. O'Neill was the only Rough Rider officer killed during the war. That made him a national hero, but he was already a hero in Arizona.

Born in St. Louis, O'Neill came to Phoenix in 1879, where he worked as a newspaper reporter. Moving to Cochise County, he reported for the *Tombstone Epitaph* before returning to Phoenix to serve as a deputy marshal. In 1882 he moved to Prescott and founded a livestock newspaper. Four years later, he became a captain in the Prescott Grays, part of the Arizona Militia. On

February 5 that year, his unit provided security at the hanging of convicted murderer Dennis Delda. When the trap sprang and Delda dropped to his death, O'Neill fainted. In 1888, after a time as county judge, O'Neill was elected sheriff.

When four men robbed a train near Canyon Diablo on March 21, 1889, O'Neill led a posse in pursuit of the bandits. In doing that, the sheriff proved that while he might faint at a hanging, he was not faint of heart. He and his men tracked down the robbers, had a shoot-out with them in which only O'Neill's horse was killed, and succeeded in taking them into custody. The lawmen had ridden more than six hundred miles, one of the longest pursuits in the history of the Wild West. After serving as sheriff until 1894, O'Neill was elected mayor of Prescott three years later and worked to bring rail service to the Grand Canyon. When the Spanish-American War began, he joined the First US Volunteer Cavalry, better known as the Rough Riders. On July 1, 1898, Buckey O'Neill was killed in action in Cuba.

Arizona Pioneers Home

Even in territorial days, most Arizona residents preferred as little government as possible. Despite the majority's conservative leanings, in 1909 the territorial legislature did something downright liberal if not socialistic—they voted to open the nation's first government-operated retirement home. To qualify for a bed, an applicant had to be destitute, sixty years old or older, and an Arizona resident for at least twenty-five years. Only two other states have similar homes, and though different in their own ways, they were based on the Arizona model.

Known as the **Arizona Pioneers Home**, the facility (300 South McCormick St.; 928-445-2181) stands on a bluff overlooking Prescott. A three-story, red brick building, the home opened February 1, 1911. Soon it had forty residents—old miners, Indian fighters, cowboys, and other Old West types. Buffalo Bill Cody visited during its first year to talk about the old days with several residents of his acquaintance and called it one of his happiest experiences in years. The home expanded in 1916 with an addition that could accommodate up to twenty pioneer women. A hospital wing added in 1926 brought the floor space to 53,564 square feet.

The home received national publicity that irked staff, residents, and many locals when *LIFE* magazine published an article in 1947 portraying the facility as the Wild West's last resort, claiming its whiskey-breathed oldsters often engaged in fisticuffs or whacked one another with their canes over grub, dominoes, women, or differences of opinion on the way something happened back when, like Tombstone's OK Corral street fight. A resident identified only as Six-Shooter Smith, the author said, had ten notches on his walking stick for every man he had killed in his salad days. While that particular piece surely contained exaggeration if not outright fiction, it is the truth that the home had some notable residents in its earlier days, including Mary Katherine Horony-Cummings (1850–1940), far better known as Big Nose Kate, the consort of one Doc Holliday.

The unique facility remains open in its original building, a structure now listed on the National Register of Historic Places. Three metal plaques on the home relate to its history. Twenty-first-century residents must be at least seventy years old and have been an Arizona resident for fifty years.

Arizona Pioneers Home Cemetery (1400 West Iron Springs Rd.) is the burial place for more than 1,300 of the 3,000-plus pioneers who have lived at the home since it opened. The best-known grave belongs to Horony-Cummings (row 11, grave 4).

Not-So-Gentle Tamer

The deadliness of rattlesnakes has often been exaggerated in Western novels and movies but being bitten by one is still a painful and serious medical emergency. Dedicated in 2013, one of the West's most unusual statues depicts a pioneer woman holding a dead rattler, the shovel she used to chop off its head gripped in her other hand. The ten-foot bronze, titled **Not-So-Gentle Tamer** (7501 East Civic Circle, Prescott Valley, eight miles east of Prescott), is based on a painting by writer-artist Bob Boze Bell, who saw his grandmother calmly dispatch diamondbacks with her hoe.

Quartzsite (La Paz County)

The first settlement near future Quartzsite was a stagecoach stop called Tyson's Well. Miner Charles Tyson dug the well in 1864 and built a thick-walled adobe structure nearby that California-bound travelers called Fort Tyson. But no significant growth occurred in the area until gold mining began in the 1890s. By then the Tyson's Well post office had been shut down. When the community had enough people to merit opening a post office again, the name selected was Quartzite for the abundance of quartz in the vicinity. Someone in Washington mistakenly added an "s" to the name, and the town officially became Quartzsite. When mining waned, so did Quartzsite, but its location on I-10 keeps it a popular tourist stop.

Built in 1866 through 1867, the **Tyson's Well Stage Station** (161 Main St.; 928-927-5229) still stands and is now a museum operated by the Quartzsite Historical Society. The museum's holdings include an extensive collection of mining equipment and an assay office that was part of the nearby Margarita Mine.

The remnants of Fort Tyson's adobe walls stand at Main Street and Moon Mountain Road.

Hi Jolly Monument

One of the West's more unusual monuments honors one of its more unusual characters, **Hi Jolly**. His real name was Philip Tedro—born in 1828 in Turkey to a Syrian father and Greek mother—but when he converted to Islam, he took the name Hadji Ali.

Ali came to the US in 1856 aboard a naval supply ship that was transporting thirty-three African camels to Texas so the army could determine if the ungainly beasts of burden might be as useful in the deserts of the Southwest as in the Middle East. Using the camels either as pack animals or transportation, Lt. Edward Beale led an expedition from Texas to California, with Ali acting as chief wrangler. Ali's Muslim name was unfamiliar to most nineteenth-century Americans, so someone took to calling him "Hi Jolly" and that's how he was known from then on.

The camels proved their worth, but enough issues arose to make any further military usage impractical, not to mention expensive. Some of the camels were sold to circuses, mining companies, or private individuals, with the rest turned loose in the desert to fend for themselves. Hi Jolly ended up with some of the camels, using them to haul freight. He also served as a government packer and scout. Later he married and had three children. Unable to get any sort of pension for his military service, the Syrian-turned-Arizonan spent the last years of his life prospecting in the Quartzsite area.

When Hi Jolly died at the age of the seventy-four in December 1902, he was buried in the **Quartzsite Cemetery** (West Elsie and Hi Jolly Lane). In 1935 the Arizona Department of Transportation erected a distinctive stone monument over the old camel driver's grave—a pyramid built with layered chunks of variously colored ore topped with the metal silhouette of a camel. A plaque summarizes Hi Jolly's story, noting he had been "Camel driver – Packer – Scout – Over Thirty Years A Faithful Aid To The US Government."

Scottsdale (Maricopa County)

Scottsdale is named for Winfield Scott, an army chaplain who, with his brother George, bought land northeast of Phoenix in 1888 and helped develop it as a church-minded agricultural community. It also attracted tuberculosis sufferers who came west for the dry climate. As Phoenix grew, Scottsdale lost much of its separate identity and evolved into an upscale suburb with art galleries and resorts.

Considered one of the West's top museums, **Western Spirit: Scottsdale's Museum of the West** (3830 North Marshall Way; 480-686-9539) fills a modern two-story building owned by the City of Scottsdale. Managed by a nonprofit organization, the museum showcases Western art and artifacts. As its mission statement declares, this Smithsonian affiliate museum "boldly immerses its guests in the unique story of the Greater Western region, illuminating the past to shape our future."

Show Low (Navajo County)

One of the West's more interestingly named towns, Show Low was dealt its name in a poker game. There are a couple of versions of how that came to be. One is that Corydon Cooley and Marion Clark jointly claimed one hundred thousand acres of well-watered grazing land and then decided in 1876 that one of them had to go. The other story is that the two were neighbors who didn't like being so close to each other. Both accounts have them deciding to let the outcome of a card game determine ownership of the land in question. They had been playing Seven-Up most of the night and both were getting tired. Ready for some sleep no matter the consequences, Clark put it all on the line. "Show low you win," he declared. Cooley flipped a deuce of clubs and said, "Show low it is."

Cooley called his ranch the Showlow, but when Mormon settlers started a town in the area the post office established in 1880 was designated as Show Low. In 1888 Cooley sold his ranch and moved away but the name Show Low stuck.

Begun in 1993 and expanded in 2007, the **Show Low Historical Society Museum** (561 East Deuce of Clubs; 928-532-7115) has six thousand square feet of exhibit space in two buildings that showcases the area's history from the mid-sixteenth century to the present.

What may well be the only monument in America, if not the world, that depicts a poker game, the **Cooley-Clark Card Player Statue** stands in a small park (1025 East Deuce of Clubs) on Show Low's appropriately named main thoroughfare. The first version of the sculpture showing two seated cowboys holding their cards was made of fiberglass and was destroyed by fire in 2016. A year later, a bronze version replaced it.

Springerville (Apache County)

The town that developed around Henry Springer's trading post in the Round Valley had three other names before it was changed to honor Springer in 1876. Timber harvesting and ranching were the town's early economic mainstays, and it has continued as a trade center.

Typically, when someone was killed in the Wild West it involved settling a grudge, a robbery, or self-defense. Sometimes, however, a murder was simply gratuitous. That was the case with **James Hale**, killed December 25, 1886, in front of the Brighton Saloon. Billy Evans and Jack Timberline, newspapers reported, killed Hale because Evans "wanted to see if a bullet would go through a Mormon." The two men never faced trial in the killing, but five months later Evans also learned that a bullet—several actually—could go through *him*. He was killed near Blue River after he stole several horses. What happened to Timberline is not known. A stone marker erected in 2002 stands where the saloon had been on South Mountain Avenue (Business US 180), about three hundred feet south of East Main Street (US 60, US 180, and US 191).

Cast by St. Louis sculptor August Leimbach, a ten-foot-high, five-ton statue is one of a dozen identical monuments to pioneer women erected along the National Old Trails Road from Maryland to California in 1928 and 1929. When the ***Madonna of the Trail*** statue (182 East Main St.) was dedicated on September 28, 1928, the governor spoke, followed by a Missouri judge, then president of the National Old Trails Road Association. His name was Harry S. Truman, future US president. The monument originally stood in front of the local post office but was moved across the street in 1997 and rededicated a year later.

Four museums in one, the **Springerville Heritage Center** (418 East Main St.; 928-333-2656) occupies the old Springerville School. Operated by the White Mountain Historical Society, the center focuses on people and places of the White Mountain area; the **Casa Malpais Archeological Museum** displays Mogollon culture artifacts from the Casa Malpais archeological site in the White Mountains; the **Becker Family Collection** consists of documents and photographs related to the Becker Mercantile Company and the family's role in the development of Apache County; and the **Renee Cushman Art Museum** features fine art collected by Springerville resident and ranch owner Renee Cushman and the three wealthy husbands she had.

Tombstone (Cochise County)

Shrouded with the Wild West's most evocative town name, Tombstone is the Jerusalem for Old West history buffs. Not that Tombstone has the greatest number of historic sites, but thanks to popular culture and the recognition factor of the name Wyatt Earp, Tombstone (though closely followed by Dodge City, Kansas, and Deadwood, South Dakota) is the best known of all the hundreds of historic places west of the Mississippi.

The town's name isn't as sinister as some may think. It's actually owed to army scout **Ed Schieffelin**. While Schieffelin did his job keeping a wary eye out for unfriendly Apaches, he also paid attention to the geology of the area. The Pennsylvanian-turned-Westerner often wandered off by himself looking for gold prospects. He worked out of Camp (later Fort) Huachuca where a soldier warned him that all he was likely to find in the desert would be his tombstone. Instead, the lone-wolf scout discovered a rich deposit of silver-bearing ore at a place called Goose Flat. When he filed a claim, he called it Tombstone. Later he found two other deposits he called the Lucky Cuss and Toughnut. The mining town laid out in 1879 took its name from the first of Schieffelin's claims, Tombstone.

A year later, having made good money, Schieffelin left Arizona for California. Before his death in Oregon in 1897, he had stipulated in his will that he wanted to be buried near Tombstone in his miner's clothing with his pick and canteen. That wish was carried out. His grave (895 Monument Rd.; GPS coordinates: N31° 43.85', W110° 06.20'), marked by a pyramid-shaped piled-stone monument, is located two miles northwest of town.

Tombstone has always been about making money. In its wild early days, that money came from the silver ore and the many business enterprises that catered to miners and the mine operators. Later, after the mining boom had gone bust, Tombstone reinvented itself as a tourist town. Some places catering to the town's many visitors are simply tourist traps, and its claim to be "the most authentic western town left in the US" is overstated, but Tombstone still has much to offer the Wild West history buff.

Explorations are best started at the **Tombstone Visitor Center** (395 East Allen St.; 520-457-3929), which can provide a self-guided walking tour and publications on Tombstone's historic sites and other attractions.

The privately owned **Tombstone Western Heritage Museum** (517 East Fremont St.; 520-457-3800) holds the best collection of Tombstone artifacts and ephemera. Among its holdings are artifacts that once belonged to Wyatt and Virgil Earp, photos of the brothers Earp and Tombstone's more noted outlaws, and original documents dating to the early 1880s.

Another private museum, **Rose Tree Inn Museum** (118 South 4th St.; 520-457-3326) is centered around the world's largest rose tree. While roses and Tombstone seem a strange match, the tree does date to the town's wild days. The museum features vintage furnishing from Tombstone's heyday.

Bird Cage Theater, 1881

The **Bird Cage Theater** (535 East Allen St.; 800-457-3423) opened as the Elite Theater on Christmas Day 1881 and for the next eight years never closed, operating around the clock every day throughout the year. The venue featured a saloon, gambling parlor, theater, and brothel. The popular establishment became the Bird Cage following the release of Broadway composer Arthur J. Lamb's hit, "She's Only a Bird in a Gilded Cage." The *New York Times* reported in 1882 that "the Bird Cage Theatre is the wildest, wickedest night spot between Basin Street and the Barbary Coast." Many of the Wild West's most famous characters spent time here and some of the nation's best-known performers appeared here. Legend has it that a nonstop poker game continued at the Bird Cage until it closed in 1889 when Tombstone went into decline. One of Tombstone's best-preserved buildings, the Bird Cage opened as a tourist attraction in 1934.

Boot Hill Cemetery

Covering a slight hill just northwest of the city, from 1878 to 1884 **Boot Hill** (408 North Fremont St.) was the burial ground for many of Tombstone's early residents, good and bad. But only since the 1920s, when Tombstone civic leaders began to appreciate the tourism value of the historic graveyard, has it been known as Boot Hill. During the town's heyday, it was simply City Cemetery, never Boot Hill. By the time the cemetery was abandoned, it had about 250 graves. Unfortunately for history, many of the original wooden grave markers deteriorated over time. Fortunately, latter-day researchers studying available records have been able to place numerous markers reasonably close to their initial locations. The identity of some occupants of this cemetery were not even known at the time of their burial. The historic cemetery is managed by the City of Tombstone.

Lester Moore was a real person who now lies beneath a grave marker with a fake epitaph. Moore was a Wells Fargo agent killed in 1880. Decades later, when Boot Hill became a tourist destination, he was memorialized with these twelve words: "Here lies Lester Moore, four slugs from a .44. No Les, no more."

Better known as **China Mary**, Sing Choy (1839–1906) became the un-elected leader of the mining town's Chinese community and their liaison with Tombstone's white residents. Well respected by both segments of the population, she supplied Chinese labor and guaranteed their work. She made her money by taking a percentage of the wages they received. That income enabled her to invest in laundries and eateries as well as opium dens and bawdy houses. She also owned a general store. Most of Tombstone showed up for her funeral after she died of a heart attack in 1906. Her grave marker is one of Boot Hill's more prominent ones.

Crystal Palace Saloon

Built in 1879 and originally known as the Golden Eagle Brewing Company, the **Crystal Palace Saloon** (436 East Allen St.; 520-457-3611) is one of the few buildings that survived the fire in 1881 that destroyed much of Tombstone's business district. Owner Benjamin Wehrfritz later added a second floor. US Deputy Marshal Virgil Earp and others officed in the building. The historic red brick building still accommodates a bar and restaurant.

OK Corral

The October 26, 1881, event known as the "Gunfight at the OK Corral" is the Wild West's most famous shoot-out, but the frontier era saw numerous shootings that lasted longer and claimed more victims than the dustup in Tombstone. But thanks to writer Walter Noble Burns and his *Tombstone: An Iliad of the Southwest* (1927), followed by a succession of movies and television shows, the events of that distant day ascended to the figurative Parthenon of Old West history.

Gunplay erupted that afternoon when city marshal Virgil Earp, enlisting the aid of brothers Wyatt and Morgan and Doc Holliday, tried to disarm Billy Clanton and Frank McLaury. It didn't go well. Thirty rounds were fired in as many seconds, leaving Clanton and brothers Frank and Tom McLaury dead and Virgil, Morgan, and Holliday wounded. The shooting occurred in a vacant lot at the southeast corner of Fremont and 3rd Streets, behind the OK Corral. All three of the gunfight fatalities were buried in Boot Hill.

The **OK Corral and Historama** (326 East Allen St.; 520-457-3456) is a privately owned museum and stages daily reenactments of the gunfight.

Tombstone Epitaph

With his printing press in a large canvas tent on Fremont Street, John P. Clum put out the first issue of the *Tombstone Clarion* on May 1, 1880. Perhaps because he was competing with a paper called the *Nugget*, at some point it came to Clum that *Epitaph* was a far more fitting name for a newspaper published in a place called Tombstone. His standing quip was that every Tombstone needed an *Epitaph*. While editor of the newspaper, Clum also served as Tombstone's postmaster and mayor. In 1882, he sold the newspaper and left town.

Since Clum's time, the newspaper has had numerous owners. In 1927 it relocated from a two-story adobe building on Fremont Street to its current location. Harold Love bought the newspaper in the 1960s and it is still owned and operated by the Love family. Fortunately, for the history of the Wild West, the *Epitaph*'s back issues survived all the changes of ownership and constitute one of the better sources of research on Tombstone. Now a National Historic Journalism Site, the ***Tombstone Epitaph*** building (11 South 5th St.; 520-457-2211) includes a museum.

Tombstone Courthouse State Historic Park

When Cochise County was organized in 1881, Tombstone became its county seat. A two-story, red brick Victorian courthouse was built a year later. It continued in use until 1931, when Bisbee took over as county seat. In 1941, the county conveyed the twelve-thousand-square-foot building to the City of Tombstone, which went on to lease it to the Tombstone Restoration Commission. That group restored the first floor and opened it to the public in 1956. The courthouse became the centerpiece of Arizona's first state park, the **Tombstone Courthouse State Historic Park** (223 East Toughnut St.; 520-457-3311), in 1959. Here, visitors will find exhibits and artifacts that capture one of Arizona's most notorious chapters.

Wyatt Earp House

A small adobe house that may once have been the home of Wyatt Earp was restored a few years ago. Privately owned, the old house (102 East Fremont St.; 520-457-3111) now serves as a small art gallery. In the yard, surrounded by an iron fence, is a bronze statue of Earp by artist Tim Trask. Historians continue to debate whether Wyatt and his wife Mattie ever actually lived here, but the sculpture outside ensures its status as an Earp-related attraction.

How Tombstone Celebrated Washington's Birthday in 1884

The second act in the 1883 **Bisbee Massacre** (see Bisbee) occurred in Tombstone on February 22, 1884. Concerned that the man who planned the Bisbee robbery might live to a ripe old age while serving his life sentence at the territorial prison in Yuma, a mob of miners armed themselves and appointed a delegation of seven to remove John Heath from the county lockup—and civilized society. With no harm done to the sheriff or his deputies, the mob took Heath from the jail and marched the prisoner down aptly named Toughnut Street for the final adjudication of his case.

Heath protested that they were about to hang an innocent man, but his plea left the mob unmoved. Finally accepting his fate, Heath did have one favor to ask, "that you will not mutilate my body by shooting into it after I am hung." That seemed reasonable enough. The ex-officio executioners were even kind enough to tie Heath's handkerchief around his eyes at his request. But the humanity ended there. Once the rope had been placed around his neck, several members of the mob hoisted Heath from the crossbar of a telegraph pole, and he slowly strangled as they looked on approvingly.

After Heath quit kicking, a member of the group tacked to the pole a placard that read:

> JOHN HEITH [sic]
> Was hanged to this pole by the
> CITIZENS OF COCHISE COUNTY
> for participating in the Bisbee massacre
> as a proved accessory
> AT 8:00 A.M., FEBRUARY 22, 1884
> (Washington's Birthday)
> ADVANCE ARIZONA!
> The lynching occurred at 1st and Toughnut Streets.

Legal Hangings Were Not Always Well Executed

On March 28, 1884, just over a month after the lynching of John Heath, the five men sentenced to death for their role in the Bisbee Massacre were afforded a legal hanging. Unfortunately for them, legal did not always mean well executed. When Sheriff Jerome Ward sprung the trap beneath them, he assumed the fall would break their necks. But that happened for only one of them; the other four strangled. A reconstruction of the gallows stands behind the courthouse in **Tombstone Courthouse State Historic Park** (223 East Toughnut St.; 520-457-3311).

Tucson (Pima County)

European settlement in the area that would become Tucson began with the establishment of a Spanish mission on the Santa Cruz River in the 1700s, followed by the building of a presidio to protect the mission. Construction of **San Xavier Mission** (1950 West San Xavier Rd.; 520-294-2624) began in 1783 and continued until 1797. It is the oldest European structure in Arizona and still operates as a Catholic church. The mission has interpretive historical exhibits and is open to the public.

Following the Republic of Mexico's independence from Spain in 1821, Tucson continued as a small Mexican settlement. With completion of the Gadsden Purchase in 1854, Tucson became an American community. Following the opening of the Butterfield Overland Mail Company, Tucson was a stagecoach stop. After the Civil War, Tucson developed as a trade center and from 1867 to 1877 was the territorial capital. Despite having lost the capital, Tucson grew rapidly after completion of the Southern Pacific Railroad to that point in 1880. Eleven years later it became the home of the University of Arizona and in the twenty-first century is Arizona's second-largest city.

John Charles Fremont, the so-called Great Pathfinder, was Arizona's first territorial governor. The **Sosa-Carrillo-Fremont House** (151 South Granada Ave.; 520-622-0956), the 1870-vintage adobe house where he lived while serving that role, was added to the National Register of Historic Places in 1971. Today it is operated as a museum by the Arizona Historical Society.

The US Army established Camp Lowell in 1866 near Tucson's downtown. In 1873, the military relocated to a site near the Rillito River, seven miles out of town. Soon designated a fort, the post continued in operation through the long Apache Wars until its abandonment in early 1891. With no maintenance, Fort Lowell's adobe buildings deteriorated rapidly. Following a succession of government, private, and nonprofit landowners, most evidence of the post had disappeared by the 1930s. The Arizona Historical Society restored what remained of the post commander's residence in 1963 and opened it as a museum at what is now **Fort Lowell Park** (2900 North Craycroft Rd.; 520-885-3832). Portions of the post hospital still stand, its adobe walls protected from heavy rain by an open-sided shelter. In addition to older historical markers, interpretive signs relate the fort's history. In 1991 a fourteen-foot bronze statue of a cavalry bugler astride an alert horse, ***Chief Trumpeter***, was dedicated at the twenty-nine-acre site. A historical marker in the southwest corner of **Armory Park** (221 South Sixth Ave.) at the site of Camp Lowell details the history of the original post.

Dead at the Depot

Trouble hissed to a stop at the Tucson depot on the evening of March 20, 1882, when the westbound Southern Pacific passenger train arrived. On board were Virgil Earp and his wife on their way to California to avoid possible retribution stemming from the shoot-out near the OK Corral the previous October in Tombstone. Also on the train were Virgil's younger brothers Wyatt and Warren, Wyatt's pal Doc Holliday, "Turkey Creek" Jack Johnson, and Sherman McMaster. All of them, and additional recruits, would take part in what became known as the **Vendetta Ride**—the series of killings attributed to Earp and his men of some of those responsible for the murder of his brother Morgan at the OK Corral. Wyatt's intention on this trip was to protect Virgil and his wife until they could get out of Arizona Territory. The Earps were not being unduly cautious.

When Virgil and his wife returned to their Pullman car after having supper at the nearby Porter's Hotel, Wyatt saw two men with rifles running toward the train. Wyatt rushed to confront the men, one of whom was Frank Stillwell, the man who had killed Morgan Earp. Wyatt charged toward Stillwell, who tried to grab his double-barreled shotgun. In the process, as Wyatt later told an interviewer, "I let go with both barrels, and he tumbled dead at my feet." Wyatt, Warren, Holliday, Johnson, and McMaster were all considered accomplices and charged with murder, but by April 1882, Earp was gone from Arizona and two other men connected with Morgan Earp's murder were dead.

The original Southern Pacific depot, along with Porter's Hotel, were razed prior to the construction of the present depot (414 Toole Ave.) in 1907. In 1941, and again in 2004, the depot was substantially remodeled. It remains in use as Tucson's Amtrak station.

Frank Stillwell is buried in an unmarked grave at **Evergreen Cemetery** (3015 North Oracle Rd.; 520-257-4831).

A **bronze statue of Wyatt Earp and Doc Holliday** stands on the spot where Earp killed Stillwell. The statue, done by artist Dan Bates, was dedicated March 20, 2005—the 123rd anniversary of the shooting and the 125th anniversary of the arrival of Tucson's first train.

Opened in 2004, the **Southern Arizona Transportation Museum** (414 North Toole Ave.; 520-623-2223) occupies a small building adjacent to the depot originally used by the Southern Pacific for record storage. The museum explores the impact the 1880 arrival of the nation's second transcontinental railroad had on the then small village of Tucson.

Next to the museum, under a protective metal canopy, stands **Southern Pacific Locomotive 1623**, a freight train engine manufactured in 1900 and used for the next fifty-five years. The locomotive "starred" in the 1956 film *Oklahoma*.

Arizona did not become a state until 1912, but it has had an organization dedicated to its history since 1864 when the First Territorial legislature established the Arizona Historical Society. The society's **Arizona History Museum** (949 East 2nd St.; 520-628-5774) covers the Arizona story from the days of Spanish colonization forward, including its American Indian conflicts and mining era. In addition to interpretive exhibits and artifacts, the society maintains a research library and archive in the building.

Established in 1893, the **Arizona State Museum** (1013 East University Blvd.; 520-621-6302) has an extensive collection of Southwestern American Indian artifacts representing thirteen thousand years of history. The largest anthropological research museum in the Southwest, the museum is part of the University of Arizona.

The **Downtown History Museum** (140 North Stone Ave.; 520-770-1473) also is operated by the Arizona Historical Society. Housed in the old Wells Fargo Bank building, its exhibits and artifacts relate Tucson's history from its origin as a Spanish mission and presidio up to the twentieth century.

Old Tucson

With the passage of time, even faux history becomes real history. That's the case with **Old Tucson**, a Wild West tourist attraction dating to 1939. On property owned by Pima County, Columbia

Pictures built a fifty-building Hollywood version of 1860s Tucson for the movie *Arizona*. Released the following year, the film starred Jean Arthur and William Holden. By then, the set had become a modern-day ghost town that did not see further use until 1945, when a second movie was shot there. From then on, Old Tucson served as the backdrop for scores of other productions starring some of screen land's biggest names, including John Wayne, Lee Marvin, Robert Mitchum, Gregory Peck, Paul Newman, and Clint Eastwood.

In 1947, when former Texas Ranger Jeff Milton died at eighty-five, the old lawman's ashes were scattered at the movie set. In 1959, at the peak of the golden era of TV Westerns, Robert Shelton leased the property from Pima County and transformed Old Tucson into a tourist attraction. With more period structures and a state-of-the-art sound stage added in 1968, the site continued as a popular movie set.

Fire ravaged many a real Wild West town and that's what happened to Old Tucson on a windy day in 1995. Most of the town's original buildings were destroyed in the blaze, which proved to be the work of an arsonist. A new Old Tucson (201 Kinney Rd.; 520-883-0100) arose, and by the second decade of the twenty-first century, more than four hundred movies, TV shows, or commercials had been shot there.

The 360-acre theme park lies beneath the Tucson Mountains near Saguaro National Park just west of the city.

Tubac (Santa Cruz County)

For centuries, the O'odham people (later known as the Pima) had lived in the fertile, mountain-flanked valley of the Santa Cruz River in what is now southern Arizona. Then the Spanish came.

That happened in 1691 with the opening of Mission San Cayetano de Tumacacori by a European nation intent on expanding its empire and Christianizing American Indians. Sixty years later, chaffing at the diminishment of their old lifeways, the Pima revolted against the Spanish, and Spain responded militarily. In 1752, about four miles from the mission, soldiers established Presidio San Ignacio de Tubac and garrisoned it until 1776, when a presidio was built near what is now Tucson. The Tubac presidio was reestablished in 1787 and continued as a Spanish outpost until Mexico violently separated itself from Spain in 1821. By the 1840s, the settlement was abandoned due to constant raiding by Apaches. Tubac came back to life when the US gained control of the area through the Gadsden Purchase of 1853. Arizona pioneer Charles Poston based his mining operations in Tubac in 1856 and for a time it thrived, but when Tucson got rail service, the old town quickly declined. In the late 1940s Tubac came back to life as an artist's colony.

The partially restored mission is now the centerpiece of the **Tumacacori National Historical Park** (1891 East Frontage Rd. off I-19; 520-377-5060). A visitor center and museum interpret the area's long history. Ruins of the old presidio are preserved at **Tubac Presidio State Historic Park** (1 Burruel St.; 520-398-2252). The park also has a museum focused on Tubac as a cultural crossroads.

Wickenburg (Mariposa County)

German-born Henry Wickenburg found gold near the Hassayampa River in 1863. The site became the Vulture Mine, which would produce more than $30 million in gold. The town that developed near the mine was named for the man whose discovery set off the boom.

As for Henry Wickenburg, he may have found gold, but not lasting prosperity. Despondent over his financial condition, the eighty-five-year-old shot himself on May 14, 1905. Listed on the National Register of Historic Places, the restored **Henry Wickenburg House** (225 South Washington St.) is owned by the Wickenburg Historical Preservation Society and is used as a museum dedicated to local history. Wickenburg is buried in **Henry Wickenburg Pioneer Cemetery** (315 Sylvan Rd.; 928-684-5603), also maintained by the society.

Wild West Whodunit

Apache Indians attacked the Wickenburg to Ehrenburg stagecoach on November 5, 1871, killing the driver and five passengers. At least that's what the two survivors, an army paymaster named William Krueger and a bawdy house madam named Mollie Shepherd, claimed. But the only two things missing from the stage were the cash in its strongbox and a shovel. Since horses and tack meant more to American Indians than money, suspicion turned on Krueger and Shepherd. But nothing could be proven and what happened that day remains a mystery. The Arizona Highway Department in 1937 placed a fieldstone monument nine miles west of Wickenburg at the site of what came to be known as the **Wickenburg Massacre**. Topped by a metal silhouette of a running stagecoach, the marker stands near the intersection of US 60 and Flying E Ranch Road (GPS coordinates: N33° 57.79', W112° 47.83').

Jail Tree

Why waste tax dollars building a jail when felons and miscreants could simply be chained to a mesquite tree? Prisoners sometimes sweltered in the desert sun and shivered in the cold night air for up to five days before being transferred to a more traditional calaboose in Phoenix. Wickenburg finally constructed a real jail in 1890.

The tree, an estimated two centuries old, still stands in a parking lot at the corner of East Wickenburg Way and North Tegner in Wickenburg, and a marker tells the story of the tree. Sitting nearby is a lifelike sculpture of a forlorn prisoner in convict stripes with a chain locked around an ankle and toes sticking out of his socks.

A Smithsonian affiliate, the **Desert Caballeros Western Museum** (21 North Frontier St.; 928-684-2272) curates an extensive photo collection, with images dating to the 1880s, as well as an oral history and art collection.

Willcox (Cochise County)

Founded as a railroad town in 1880, Willcox became a major cattle shipping point and, like so many other southwestern towns, acquired the reputation as a great place for undertakers. Willcox fell a bit short of Tombstone in that category, but during the town's heyday gunplay was not unknown.

The **Cochise Regional Visitor Center** (101 South Railroad Ave.; 520-384-4271) is operated by the Willcox Chamber of Commerce and Agriculture. The center has brochures and guides related to southeastern Arizona and a self-guided walking tour of historic downtown Willcox.

The **Chiricahua Regional Museum** (127 East Maley St.; 520-384-3971) focuses on area history.

The **Rex Allen Museum** (150 North Railroad Ave.; 520-384-4583) documents the life and accomplishments of the noted cowboy actor and singer, Rex Allen (1920–1999), who grew up on a ranch outside Willcox.

The two-story, 1881-vintage **Southern Pacific Railroad Depot** (101 South Railroad Ave.) houses the city's administrative offices, but there's a railroad interpretive display in the lobby. It is the only surviving depot built during the construction of the nation's second transcontinental railroad.

Bullets for a Bully

Johnnie Boyett, as he was known locally, apparently was not much of a shot, but no one could fault his perseverance. In the early morning hours of July 6, 1900, bad blood between Boyett and Warren Baxter Earp—Wyatt Earp's querulous little brother—boiled over to the shedding of real blood when Boyett fired twice at Earp inside the Headquarters Saloon, and missed. Boyett got off two more shots at Wyatt's brother, and missed again. Finally, the fifth time Boyett pulled the trigger, the bullet hit Warren beneath his left collar bone and ranged down into his heart. The forty-five-year-old Earp, though he earlier had intimated that he was "fixed" (armed with a pistol), had made the mistake of taking a knife to a gunfight.

Despite workmanlike local newspaper coverage, more sensational, out-of-state papers turned the shooting into a conspiracy tracing back to the Tombstone troubles nearly two decades earlier. Later-day writers also have taken their shot at finding the "real" reason behind the pistol affray. Theorists posited that someone paid Boyett to assassinate the younger if irascible Earp. The legend also arose that Wyatt Earp hired someone to kill Boyett or the person who allegedly retained his services. Another tale has brother Virgil Earp coming to town to avenge his younger brother's killing. If either were the case, the effort failed. Boyett died of natural causes back in his native Texas in 1919. All those stories make for fun reading, but the truth is both obvious and simple: Alcohol having suppressed their better judgment, Earp and Boyett got into a barroom fight and Boyett won even if it took him five shots. Some say jealously over a local prostitute may have played a role in their enmity, but the shooting was just another Wild West difficulty, not a murder-for-hire.

The Headquarters Saloon stood at the corner of Railroad and East Maley Streets. While that building was destroyed by fire in 1945, visitors can still get a drink in the same spot at the **Flying Leap Vineyard and Distillery** (100 North Railroad St.).

Earp was buried in then-unnamed Willcox cemetery the afternoon of the day he died. By the time the name Earp had become legendary, no one remembered exactly where in the cemetery Warren had been laid to rest. A later-day tombstone now stands in what is now known as **Willcox Pioneer Cemetery** (454 North 3rd Ave.), but only in the vicinity of Earp's final resting place. Wherever his bones repose, he does have the distinction of being the only Earp brother buried in the territory-turned-state where they became famous.

Ringo

A basic forensic tool until the 1970s, the so-called paraffin test—a way to detect the presence of gunpowder residue on skin—was first used in 1933. That made it roughly a half-century too late to shed light on one of the Wild West's most compelling mysteries: Did **John Peters Ringo** commit suicide or was he murdered?

A player in Texas's bloody Mason County War, Ringo ended up in Arizona and became associated with the Cowboys, the loose-knit group of rustlers and robbers who operated in Cochise and Pima Counties in the 1880s. On July 13, 1882, someone found Ringo dead, sitting under a tree with his revolver in his hand. The coroner ruled the single gunshot wound to his head as self-inflicted, which would be consistent with his known heavy drinking and bouts of depression. But from that day forward, conspiracy theorists have argued that he was killed, the crime scene staged to make his death look like a suicide. Had the simple chemical process of using diphenylamine to detect the presence of nitrate on skin been available to law enforcement back then, history would know for sure, one way or the other. The test is susceptible to false positives and has since been replaced by a gunshot residue test using scanning electron microscopes, but in the Ringo case it would have been better than nothing. There's one incontrovertible thing about John Peters Ringo—he had a memorable last name that guaranteed his place in Wild West history.

Ringo's grave lies in the Chiricahua Mountains, part of the Coronado National Forest about thirty miles southeast of Willcox. From Willcox, take State Highway 186 southeast until it becomes State Highway 181. Roughly twelve miles from this point, turn right on Turkey Creek Road and continue five miles (GPS coordinates: N31° 51.96', W109° 25.13').

A historical marker placed by the Cochise Archaeological and Historical Society and the Arizona Historical Society stands just behind the outlaw's white stone grave marker. Though the grave is on the Jerry Sanders Ranch, the owner has established a parking lot with a trail to the site. Visitors are allowed from 8 a.m. to 6 p.m. daily.

Williams (Coconino County)

Bill Williams may have had a common name, but the tall, red-headed mountain man was uncommonly good at scouting, trailblazing, fur-trapping, shooting, drinking, running, and living a solitary life. But on March 21, 1849, neither his marksmanship nor fleet-footedness could save him from a Ute war party he ran into on the upper reaches of the Rio Grande in what is now Colorado.

When a few settlers put down roots in future Coconino County in 1876, someone decided that the highest mountain in the area should be named Bill Williams Mountain to honor the slain mountain man. When a town developed a few miles north of the peak, it became Williams. A name was about all the community had until 1882 when the Atlantic and Pacific Railroad came through. In 1901 the Santa Fe Railroad began running from Williams to the South Rim of the Grand Canyon and the town grew as a tourist waypoint billing itself as the Gateway to the Grand Canyon.

The **Williams Visitor Center** (200 West Railroad Ave.; 928-635-4061) is a good place to start exploring the area. The **Williams Historic Business District**, listed on the National Register of Historic Places, includes twenty-six buildings dating from the late nineteenth or early twentieth centuries. The two oldest structures reflect Williamson's early days as a rowdy railroad town—the circa-1893 **Cabinet Saloon** (121 West Railroad Ave.) and the circa-1897 two-story **Tetzlaf Building** (137 West Railroad Ave.), which served as a bordello, a saloon, a gambling venue, and an opium den. Despite its questionable early-day occupants, the brick building is credited with having served in the early 1900s as a firewall during two devastating blazes along Saloon Row that could have spread to the rest of downtown.

Built by the Santa Fe Railroad in 1908, the **Williams Depot** (233 Grand Canyon Blvd.; 928-635-4010) is the southern terminus of the Grand Canyon Railway, which runs a daily passenger train from Williams to the Grand Canyon's South Rim (see Globe). The train station fell into disrepair after the Santa Fe discontinued passenger service in 1968 but was restored when the Grand Canyon Railway once again started carrying people to the canyon in 1989.

Winslow (Navajo County)

Like so many Old West towns, Winslow was born of the railroad, but the Hopi and Navajo people and their Puebloan ancestors had been living in northern Arizona for centuries before the Atlantic and Pacific Railroad surveyed a townsite here in 1880. Named in honor of Atlantic and Pacific president Robert Winslow, the town became a transportation crossroads.

Steam locomotives reigned as the fastest machines of the age, but determining the route they would take across the continent took decades. In 1853 US Army Lt. Amiel W. Whipple passed through the area while mapping a potential east-west rail route along the thirty-fifth parallel. Four years later, Lt. Edward F. Beale blazed a wagon road along the route. The trail Beale blazed, the predecessor of the famed Route 66, passed through what became Winslow.

The first Euro-Americans to settle the area were Mormons, who in 1876 built an adobe fort and established the town of Brigham City a mile north of future Winslow. Flood and drought led to the abandonment of the community, but with the arrival of the railroad the new town of Winslow flourished as a ranching and American Indian trading post center. When the Santa Fe Railroad became the town's second carrier, the community saw more growth. And thanks to the Santa Fe, which in 1929 built the Pueblo-style La Posada Hotel near its tracks, Winslow evolved as a tourist destination.

Homolovi State Park (State Highway 87, one and three-tenths miles north of I-40 exit 257; 928-289-4106) focuses on the area's Hopi culture. The Hopi Reservation is an hour's drive from Winslow.

Though closed for years, the **La Posada Hotel** (303 East 2nd St.; 928-289-4366) has been restored and once again is accommodating travelers.

The **Old Trails Museum** (212 North Kinsley Ave.; 928-289-5861), with a focus of Winslow as a longtime transportation crossroads, explores the history and culture of the town and region.

Decades after the taming of the West, in 1972 seven words in the classic rock song "Take It Easy" by the Eagles led to Winslow's most-visited attraction: The downtown intersection of old Route 66 and North Kinsley Ave. Here, at what since 1999 has been **Standing on the Corner Park**, tens of thousands of tourists annually pose for photos of themselves while . . . well, you know the rest.

Young (Gila County)

The small community of Young, northwest of Globe, was not named in honor of all the people who died young in the area around it, but that would have been fitting. Now surrounded by the Tonto National Forest, Young stood at ground zero during one of the Wild West's bloodiest—if little-known—feuds.

The so-called **Pleasant Valley War** resulted in an extraordinarily high mortality rate from 1883 to 1892. Legend has it that thirty to fifty people died during the unpleasantness, but the most recent scholarly study of the feud has the provable body count at eighteen. To put either number into perspective, only about 250 people lived in the 7,600-acre Pleasant Valley at the time. In addition to those killed, new research shows that several others suffered permanent disabilities during the violence. Beyond that, other participants had to deal with depression and other mental health issues. Some ended up killing themselves. The circumstances leading to the conflict are complicated and highly nuanced, but essentially it was a range war pitting cattlemen (James Stinson and his hirelings along with Tom Graham and his family) versus sheep ranchers (the Tewksbury family). The outbreak of violence, which eventually pulled in other factions and law enforcement, claimed more than twice the lives lost in the much more famous gunfight near the OK Corral and its bloody aftermath.

Somewhat fittingly, considering all the funerals associated with the Pleasant Valley War, the **Pleasant Valley Museum** (48382 State

Highway 288; 928-462-7847) is housed in a former church built in 1925. The Pleasant Valley Historical Society was given the building in 1993 when the congregation moved to a new place of worship. A historical marker summarizing the war stands outside the museum.

The **Young Cemetery** (48412 State Highway 288), located two miles east of Young, has 339 recorded graves, six of them being the final resting place of Pleasant Valley War casualties. Five other victims are buried in the vicinity of Young, but the graves are either on private property or in an extremely remote area in the Tonto National Forest.

The grave of a Navajo sheepherder killed by Tom Graham during the war lies just outside Young, in the Tonto National Forest. Shortly before reaching Young on Forest Road 512, the road becomes Arizona 288. Turn right off 288 on Forest Road 200 and follow one mile. The grave is under a tree just down an embankment from the road.

Yuma (Yuma County)

First known as Colorado City, and then Arizona City, Yuma developed on the Colorado River's east bank just below its confluence with the Gila River. The discovery of gold in California lured multiple thousands westward, and future Yuma became a busy crossing point with several commercial ferries doing a brisk business. After the Gadsden Purchase added the area to US territory, despite periodic devastating floods on the Colorado, Yuma grew as a transportation and supply center. Goods arriving on steamboats coming up the Colorado from the Gulf of California were distributed by twenty-mule-team freight wagons across the Southwest.

From 1864 to 1883 the army maintained a quartermaster depot at Yuma, shipping supplies to military posts in Arizona, Nevada, Utah, New Mexico, and far west Texas. Yuma's status as a riverboat town faded after the railroad arrived in 1877, but after the army left, the US Weather Service, US Customs Service, and Federal Bureau of Reclamation continued to use the facility. Here engineers oversaw the construction of dams to prevent floods, generate power, and provide irrigation water. The City of Yuma acquired the old military post and surrounding property in 1957 and later conveyed it to the State of Arizona, which opened the site as **Colorado River State Historic Park** (201 North 4th Ave.; 928-783-0071) in 1997. Five of the original military structures still stand and four contain historical exhibits. The park visitor center also has interpretive displays.

Territorial Prison

The Arizona Territorial Prison at Yuma generally gets a bad rap in print and on screen. It was said to be a burning-hot hellhole, impossible to endure and even more impossible to escape. Even if an inmate managed to break out, the nearby Colorado River had pockets of quicksand along its banks. Someone making it beyond the river next had to contend with a desert landscape. Getting over the wall and making it very far was not easy, but also not impossible.

Despite its reputation, in truth, the facility was state-of-the-art for its time. Amenities included electricity, ventilation, two bathtubs, three showers, and a library with two thousand books—the largest in Arizona at the time. The facility even had a prison band. On the other hand, no prison is a resort.

The first seven inmates entered the prison on July 1,1876, and had the honor of being locked into cells they had built themselves. During the prison's thirty-three years of operation, 3,069 prisoners (including twenty-nine women) lived within its walls. Of those, despite the prison's remote location, twenty-six prisoners managed to escape and were never captured.

One of the prisoners who broke out was Joe Boot, erstwhile lover of lady bandit Pearl Hart, who also did time at the prison. She was released after serving eighteen months of her five-year sentence. Following a brief, unsuccessful attempt to put on a traveling stage show based on her short career as a stage robber, she soon disappeared into history (see Globe).

Other famous inmates included "Buckskin" Frank Leslie and Barney Riggs. Leslie was an Indian scout, prospector, and gunfighter who claimed to have killed fourteen people. One person he for sure did murder was his common-law wife, Mollie Bradshaw. The crime resulted in a twenty-five-year prison sentence, but Leslie gained parole after only seven years. Riggs was sent to the prison on a life sentence for killing a man who had been fooling around with his wife. When a group of prisoners tried to escape in October 1887, resulting in several deaths, Riggs saved the prison superintendent's life. That netted him a full pardon, a second chance that lasted fifteen years. Back in his native Texas, Riggs was shot and killed by Buck Chadborne in Fort Stockton in 1902.

After its closure, the old prison was used as a high school. By 1939, during the Great Depression, it served unofficially as free housing for vagrants. A year later, the City of Yuma took over the property and with New Deal funds built a museum on the site of the old mess hall. In 1961 the State of Arizona developed the site as the **Yuma Territorial Prison State Historical Park** (220 Prison Hill Rd.; 928-783-4771).

The **Yuma Territorial Prison Cemetery** (50 Prison Hill Rd.) is the burial place for 104 of the 111 inmates who died while serving time at Yuma. Tuberculosis was the leading cause of death. A state historical marker stands at the site.

The **Sanguinetti House Museum and Gardens** (240 South Madison Ave.; 928-782-1841) is the restored adobe home of E.F. Sanguinetti, longtime businessman known as the "Merchant Prince of Yuma."

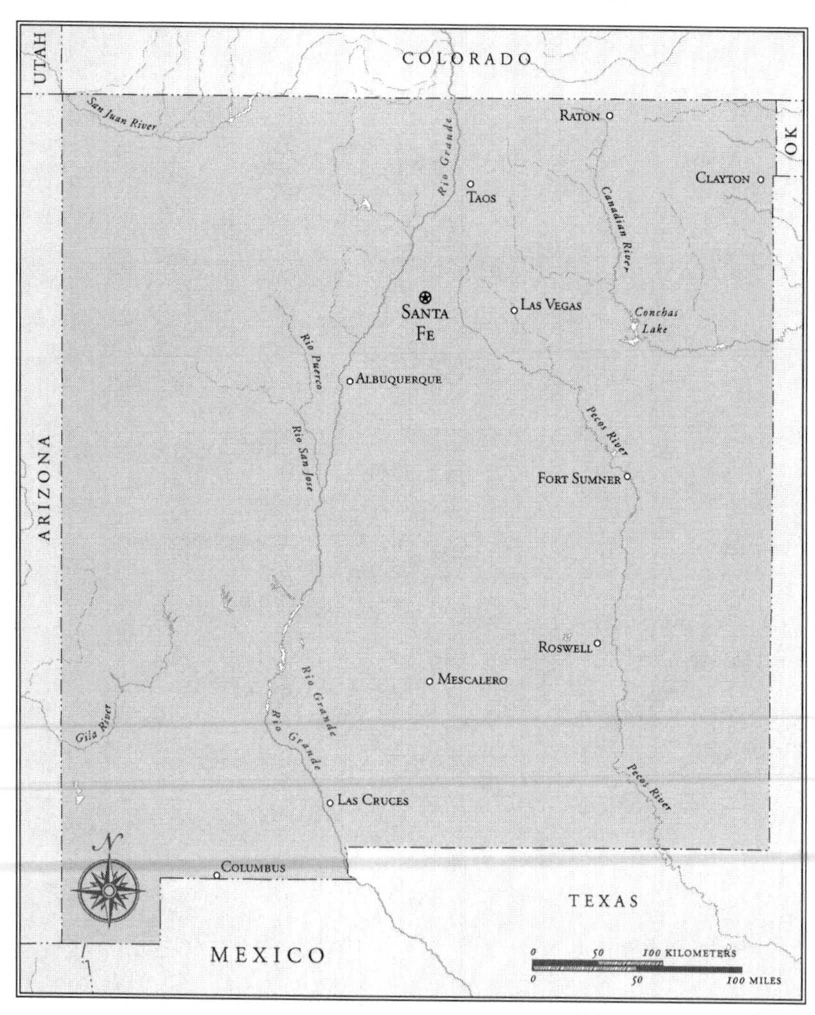
UTAH
COLORADO
OK
ARIZONA
TEXAS
MEXICO
San Juan River
Rio Grande
Raton
Taos
Clayton
Canadian River
Santa Fe
Las Vegas
Conchas Lake
Rio Puerco
Albuquerque
Rio San Jose
Pecos River
Fort Sumner
Roswell
Mescalero
Rio Grande
Rio Grande
Gila River
Las Cruces
Pecos River
Columbus
N
0 50 100 KILOMETERS
0 50 100 MILES

NEW MEXICO

Alamogordo (Otero County)

Founded in 1898 when the El Paso and Northeastern Railroad extended across New Mexico Territory, Alamogordo is the county seat and the largest city in the vast Tularosa Basin. For a late nineteenth century town, a lot of history happened around it.

Oliver Milton Lee

A fellow who makes a watch fob out of a bullet extracted from a dead man bears watching. That man was cattleman, suspected rustler, erstwhile lawman, successful businessman, and longtime New Mexican politician **Oliver Lee** (1865–1941). The piece of lead Lee kept with him came from the body of one of his closest friends, killed by another cattleman in a time and place where a life could be worth less than a stolen steer and certainly cheaper than title to well-watered grassland.

Driving a herd of horses, nineteen-year-old Lee and his older half-brother Perry Altman came to New Mexico Territory from Texas in 1884. They liked what they saw in the Tularosa Basin, a huge expanse bordered on the east by the Sacramento Mountains and on the west by the San Andreas and Oscura Mountains.

The following year the brothers returned to Texas and brought their mother. Lee and Altman hired out as cowboys until 1893 when Lee bought land in Dog Canyon, a long gash in the flank of the Sacramento Mountains about twelve miles south of present Alamogordo, and established a ranch. As his holdings grew, so did his power—and his ruthlessness. He didn't smoke, drink, or use harsh language, but he was a fine shot.

The murder of his old friend and in-law George Washington McDonald in 1888, followed by Lee's bloody reprisal, triggered a feud that evolved into a war for land control and political dominance in southeastern New Mexico that continued for years. The peak of Lee's suspected criminality came in 1896 when he and two of his ranch hands were charged with the murder of a state prosecutor and his young son (see Las Cruces). In one of the Wild West's more sensational murder trials, a jury acquitted Lee and his co-defendants. But in the court of public opinion almost everyone but his family and closest allies considered him guilty.

However, Lee's legacy wasn't all bad. He played a significant role in the creation of Otero County and in attracting the railroad line that brought the development of Alamogordo in 1898.

Lee died in 1941 and is buried in Alamogordo's **Monte Vista Cemetery** (1590 East 1st St.; 575-439-4350).

Oliver Lee may be the only man implicated in a murder—actually, three and possibly four—with a state park named in his honor. The centerpiece of the 640-acre park **Oliver Lee Memorial State Park** (409 Dog Canyon Rd.; 575-437-8284) is Lee's restored Dog Canyon adobe ranch house. After Lee sold the ranch in 1907 it went through a series of owners before becoming part of the White Sands National Monument in 1939. New Mexico began developing the former ranch into a park in 1980, acquiring title to the land from the federal government in 1983 and an additional tract in 1998. The old ranch house stood in ruins until restored by the state. It is accessible only through guided tours. A visitor center has exhibits on the canyon's geologic and cultural history.

Au revoir, Frenchy

Emigrating to New Mexico Territory in the mid-1880s, French-born **Francois-Jean (Frenchy) Rochas** (1843–1894) settled at the mouth of Dog Canyon nearly a decade before Oliver Lee. Living in a small, two-room rock and adobe cabin he built, he ran four hundred head of cattle, owned six horses, and planned to start an orchard. With water diverted from a spring farther up the canyon, he hoped to grow olives, figs, apples, cherries, plums, and peaches.

In 1893, when Lee established his ranch headquarters on the flats about a mile and a half to the south, he and Rochas put in a wooden dam and built a concrete flume that carried water to irrigation ditches that provided ample water for both places. But the Frenchman did not live to enjoy the literal fruits of his labor. In late December 1894, he was found dead in his blood-soaked bed, a bullet hole in his chest. Despite a not-yet-mailed set of letters to family members and a friend he had written only days before telling them that he intended to file a claim on the land he'd been squatting on, a coroner's jury ruled his death a suicide. The mystery surrounding the circumstance of his violent death endures, though Lee—having already killed a man to revenge the slaying of his friend George McDonald—is an obvious suspect, especially since he was able to take over Rochas's land. Area cattlemen who owed Rochas money also came under suspicion.

Now part of Oliver Lee Memorial State Park (409 Dog Canyon Rd.; 575-437-8284), the partially restored **Rochas Cabin** lies just west of the visitor center, easily reached over a short trail. The dry-laid stonewalls Rochas built to corral his livestock and delineate his orchard still stand nearby. An archeological dig at the site in 1977 and 1978 yielded a rich inventory of artifacts dating to the time of the Frenchman's occupation, and a sampling is displayed at the visitor center. Though known to have been buried in **Our Lady of the Light Catholic Cemetery** (15 Kearney St., La Luz) Frenchy Rocha's grave was reported lost in 1966. A gray granite gravestone was later set in the vicinity of where his grave was thought to be.

Albert Fall

Albert B. Fall, the attorney and politician who successfully defended Oliver Lee and Jim Gilliland in their trial for the murder of Albert Jennings Fountain (see Hillsboro and Las Cruces), had a house in Alamogordo and a large ranch in the Tularosa Basin he called the Three Rivers Ranch. After serving in the New Mexico legislature and the US Senate, Fall reached the pinnacle of his career in 1921 when President Warren G. Harding appointed him secretary of the interior.

Rather than faithfully serving his country, however, Fall used his cabinet post to facilitate his own enrichment. He was successful until 1929 when he was caught and convicted of accepting bribes totaling $385,000. He had helped his cronies in the oil business gain access to the naval reserves at Teapot Dome, Wyoming. The man who had risen from schoolteacher to US senator to cabinet member was fined $100,000 and sentenced to a year in prison. He lost what favorable reputation he had, most of his money, and his Three Rivers Ranch north of Ruidoso, New Mexico. The only break he got afterward came when he moved to El Paso, where he died in his sleep at age eighty-six in 1944.

Built around 1905, the two-story, Colonial Revival–style house (1205 Michigan Ave.) the Fall family occupied in the early 1900s has four bedrooms and three baths. Included in the Tularosa Basin Historical Society's self-guided tour of Alamogordo historic homes, the house is privately owned but can be viewed from the street.

Housed in a Pueblo Revival–style building constructed by the federal Works Progress Administration in 1938, the **Tularosa Basin Museum** (1004 North White Sands Blvd.; 575-434-4438) focuses on the basin's cultural history; the story of Alamogordo; and the nearby villages of Tularosa, La Luz, and Blazer's Mill.

Albuquerque (Bernalillo County)

Founded along the Rio Grande west of the Sandia Mountains as a Spanish colonial villa in 1706, Albuquerque developed around a central plaza that came to be known as Old Town. Later the Mexican flag flew over the town and though Anglos traveling the Santa Fe Trail began arriving earlier, Albuquerque did not fall under US control until the Mexican War of 1846 to 1848. The arrival of the Santa Fe Railroad, which in 1880 built a depot two miles from the plaza, resulted in the creation of a new town, now downtown Albuquerque. The railroad also stimulated a boom and the accompanying rowdiness common throughout the Old West. Old Town lapsed into decline until the 1930s when civic leaders realized Albuquerque could capitalize on its long history and the area began to redevelop as a tourist attraction. Despite its name, today **Old Town** is a mixture of modern and historic structures including museums, shops, art galleries, and eateries. Five structures in Old Town are listed on the National Register of Historic Places.

Covering almost a square mile, Old Town is bordered by Rio Grande Boulevard, Mountain Road, 19th Street, and Central Boulevard. The **Albuquerque Visitor Information Center** (522 Romero St. NW; 800-284-2282) is a good place to start a visit.

Founded in 1967 and in its present building since 1979 (with an expansion completed in 2005), the **Albuquerque Museum** (2000 Mountain Rd. NW; 505-243-7255) features Southwestern art and interprets the area's four-hundred-year history.

The **Indian Pueblo Cultural Center** (2401 12th St.; 505-843-7270) focuses on all aspects of New Mexico's nineteen pueblos, from their history to their food to their art.

Opened in 2000, the **National Hispanic Cultural Center** (1701 4th St. SW; 505-246-2261) stands near a natural ford of the Rio Grande crossed by the Camino Real, the Spanish trail between Mexico and New Mexico that continued as an important trade route into the nineteenth century. Exhibits and activities at the center focus on all aspects of Southwestern Hispanic culture, from art to history.

A Succession of Marshals

Milton Yarberry, the first man to wear the city's marshal badge, had previous experience. Unfortunately, it was as an outlaw said to have already killed several men. Given the town's high incidence of crime, civic leaders decided not to hold Yarberry's past against him. The newly commissioned lawman soon got in an argument with a man named Harry Brown. That March 27, 1881, difficulty, which ended when Yarberry shot and killed Brown, had not been in the performance of his duties. The two had been arguing over a woman. The county sheriff duly charged the marshal with murder, but at the former lawman's trial, his lawyer argued that Yarberry had only shot Brown in self-defense and the jury concurred. However, the following June when the marshal shot Charles D. Campbell, an unarmed railroad worker, in the back, the local judicial system did not extend him a bye. He was convicted and sentenced to hang.

Michael Robert (Bob) McGuire succeeded Yarberry as marshal. On November 20, 1886, he and deputy **E.D. Henry** went to a rough area north of downtown to arrest two outlaws—**John (Kid) Johnson** and **Charlie Ross**. According to one researcher, Johnson also went by the name Joe Chancellor but his righteous name was Joe Evans, son of an Albuquerque railroad agent. Ross was said to have at least one redeeming trait—a sense of humor.

The officers' encounter with the accused horse thieves did not end well. When the arrest attempt devolved to gunfire, Deputy Henry fell dead with two bullets in the chest and one in a leg while Marshal McGuire suffered wounds that claimed his life six days later. While the officers had managed to wound the wanted men, they were able to get away. Ross did not make it far before being taken into custody by other officers. He recovered and, possibly with the help of a girlfriend, escaped from the county jail on January 3, 1887. Before he left, he scribbled a note addressed to the editor of the local *Daily Democrat*: "Please say in your paper that hearing there is a reward offered for my partner, Johnson, that I have gone to find him." The "Kid" was later arrested in El Paso, but New Mexico prosecutors decided they didn't have enough evidence to get him convicted and dropped the murder charges against him.

The first Albuquerque police officer to die in the line of duty, Deputy Henry is buried in **Fairview Memorial Park** (700 Yale Blvd. SE; section 16B, row F East, grave 30). The Historic Fairview Foundation placed a gray granite marker over his grave with an engraving of a marshal's badge.

Perfecto Armijo

Francisco Perfecto Armijo de Jesus (1845–1913), one of the Wild West's toughest but lesser-known lawmen, was Bernalillo County's first sheriff. He served from 1879 to 1886 and then again from 1905 to 1908. In February 1883 he oversaw the hanging of the man who had been Albuquerque's first city marshal, Milton Yarberry. Legal hangings generally were accomplished by dropping the condemned person through a trapdoor so that the rope around his neck would break it. In Yarberry's case, the county took an innovative approach and constructed gallows designed to break the prisoner's neck by jerking him upward. But it didn't work quite right. When Yarberry shot skyward that February 9, 1883, his head hit the crossbeam hard. Because of that, officials were not certain whether the upward thrust or the collision with the timber did him in. No matter, Yarberry would not be shooting anyone else.

Armijo is buried in **Mount Calvary Cemetery** (900 Edith Blvd. NE; GPS coordinates: N35° 06.00', W106° 38.21'). His tall marble marker stands in the northeastern corner of the cemetery's original section, first called the Santa Barbara Cemetery. Yarberry was buried in the same section, the noose still around his neck. He had a tombstone for a time (though it misspelled his name) but it later disappeared.

Artesia (Eddy County)

The Goodnight-Loving cattle trail, extending from Texas through the Pecos River valley on its way to Colorado, calved one of the first Anglo settlements in New Mexico, **Seven Rivers**. Named for seven spring-fed tributaries emptying into the Pecos at that point, the town dated to 1867. During the 1870s, Seven Rivers was rougher than a longhorn's hide, though it proved not nearly as enduring.

In its heyday, Seven Rivers supported two stores, an equal number of saloons, a post office, a schoolhouse, and a hotel. Thanks in part to the drilling of numerous robust artesian wells that would give Artesia its name, by 1880 farming had become more important to Eddy County's economy than the cattle business. That hurt Seven Rivers, as did the growth of Eddy (later Carlsbad) only seventeen miles to the south. The final two nails in the proverbial coffin were the cause of death of many a Wild West town—losing a county seat election and being bypassed by the railroad. People started moving out, and by the early 1900s, in a figurative sense Seven Rivers had dried up. Left behind was a cemetery, but even it would not last.

By the 1920s even Artesia's fate seemed uncertain due to a significant drop in the water table from overuse. The discovery of oil and gas in the area helped sustain the economy, and the development of Brantley Reservoir in the 1980s made Artesia a recreational destination.

When it became clear that the creation of the reservoir would destroy the old **Seven Rivers Cemetery**, the federal government contracted to have all the identifiable graves exhumed and the remains reburied in Artesia. Led by archeologist Bobbie Ferguson, the 1988 project resulted in the removal of fifty-two skeletons. Archeologist and forensic experts examined the bones and found something they had not expected: of the fifteen men ages eighteen to forty-five buried at Seven Rivers, ten had died violently.

Among that unfortunate two-thirds who died hard were Texas cowhand **Zack Light**, his skull penetrated by a bullet just above the left eye, the result of having been shot in a saloon owned by the sheriff; **K.S. Keith**, killed by American Indians who tortured him first by cutting off half his right leg; **William Johnson**, his head removed by a close-range shotgun blast at the dinner table when he happened to mention to his father-in-law that he had been a Yankee soldier during the Civil War; newly married **John Northern**, shot dead in the saloon where he worked, and an unknown thirty-year-old who lived about a year with a knife blade embedded in his shoulder until someone filled his chest with buckshot.

The remains and the tombstones associated with these men and others were relocated to the rear of **Twin Oaks Memorial Park** (59 Lake Arthur Hwy.).

History in Bronze

Since 2003, a public-private partnership has been telling the area's story in a series of larger-than-life bronze statues. The statues cover two eras, the time of the cattle drives along the Goodnight-Loving Trail and the development of oil production around Artesia. Statues related to the cattle days include *The Trail Boss, The Vaquero, The Rustler,* and *Sallie Chisum.* She was the niece of cattle king John S. Chisum and a significant figure in Artesia's history. The statues are along Main Street in downtown Artesia.

Focusing on the history of Artesia and the Pecos Valley, the **Artesia Historical Museum and Art Center** is in the cobblestone **Moore-Ward House** (505 West Richardson Ave.; 575-748-2390). The 1905-vintage house is listed on the National Register of Historic Places.

Carlsbad (Eddy County)

Founded on the Pecos River in 1888, Carlsbad was first named Eddy for rancher Charles B. Eddy, its developer. Eddy conceived the new town as an agricultural and ranching community, and that's what it became. But in 1898 a cowboy named Jim White discovered a huge cave about twenty miles south of town. The cavern proved so large and geologically interesting that it came to be considered a national treasure and in 1930 was opened as a national park. Meanwhile Eddy had been renamed Carlsbad, for the German resort of Karlsbad, and the cave found by White became known as Carlsbad Cavern.

Check out the **Carlsbad Caverns National Park Visitor Center** (727 Carlsbad Cavern Hwy.; 575-785-2232) and **Carlsbad Museum and Art Center** (418 West Fox St.; 575-887-0276).

Mean as Hell

Eddy developed as a decent, law-abiding town, but soon had an evil twin named Phenix (with no "o"). Located just south of town, Phenix had the saloons, gambling houses, and brothels that Eddy did not. One of the watering holes was owned by the sheriff, another was run by **Daniel R. (Dee) Harkey** (1866–1958). Originally from Texas, he came to New Mexico Territory in 1890 and served as a lawman from 1893 to 1911. In 1948, at eighty-three, his book *Mean as Hell* was published. In that book, he claimed to have been shot at more times than any man other than in war—fifty times.

Harkey is buried in Carlsbad Cemetery (1506 Boyd Dr., in the International Order of Odd Fellows section, block 24, lot 1, space 4). The old former lawman died in his residence (409 North Canyon St.), his home since 1903. An insurance company office now stands at the site.

The southern portion of Carlsbad covers where Phenix once stood until fire destroyed most of the town. One old disreputable house did survive until 1989 before being razed.

Chloride (Sierra County)

New Mexico has roughly four hundred ghost towns. Around a score have remained relatively well preserved. Of those, Chloride is one of the best. So far as known, no one has ever counted how many Englishmen arriving in the Old West ended up as mule skinners, but it could not have been many. Harry Pye was one. He made his living transporting supplies for the military via mule train.

In 1879, in the Black Range of southwestern New Mexico, Pye discovered a rich vein of silver chloride. Figuring his mule skinning days were over, he tried to keep his find a secret. Unfortunately, word got out and miners descended on the area to stake claims. Pye might still have come out ahead, but it wasn't to be. A few months after striking it rich, Apaches killed him.

Despite the ongoing threat from unfriendly American Indians, mining activity continued at a frenzied pace. What began as a collection of tents developed into a boomtown. Chloride seemed an obvious name choice. It was like most Wild West mining towns, with a couple of interesting exceptions: Hoping to attract women, the town's governing body offered a free lot to the first female who moved there. Not only that, whoever fathered the first child, assuming it was legitimate, could have a seat on the town council. By the mid-1880s the town had three thousand residents and the usual spectrum of businesses, from saloons to stores to a laundry. Beginning in 1882 and continuing until 1897, it also had a weekly newspaper, the *Black Range*.

What Chloride lacked was rail service, so for most of its life the ore coming out of the numerous mines around it had to be hauled out by wagon. Before the price of silver tanked in 1893, the mines had produced a half a million dollars in silver. Copper, lead, and zinc mining continued in the area until the early 1930s, but the town's last business closed in the early 1920s.

The former **Pioneer Store** (300 Wall St., Winston; 575-743-2736) built in 1880, operated until 1923. With most of the merchandise that remained on the shelves still there, it is now a museum run by longtime resident Don Edmund. The store is listed on the New Mexico State Register of Cultural Properties.

Cimarron (Colfax County)

Names alone do not define most Old West towns, but Cimarron—the Spanish word for "wild and unruly"—is a perfect fit for this historic northeastern New Mexico town. A stopping place on the Santa Fe Trail, Cimarron later became the center of a land empire and therein lay trouble.

The 940-acre **Cimarron Historic District** (709 State Highway 21) listed on the National Register of Historic Places, includes fifteen historically significant structures, including the 1872-vintage former Colfax County courthouse and a once-well-used jail built the same year. A self-guided walking tour of Old Town Cimarron is available at the **Cimarron Chamber of Commerce** (104 North Lincoln Ave.; 575-376-2417).

Colfax County War, 1875

In 1841, Mexico granted Charles Beaubien and Guadalupe Miranda nearly two million acres in northeastern New Mexico and southwest Colorado. Lucien Maxwell married Beaubien's daughter and eventually became owner of the grant. That made him the largest single landowner in the nation. In 1870 he sold most of the land to a syndicate whose shareholders and officers included members of the so-called Santa Fe Ring, office holders who maintained ruthless control over the territory, their own political and financial benefit overriding any other concern. The **Colfax County War** was a violent struggle between newly arrived ranchers and others who considered the former Maxwell grant public land open for settlement and the powerful establishment, which felt it was their land to dispose of as they pleased. The first victim of this war was Rev. Francis J. Tolby, a Methodist preacher who sided with the settlers and vigorously argued their position. His body was found September 14, 1875, killed from ambush. Violence continued for a decade with scores dying. Tolby is buried in the Cimarron Cemetery (GPS coordinates: N36° 30.01', W104° 55.69') beneath a gray granite tombstone. Between his name and date of death is only one word: Assassinated. Also known as Mountain View Cemetery, the old graveyard is on a hill three-quarters of a mile south of US 64 off State Highway 21, a mile southwest of town. Turn west and go two-tenths of a mile to the cemetery gate.

St. James Hotel

Believers say the **St. James Hotel** (617 South Collison Ave.; 575-376-2664) is the most haunted overnight accommodation in the West, if not the nation. The claim is that twenty-six people have been shot to death there. While that purported body count is surely exaggerated, enough killings have been documented to make the ghost legends understandable. Bullet holes are still visible in the ceiling of the hotel's restaurant/bar.

The hotel's story begins with Henri Lambert (1838–1913), who had been President Abraham Lincoln's chef. Lambert later came west, settling in the Colfax County gold mining town of Elizabethtown, hoping to strike it rich. That failing, he returned to what he was good at—cooking. At the suggestion of land baron Lucien Maxwell, Lambert moved to Cimarron and opened the Lambert Inn in 1872. Later the two-story, Spanish Colonial–style hotel was renamed the St. James. Numerous famous Wild West characters, from the Earps to Buffalo Bill, are said to have stayed there. New owners renovated the old hotel and its restaurant in 2009. Founder Henri Lambert is buried in Cimarron Cemetery (GPS coordinates: N36° 30.01', W104° 55.69').

Clay Allison

Robert Clay Allison (1841–1887) and his brother came to New Mexico with a cattle drive along the Goodnight-Loving Trail and in 1870 the brothers started ranching near Cimarron. Allison soon got caught up in a strange case. It began one night when Charles Kennedy's tearful wife barged into a saloon in **Elizabethtown** (now a ghost town) to report that her husband had been robbing and murdering travelers who stayed at their roadside inn. Now, she wailed, he had killed their infant child. Bones were found around their place and Kennedy was arrested and charged with murder. While there was some doubt whether all the bones were human, Allison and others decided to liberate Kennedy from jail and lynch him. Legend has it that Kennedy owned up to having killed twenty-one people before receiving final adjudication at the hands of the mob. If Kennedy gave as many overnight lodgers eternal rest as is usually claimed, he ranks as one of the Wild West's more notorious serial killers.

On January 7, 1874, a disagreement between Allison and Charles Colbert was settled moments after Colbert took a shot at Allison and missed. Allison did not miss. While that killing had been personal, soon Allison became involved in the Colfax County War. On October 30, 1875, he led the mob that lynched the supposed killer of Rev. Francis J. Tolby, though they likely hanged the wrong man. The next day in the St. James Hotel, Franciso Griego, a relative of the man lynched the night before, accused Allison of involvement. While he was right about Allison's complicity, he was wrong in thinking he could get to his gun faster than Allison. Though charged with the Colbert and Griego killings and suspected in the disappearance of a friend of Colbert's, Allison escaped indictment and left New Mexico to further his growing reputation elsewhere.

The ruins of Elizabethtown are five miles north of Eagle Nest on State Highway 38. A historical marker at the northeast corner of the intersection of Therma Way (US 64) and State Highway 38 summarizes the ghost town's history.

David Crockett

His granduncle may have been "King of the Wild Frontier," but this **Davy Crockett** (1852–1876) did not die a martyr. Born in Tennessee, he grew up in Texas. In 1870, he sold a small herd of cattle and, with a pal named Gus Heffron, rode west to Cimarron. Squatting on land owned by the Maxwell Land Grant and Railroad Co., Crockett and Heffron started ranching.

Unfortunately, the Alamo hero's nephew—normally a mild-mannered sort—had a weakness for drink. That became quite evident in the early spring of 1870 when he and Heffron got drunk at Lambert's Inn and shot and killed three African-American soldiers. As the March 25 *Santa Fe Daily New*

Mexican reported, "From what we can gather from the bartender there was no provocation whatever. No arrests have been made, but the guilty parties are being searched for." Everyone in Cimarron, of course, knew that the shooters were Crockett and Heffron. Soon both men sat in the county jail, but that summer a justice of the peace found insufficient evidence to merit prosecution and they went free. Crockett, however, did not reform.

The two cowboys soon went on another toot, riding their horses into saloons and assorted businesses. Brandishing double-barreled shotguns, they made it known generally and to the sheriff particularly that they did not intend to spend any more time in the county lockup. Not intimidated, Sheriff Isaac Rinehart organized a posse to corral the pair. The county lawman and his contingent of deputized citizens cornered them in a barn and ordered them to surrender. When instead Crockett and his pal pointed their scatterguns at the lawmen, the posse opened fire on the duo. At that, the pair wheeled their horses and splashed across the nearby Cimarron River. The posse gave chase, finding Crockett dead just across the stream. A few hundred yards farther, they took Heffron into custody. He had been wounded, but not mortally.

Crockett is buried in Cimarron Cemetery (GPS coordinates: N36° 30.01', W104° 55.69'). In time, the wooden marker on Crockett's grave deteriorated. A modern tombstone has since been placed at the presumed location of his grave.

Three museums in and around Cimarron focus on the area's history. In 1864, Lucien Maxwell had a four-story stone mill built in Cimmaron. It provided grain for his ranch, the Jicarilla Apache Indian Reservation, and Santa Fe Trail travelers. Operated until 1870, it is now owned by the CS Cattle Co., which allows the Cimarron Historical Society to use it to house the **Old Aztec Mill Museum** (just off State Highway 21 on 17th Street; 575-376-2417).

In 1950, the Boy Scouts of America, which has a large campsite on nearby Philmont Ranch, built an adobe museum eleven miles south of Cimarron at Rayado to interpret the lives of Lucien Maxwell and legendary scout Kit Carson, who worked for Maxwell in 1849 (see Taos). Each room of the **Kit Carson Museum** (State Highway 21, Rayado; 575-376-1136) features reproduction furniture and artifacts typical of New Mexico in the 1850s. Staff wear period clothing and demonstrate frontier skills from blacksmithing to marksmanship.

Housed in the old county courthouse, which has built-in gallows, the **Santa Fe Trail Museum** (612 Colbert Ave., Springer; 575-483-2682) has artifacts and exhibits relating to the trail and the area's early railroad history. Built in 1881, the courthouse was used until 1897 when the county seat was moved to Raton. During the Colfax County War, two men died in a gunfight on the courthouse grounds in 1885.

Clayton (Union County)

With twin peaks known as the Rabbit Ears looming above the prairie to serve as a waypoint, William Becknell blazed a branch of the Santa Fe Trail called the Cimarron Cutoff through the northeastern corner of New Mexico in 1822. Travelers often camped at a water hole eight miles south of the Rabbit Ears and after the Civil War passing cattle drives overnighted there. Nearby, a hardy entrepreneur sold drovers supplies out of a tent, but while ranching began in the area in the 1870s, no development occurred until the Fort Worth and Denver Railway approached in 1887. Seeing an opportunity, rancher Stephen W. Dorsey acquired land along the route and had a townsite surveyed. Named Clayton for Dorsey's son, the town flourished as a cattle shipping point. With the organization of Union County, it became county seat.

"Black Jack" Loses His Head

Clayton's status as county seat assured its place in Wild West lore when a Texas cowboy-turned-bad-man named **Tom "Black Jack"**

Ketchum went on trial in 1900 for train robbery, the technical charge being "felonious assault upon a railroad train." Train robbery was a dangerous undertaking for all concerned, but in most places, it was not considered a capital crime unless someone got killed in the process. In New Mexico Territory, however, it was.

A Union County jury found Ketchum guilty of a botched train robbery that occurred on August 16, 1899, near Folsom that ended when a conductor nearly blew off Ketchum's right arm with a load of buckshot. The judge sentenced the outlaw to death, his appeal went nowhere, and after three stays, his hanging was set for April 26, 1901.

Ketchum—his nickname "Black Jack" apparently the result of some people confusing him with outlaw William "Black Jack" Christian—had gained some degree of notoriety for his exploits, but what happened the day of his hanging assured him lasting fame.

Dressed in a fine suit, his shoes polished, Ketchum walked up the steps to the gallows, stood stoically as the rope was adjusted around his neck and a black hood was pulled over his head. His only request was to be buried deep. Asked by Sheriff Salome Garcia if he was ready, Ketchum said, "Let 'er go." That would have been that, just another legal hanging, but when Ketchum shot through the trapdoor, instead of breaking his neck, to the horror of all present, the force of the fall decapitated him. As if that were not enough to give the hapless outlaw an unenviable form of immortality, a photographer captured the grisly aftermath in graphic detail.

A historical plaque on the side of the old Union County Sheriff's Office (575-374-2583) at Adams and South 2nd Street in Clayton marks the site of the hanging. Ketchum is buried in Clayton Cemetery, one mile southeast of town midway between Dorsey and Water Streets off Princeton Avenue. For years the grave was unmarked, but it now has a tombstone.

Operated by the Union County Historical Society, the **Herztein Museum** (22 South 2nd St.; 575-374-2977) has an extensive exhibit on Ketchum and artifacts relating to the botched hanging.

Eklund Hotel

Once touted as the finest hotel between Fort Worth, Texas, and Trinidad, Colorado, the **Eklund Hotel** (15 Main St.; 575-374-2551) dates to 1892 when the two-story stone building was constructed as a combination store and rooming house. Two years later Carl Eklund opened a saloon where the store had been, putting in an ornate, carved bar. In 1897, Eklund and wife Gerda bought the property and added another two-story section to the building to accommodate a lobby, dining room, and the saloon. A final expansion came in 1905 with the addition of a third floor. Eklund must have done well, because by 1913 he had a thirteen-thousand-acre ranch near the Rabbit Ears formation, a landmark on the old Santa Fe Trail. Under different management, the hotel closed in 1975 but was refurbished and reopened in 2004, its original forty-two rooms reduced to twenty-six larger units. It closed again five years later but opened once again in 2011. The old hotel was listed on the National Register of Historic Places in 2002. Like most old hostelries, it is reputed to be haunted.

Columbus (Luna County)

Nearly two decades after most of the West had ceased being particularly wild, in the pre-dawn hours of March 9, 1916, some five hundred mounted Mexican revolutionaries led by Pancho Villa raided the small railroad town of Columbus, killing ten American civilians and eight US soldiers. It was the first ground invasion of the continental US since the War of 1812 and sparked the last large-scale cavalry campaign in the long history of the American horse soldier—the punitive expedition into Mexico led by Gen. John (Black Jack) Pershing in pursuit of Villa.

The village of Columbus and the site of the army's Camp Furlong is a National Historic Landmark, part of it located in **Pancho Villa State Park** (400 State Highway 9; 575-531-2711). A visitor center in the 1902-vintage US customs house has interpretive exhibits and artifacts related to the raid and subsequent US military pursuit. The **Columbus Historical Society Museum** (State Highway 9 at State Highway 11; 575-531-2414) occupies the old railroad depot. Columbus's historic buildings include the old Hoover Hotel, the Camp Furlong headquarters, the post recreation hall, the guard house, Columbus village jail, and others.

Deming (Luna County)

Deming began when the nation's second transcontinental railroad, the Southern Pacific, was completed nearby on March 8, 1881. The thirty-acre Downtown Deming Historic District includes sixty-five structures listed on the National Register of Historic Places.

The Man Who Killed the Man Who Killed John Wesley Hardin

George Adolphus Scarborough (1859–1900) started his law enforcement career as sheriff of Jones County, Texas. While serving as a deputy US marshal in El Paso, Texas, on April 6, 1896, he killed constable John Selman, the man who had shot and killed the notorious John Wesley (Wes) Hardin the previous August 19 in El Paso's Acme Saloon.

In 1900, working in New Mexico as a detective for a cattleman's association, Scarborough and lawman Walt Birchfield were ambushed while on the trail of outlaws in the Chiricahua Mountains. Shot in the thigh, Scarborough was taken to the Santa Fe Railway Hospital in Deming, where his leg had to be amputated. He died there on April 6, four years to the day after he had gunned down Selman. Not everyone mourned the lawman's death. Shortly after Scarborough ended Selman's career, the *Western Liberal* in Lordsburg, New Mexico, had opined that if Scarborough "should die of pneumonia, El Paso would be left without a professional killer."

Scarborough is buried in Deming's **Mountain View Cemetery** (International Order of Odd Fellows section). The cemetery is three miles east of Deming, on the south side of US 80 (GPS coordinates: N32° 16.07', W107° 43.16').

Mrs. Thurmond's Secret

Carlotta (Charlotte) J. Thompkins Thurmond (1844–1934) and her husband Frank settled in Deming in 1882 shortly after the arrival of the Atchison, Topeka, and Santa Fe Railway made it a boomtown. The Thurmonds became pillars of the community, he a prosperous miner and banker, she active in society and a devout Episcopalian.

Not until after her death did it become generally known that Mrs. Thurmond had a shady past. As a young, attractive redhead, she had been known as Lottie Deno (though she had other aliases as well). A professional gambler, and likely a prostitute, she, along with husband Frank, spent time in Fort Griffin, Texas, and other wild towns in the Southwest before putting their nefarious past behind them. The famous radio and television character Miss Kitty of *Gunsmoke* fame was supposedly inspired by Lottie Deno.

Mrs. Thurmond is buried in Deming's **Mountain View Cemetery** (Knights of Pythias section, row C, lot 2). Her grave is next to that of husband Frank, who died in 1908. The cemetery is three miles east of Deming, on the south side of US 80 (GPS coordinates: N32° 16.07', W107° 43.16').

The Thurmonds had a ranch forty miles from Deming but lived in town at 408 West Pine St., just down the street from the **Old Deming National Bank** (122 East Pine St.) where Frank Thurmond was vice president. Mrs. Thurmond continued to live at the house after her husband's death and it still stands, though extensively remodeled. Mrs. Thurmond was a founding member of **St. Luke's Episcopal Church** (419 West Spruce St.), which was built in 1891 and remains in use. She attended services there for decades.

The **Deming Luna Mimbres Museum** (301 South Silver St.; 575-640-0379) has, since 1977, occupied the old national guard armory, built in 1916 not long after Mexican revolutionary Pancho Villa's raid on Columbus, New Mexico.

Fort Craig (Socorro County)

Established in 1854, Fort Craig became one of the largest and most important military posts in the West. For most of its history, the Stars and Stripes flew over its parade ground, but for a time during the Civil War, the post was under Confederate control and was the scene of the largest military engagement between the North and the South in the Southwest. After the war, regarrisoned by federal troops, the post resumed its role in the Indian Wars until abandoned in 1885. Nine years after the army marched away, the military reservation went on the auction block. The property was donated to the federal Bureau of Land Management in 1981 and is maintained as the **Fort Craig National Historic Site** (Fort Craig Road, San Antonio; 575-835-0412). The old fort is thirty-five miles south of Socorro.

Fort Seldon (Dona Ana County)

Established on the Rio Grande, thirteen miles north of Las Cruces, in 1865 to protect the Mesilla Valley, Fort Seldon remained strategically important throughout the Apache Wars. Beginning in the 1870s, troops from the fort manned a heliograph station on nearby Robledo Mountain, using a mirror to flash signals to Fort Bliss, fifty miles away.

In 1884 a cavalry captain named Arthur MacArthur arrived with his family at the post as its new commander. There his four-year-old son Douglas learned to ride and shoot before he knew how to read or write. When he was older, years after the army had abandoned Fort Seldon in 1891, Douglas MacArthur attended West Point and would rise to five-star general as supreme allied commander in the Pacific during World War II. Named to the National Register of Historic Places in 1970, the adobe ruins of the old fort have been maintained as **Fort Selden Historic Site** (1280 Fort Selden Rd.; 575-526-8911) since 1974. A visitor center has exhibits on the area's frontier and military past.

Buffalo Soldier Monument

At one point the US Army maintained sixteen forts in New Mexico. Eleven of them were garrisoned at various times from 1866 to 1900 by African-American soldiers of the Twenty-fourth, Fifty-seventh, and 125th Infantry regiments and later, the Ninth and Tenth Cavalry. American Indians called them **Buffalo Soldiers** and the name has endured. In commemoration of their contribution to the settlement of the West, *The Sentinel*, a larger-than-life bronze statue of a Buffalo Soldier by sculptor Reynaldo Reyes, stands lasting guard at the **Fort Selden Historic Site** (1280 Fort Selden Rd.; 575-526-8911).

Fort Sumner (De Baca County)

"My dear wife," Lt. George H. Pettis wrote, "this is a terrible place; it is intended to make it the final home of all the Indians in this country; there are about fifteen hundred here now,—Navajos and Apaches . . ." Assigned to Company K, First California Infantry, Pettis was at Fort Sumner, finishing a letter home, on February 26, 1864. The junior officer described what would come to be recognized as one of the darker chapters of Wild West history, the forced relocation of several thousand American Indians during the Civil War.

Construction of the military post began in the late fall of 1862. Though initially intended to protect settlers in the Pecos Valley, the fort's mission changed: Its troops would oversee the forced relocation of thousands of Navajo and Mescalero to a million-acre reservation, the **Bosque Redondo**. During their internment, which began in 1863, American Indians were prohibited from practicing long-standing rituals, afforded only meager rations, and forced to provide their own shelter. With little or no firewood, the two tribes suffered from exposure, starvation, and disease. Roughly 1,500 people died. Groups from both tribes managed to escape and return to their land, but most stayed.

An 1868 treaty allowed the surviving Navajo to return to their traditional homelands and gave them national sovereignty. Five years later the Mescalero signed a treaty creating their reservation. Even so, the culture of both peoples had been forever changed.

Over time, Fort Sumner became increasingly better known for its connection to Billy the Kid, one of the Wild West's most noted outlaws (see Las Cruces, Lincoln, Mescalero, Santa Fe, and Silver City), and what happened to the Navajo and Mescalero people was all but forgotten—except by the Navajo and Mescalero.

The Fort Sumner property became a state park in the 1930s. In 2005, partnering with the Navajo and Mescalero, the New Mexico State Monuments Division and the Museum of New Mexico developed the **Bosque Redondo Memorial** (3647 Billy the Kid Dr.; 575-355-2573) at the **Fort Sumner Historic Site**. With stylized elements of Navajo architecture and a teepee-like feature representative of the Mescalero culture, the museum tells the tragic story through permanent and temporary exhibits and an interpretive trail around the fort site.

Billy the Kid's Death Site

The federal government closed Fort Sumner in 1868, and in 1870 sold its buildings to prominent New Mexico landowner Lucien Maxwell, who established a ranch on the land and lived in one of the old officer's quarters. Following Maxwell's death in 1875, his son Pete lived in the house. By then, a small settlement, also known as Fort Sumner, had developed on their property. At one point, roughly two hundred people lived there.

The Maxwell family sold their property in 1884 and the new owners required all the people living at Fort Sumner to leave, which ended it as a community. The adobe ranch house in which the Maxwells had lived, and where Pat Garrett killed Billy the Kid on the night of July 14, 1881, fell into disrepair. Low, stubby traces of its earthen walls were still visible until washed away by a Pecos River flood in 1937. Located behind the Bosque Redondo Memorial, a flat engraved stone and an interpretive plaque mark the site of the ranch house (GPS coordinates: N34° 24.24', W104° 12.00').

Fort Sumner Cemetery

One of the most historic graveyards in the Old West, the **Fort Sumner Cemetery** (3501 Billy the Kid Dr.; 575-355-7705) has 112 documented burials and likely dozens more. But only twenty-five graves are marked, the most famous being Billy the Kid's. Sixteen other plots belong to people associated with him in one way or another, from fellow outlaws Charlie Bowdre (1848–880) and Thomas O'Folliard, Jr. (1858–1880) to Paulita Maxwell Jaramillo (1864–1929), the woman many believe was his girlfriend.

The most impressive grave marker, and the one belonging to the most historically significant occupant of the cemetery other than The Kid, is that of Lucien Maxwell (1818–1875). The Kid did not get a stone marker until 1931, when it was evident his burial site had become a tourist destination. That stone bore his name, Bowdre's, and O'Folliard's, under the single word, "Pals." He got his own tombstone in 1940, a marker stolen and recovered twice, in 1950 and again in 1981. Now an iron cage protects the grave, but even it was damaged by vandals in 2012. The kicker is that no one knows for sure whether the markers stand at the right spots because a flash flood in 1904 washed away The Kid's original wooden cross.

The cemetery is just off Billy the Kid Drive, three miles south of US 60/84 and a half-mile from the Bosque Redondo Memorial (GPS coordinates: N34° 24.23', W104° 11.57').

Billy the Kid Museum

Four-year-old Ed Sweet came to New Mexico in 1908 on an immigrant train with his family. He grew up in Melrose, thirty-six miles east of Fort Sumner. Though as a young man he struggled to make a living doing everything from selling apples to making brooms, he became interested in Wild West history and began collecting relics. By the early 1950s he had acquired a sizable collection and decided to open a museum dedicated to Billy the Kid. Since January 1953 the **Billy the Kid Museum** (1435 East Sumner Ave.; 575-355-2380) has attracted hundreds of thousands of visitors from across the world and continues in operation under the stewardship of Sweet's son and grandson. Artifacts on display include a rifle that belonged to The Kid, his chaps and spurs, curtains from the room where he was killed, and locks of his hair.

Fort Stanton (Lincoln County)

Established in 1855, **Fort Stanton** (401 Kit Carson Rd.; 575-354-0341) is one of the West's best-preserved frontier military posts. Eighty-eight historic buildings, some dating to the fort's antebellum days, still stand. Located on 240 acres in the heart of the Lincoln National Forest, the fort saw occupation by both the Confederacy and federal troops under the legendary Kit Carson during the Civil War. After that conflict, the fort continued to play an important part in the Indian Wars. Though its military usage ended in 1896, over the years the old fort served variously as a Merchant Marine tuberculosis hospital, Civilian Conservation Corps camp, a World War II internee camp, a training school for the mentally disabled, and a low-security women's prison. The fort became a state historic site in 2008. With support from a nonprofit group, the state operates a museum in one of the old buildings.

Fort Union (Mora County)

From 1851 to 1891, **Fort Union** stood watch over New Mexico Territory. It was established only three years after the end of the Mexican War of 1846 to 1848 and stood where the two branches of the Santa Fe Trail came together. Over the years, three different forts were built at the site and eventually Fort Union was the largest army garrison west of the Mississippi. In addition to its tactical missions during the Indian Wars, the fort maintained a large commissary depot that supplied numerous other military posts in the Southwest. In 1954, the ruins of the fort became **Fort Union National Monument** (3115 State Highway 161, Watrous; 505-425-8025). The visitor center has exhibits on the colorful history of the old fort.

Hillsboro (Sierra County)

Two prospectors—Dan Dugan and Dave Sitzel—found high-assay gold on the east slope of the Black Range in 1877 and staked claims along Percha Creek. The story is that each man had a town name in mind, so they wrote down their suggestions and put the two scraps of paper into a hat. The name drawn was Hillsborough, which soon got melted down to Hillsboro. Despite the danger posed by unfriendly Apaches, the town boomed and became the seat of Sierra County in 1882. The mining focus eventually shifted from gold to silver, but Hillsboro continued to flourish until the value of silver tanked in 1893. Still, the town hung on as a county seat until 1936, when Hot Springs (now Truth or Consequences) became the county capital.

Sadie Orchard Grew Quite a Reputation

Sarah (Sadie) Jane Creech was a well-known madam in nearby Kingston before moving to Hillsboro in 1893, but it was here that she grew from colorful character to Wild West legend. By marrying James W. Orchard two years after hitting town, she acquired the name she would have from then on—Sadie Orchard. Even after tying the knot with Orchard, stagecoach company owner and sometimes mine operator, she ran a hotel and eventually acquired two others. While that was certainly respectable, talk was that even after getting hitched she offered male guests more than a place to spend the night. While much of what has been written about Sadie is pure legend (like her riding naked through town to advertise her business or driving a stagecoach for her husband), she was an astute businesswoman and shameless self-promoter with a definite rough side. She broke off with husband Orchard in the early 1900s and he left town, but Orchard stayed in Hillsboro the rest of her life.

Following her death on April 9, 1943, Sadie was buried in Truth or Consequence's **Hot Springs Cemetery** (100 East 8th Ave.).

Southwest's Trial of the Century

The biggest event in Hillsboro's history came in May 1899 when rancher **Oliver Lee** and hired hand **Jim Gilliland** stood trial for murder in the disappearance of Albert Jennings Fountain and his young son Henry three years earlier (see Las Cruces). Adding to the trial's sensation, one of the prime witnesses would be Pat Garrett, the lawman who killed Billy the Kid in 1881.

Lawyers for the prosecution and defense (including the late Fountain's political adversary, Albert B. Fall), reporters, and partisans of the defendants or the missing Fountains crowded the town. Hillsboro's largest hotel had no available rooms, so some out-of-towners stayed at Sadie Orchard's establishment. Others slept in tents, each faction having its own camp. Since many who showed up for the trial arrived on her husband's stage, not only did Sadie and her husband benefit financially from the trial, Sadie supposedly furnished food for the defendants (for a price, of course) as well. In addition to an influx of people and money, the trial brought modern technology to town with twenty miles of telegraph line being strung from Lake Valley to connect the mining community electronically with the outside world for the first time. The eighteen-day trial ended in acquittal. Given the lack of eyewitnesses or bodies, the jury reached its verdict in less than an hour. Garrett and Fall took the first stagecoach out of town.

The ruins of the old Sierra County Courthouse and jail, built in 1892, stand on Elenora Street. The two-story building was sold by the county in 1939 and most of its red bricks were salvaged and hauled by truck to the new county seat of Hot Springs (now Truth or Consequences), thirty-two miles away. The bricks were used to build several new storefronts.

Black Range Museum

Built prior to 1893, this building was initially Sadie Orchard's Ocean Grove Hotel and later, Tom Ying's Restaurant. Privately operated for years, the **Black Range Museum** (3 Carro Ln.; 575-895-5233) was bought by the Hillsboro Historical Society in 2016. The restored museum focuses on the ghost town's history and displays many items that belonged to Orchard or Ying. Ying's Victorian-style residence stands next to the museum.

In addition to the museum, Hillsboro has ten structures on the National Register of Historic Places and the museum lists thirty-one other locations in town that are of historical interest.

Tom Ying is buried in the Hillsboro Cemetery off Hillsboro Cemetery Road.

Kingston (Sierra County)

While gold mining spurred nearby Hillsboro's boom a few years before, it was the discovery of silver in August 1882 that led to the town of Kingston. Starting with one tent under a large cottonwood tree, by 1885 the community had several thousand residents and the usual range of boomtown businesses, from mercantile establishments to gaming halls to places selling booze and venues offering female companionship for hire. The town's best-known madam was the woman later known as Sadie Orchard. Her bordello was located on Virtue Street. As writer-historian Francis Fugate put it in his *Roadside History of New Mexico*, it eventually "occurred to someone that the town did not have a church [so] sponsors of the idea went where money flowed the easiest . . ." That would be the various disreputable enterprises, where owners, employees, and customers donated enough to build a church. Soon stone and brick buildings began to replace many of the hastily built frame structures. Mines in the area produced an estimated $7 to $10 million in silver, but as the ore began to play out in the late 1880s, so did Kingston.

The **Percha Bank Museum** (46 Main St.; 575-895-5652) is the only unaltered vintage structure in Kingston, which has become a small art colony, but a former hotel and another original building have been altered for use as private homes.

The **Old Schoolhouse Museum** (46 Water St.; 575-895-5501) occupies the former Kingston school. A brochure mapping a walking tour is available at the museums.

Las Cruces (Dona Ana County)

On the Camino Real, the old Spanish road between the Pass of the North (later El Paso, Texas) and Santa Fe, Las Cruces developed as an agricultural community along the Rio Grande in the fertile Mesilla Valley. Spanish for "the crosses," Las Cruces got its name from the weathered crosses that marked the graves of fourteen Mexican soldiers killed by Apaches in 1830 near where the town would later be founded. The area came under US control following the Mexican War in 1848, but that was not formalized until the completion of the Gadsden Purchase in 1853. The California gold rush had been bringing westbound travelers through the area and Las Cruces grew as a crossroads, trade center, and agricultural community. The town got an additional boost in 1881 when the railroad arrived and yet another in 1888 when it was selected as the site for a land grant college that became New Mexico State University.

The Las Vegas–Mesilla area has three museums bearing on its Old West heritage, the **Gadsden Museum** (1875 Boutz Rd., Mesilla; 575-526-6293), **Las Cruces Railroad Museum** (351 North Mesilla St., Mesilla; 575-528-3444), and the **New Mexico Farm and Ranch Heritage Museum** (4100 Dripping Springs Rd.; 575-522-4100).

Old Mesilla Courthouse

Originally part of Mexico, Mesilla was a significant waypoint on the Butterfield Stage Line's route from San Antonio to San Diego. The old village became part of the US with the signing of the Gadsden Purchase in 1853. Mesilla remained larger than nearby Las Cruces until the Santa Fe Railroad went through there rather than Mesilla.

Built around 1850 and first used as a general store, the adobe structure that later housed the **Dona Ana County courthouse** (2385 Calle de Guadalupe) has eighteen-inch-thick walls and a ceiling of *latillas* (layered striped branches) and *vigas* (wooden beams). The building could be as much a place of refuge as a seat of justice. The sturdy courthouse provided shelter during a political riot on the town plaza in August 1871 that left nine people dead. A decade later, Billy the Kid stood trial in the courthouse in 1881 for the murder of Sheriff William J. Brady during the bloody Lincoln County War. Found guilty, The Kid was sentenced to hang. Transferred to Lincoln to await his execution, the outlaw would not be content to accept his fate.

The old courthouse stands on the southeast corner of the Mesilla plaza. After the county built a new courthouse in 1882 in Las Cruces, the building was used for a time as a school and then as a bar-billiard hall. For years, the **Billy the Kid Gift Shop** (575-523-5561) has occupied the historic structure.

A Mountain Mystery

Peaking at 8,990 feet, the Organ Mountains tower over the desert floor ten miles east of Las Cruces. They are the setting for an enduring mystery.

El Ermitano, as he became known, was born in Italy in 1800 to well-to-do parents. Before coming to the US in 1859, Giovanni Maria de Agostini perambulated much of the world, including Europe, South America, and Cuba. In the US, he walked from New York to Kansas and from there to Mesilla in 1867. He moved to El Paso for a while, spent time in Juarez, Mexico, and then walked roughly six hundred miles through hostile American Indian country to San Antonio.

Having seen a lot of landscape in his lifetime, he was drawn back to the Organ Mountains where he lived in a natural cave—more an overhang—in the volcanic rock on the west side of the towering Organs. Friends in nearby Mesilla cautioned him against being alone in such a remote area. To ease their concerns, Agostini promised to light a fire in front of his cave every Friday night. "If the fire fails to appear it will be because I have been killed," he said. "I shall bless you daily in my prayers."

One Friday evening in late April 1869 the fire did not appear. A posse later found El Ermitano lying face down on his crucifix. Two wounds in his chest appeared to have come from a lance, but death came from a blow to the back of his skull with a rock. The murder has never been solved, though the most common theory is that American Indians killed him.

Agostini lies in the Mesilla Valley Cemetery, also known as the San Albino Cemetery (2965 Calle de Guadalupe). His original tombstone is broken and too weathered to read. A second marker, made of concrete, was added in 1949. A final tombstone, one of red granite, was put up in 2013 by parties unknown. **La Cueva**, the site of his murder, is part of the **Organ Mountains-Desert Peaks National Monument** (ten miles east of I-25, exit 1, on the western edge of the Organ Mountains).

Nearby, at a water source called **Dripping Springs**, are the ruins of an old health resort. One of the resort's regulars was Pat Garrett, the lawman who killed Billy the Kid.

Agostini's crucifix, two of his books, and several other possessions are held by the Gadsden Museum (1875 Boutz Rd., Mesilla; 575-526-6293).

Vanished in the Sand

Since 1896, a simple white marble cenotaph has stood over two empty burial plots in memory of **Albert Jennings Fountain** and his nine-year-old son, **Henry**. Their remains have never been found, but few ever doubted their fate.

The disappearance and almost certain murder of father and son remains one of the Wild West's most intriguing mysteries. Like many of the West's better stories, the Fountain case would take a book to tell in detail, and indeed it has been the subject of one volume and a major part of several others. Essentially, as attorney for the Southeastern New Mexico Stock Association, and due to competing political affiliations, business interests, and even his basic beliefs, Fountain made some powerful—and ruthless—enemies.

When local and territorial authorities seemed unable to get to the bottom of what happened (partly due to the influence of Fountain's enemies but also because of law enforcement ineptness), Fountain's friends and family induced former Lincoln County sheriff Pat Garrett to move from Uvalde, Texas, to Dona Ana County to take up the investigation. Motivated by a sense of duty and a $10,000 reward, first as a deputy and then as sheriff, Garrett began gathering a case against area rancher Oliver Lee and two of his henchmen, Jim Gilliland, and Bill McNew.

But lacking bodies, a murder weapon, or any eyewitnesses, all Garrett could put together was a circumstantial case further hampered by the political and financial influence of Fountain's enemies. The trial didn't turn out well for the prosecution or, in the end, Pat Garrett.

A state historical sign stands at Mile Marker 178 on US 70 (GPS coordinates: N32° 31.06', W106° 22.53') near the point where Fountain and his son were last seen alive on the vast wind-swept formation of glistening white gypsum crystals known as the White Sands. Their cenotaph is in Las Cruces's Masonic Cemetery (760 South Compress Rd.; section A, block 12, lots 18-19; GPS coordinates: N32° 17.99', W106° 47.04').

Pat Garrett Didn't Die Holding His Gun

The man who killed Billy the Kid unexpectedly took his eternal leave while taking a leak.

Twenty-six years after the shooting that put him in the history books and The Kid in his grave, and more than a decade after his investigation of the Albert Fountain case, **Pat Garrett** had transitioned from law enforcement to ranching. On March 1, 1908, he was riding in a rented two-horse buggy being driven by Carl Adamson. Accompanying them on horseback was Wayne Brazel. The three men were on their way to the county seat in Las Cruces to finalize the sale of Garrett's ranch. For much of the trip, Brazel and the former lawman had been arguing over the lease Brazel held on the land Garrett was selling. When Adamson stopped the buggy at the juncture of two trails, Garrett stepped down to relieve himself.

Moments later a bullet slammed into his head from behind. Then a second round hit him in the stomach, though some accounts have the order of the shots reversed. It would seem obvious that one of the two men who had been with Garrett killed him, and indeed, Brazel hastened to the sheriff's office and confessed to the crime. But he was found not guilty the year after the killing.

Since then, speculation on who killed Pat Garrett has been an ongoing topic of discussion among amateur and professional Western historians. A reasonable circumstantial case can be made against one of the Wild West's most notorious hired guns, Jim B. Miller, better known as either Deacon Jim Miller or Killer Miller. Perhaps the most damning fact is that Miller was the brother-in-law of Carl Adamson, the man in the buggy with Garrett.

Neither Miller nor anyone else was ever charged with Garrett's murder, but barely a year after it happened, a lynch mob in Oklahoma negated the possibility of any earthly prosecution of the professional hit man.

Since Garrett was six-foot-four, his family had to special order a coffin to accommodate his body. That done, he was buried with Masonic rites in the Masonic Cemetery (760 South Compress Rd.; section 7, block 11). Garrett's wife, Apolinaria Gutierrez Garrett (1861–1936) and six of their eight children are all buried nearby.

In the late 1930s, Garrett's youngest son Jarvis marked the remote place where his father died. Being during the Great Depression, apparently all he could afford to do was pour concrete around a rock with a cross carved in it, sink two pieces of angle iron into the concrete, and scratch "P Garrett" and "Feb 1908" into the mixture before it dried. Of course, Garrett was killed on the first day of March 1908, not in February.

The do-it-yourself marker now lies in a power line right of way, 1.2 miles south of a state historical marker at US 70 and South Jornada Road (GPS coordinates: N32° 21.97', W106° 43.03'). The City of Las Cruces maintains the site as a park, though there are no amenities.

Opened in 1926, the two-story, Italian Renaissance–style **Rio Grande Theater** (211 North Main St.; 575-541-2290) hosted the world premiere of the first-ever Billy the Kid movie on October 12, 1930. Directed by Texas-born King Vidor and distributed by MGM, the film was based on the first twentieth-century book about the New Mexican outlaw, Walter Noble Burns's *The Saga of Billy the Kid*.

Pat Garrett's widow, Apolinaria, and one of their children, Paulene, were special guests at the first showing of the movie, filmed twenty-two years after the lawman's death. Well reviewed at the time as an accurate telling of the outlaw's story, in truth the film was faithful only to Burns's fanciful and error-filled book. Still, the book and movie brought The Kid back to life as one of the Wild West's enduring figures.

The theater is still a movie house and the building is listed on the National Register of Historic Places.

Las Vegas (San Miguel County)

Local officials and those whose job it is to market this city like to note that it is the original Las Vegas, first settled in 1835 astride the Santa Fe Trail on a Mexican land grant and a well-established city long before that other Las Vegas had its first neon lights. While promoters of Las Vegas, Nevada, advertise that "what happens in Las Vegas stays in Las Vegas," what happened in Las Vegas, New Mexico, in frontier times did not stay there. Accounts of Wild West violence in and around town enlivened newspapers across the nation, particularly during the last three decades of the nineteenth century. What did stay in this Las Vegas were the bodies of many a man, and a few women, who died violently in gunfights, in ambushes, during the commission of crimes, or at the hands of vigilantes.

For years not only did Las Vegas rank as New Mexico's most populated city, it was the largest on the long trail from Missouri to Santa Fe. In 1879 it became an end-of-the-line railroad town when the tracks of the Atchison, Topeka, and Santa Fe reached it. The *Las Vegas Optic* chronicled twenty-nine violent deaths in town in just the first year after the railroad reached it. The arrival of rail service transformed many a Wild West town, but in Las Vegas it did something different. The railroad built its depot across the shallow Gallinas River from the old town on the west side of the river. Soon, saloons, gambling places, brothels, hotels, and other businesses oriented to a more transient population constituted a new town adjacent to the railroad tracks known as East Las Vegas. It would not merge with the old town until 1970.

Not only did enough Wild West violence take place here to provide ample fodder for nonfiction writers, novelists, and Hollywood, but Las Vegas is also one of the best-preserved of the Old West towns. Nine hundred buildings—each with a story—are listed on the National Register of Historic Places. They represent more than fifty years of nineteenth- or early-twentieth-century architectural styles, making the city particularly popular with the movie industry. More than 150 movies or television shows have been shot here.

Most windmills are supported by a four-legged wood or metal tower. But the public windmill put up in the old town plaza in 1876 spun atop a shorter tower sitting atop a tall, square platform supported by four legs. The well soon went dry, but the windmill did come in handy for lynching undesirables, sometimes more than one at a time. When kids started hanging stray dogs from the mill, it was taken down in April 1880. The windmill rose from the center of the plaza where a gazebo now stands. The city plaza has been a city park for generations.

Only two years after the well-used hanging windmill came down, the **Plaza Hotel** (230 Old Town Plaza; 505-425-3591), so named because it stands on one side of the old plaza, opened for business. Early notable guests amounted to a Who's Who of noted figures, ranging from Doc Holliday and Big Nose Kate to future president Theodore Roosevelt. Restored to its original elegance, the forty-two-room hotel still accommodates guests.

Operated by the Las Vegas Citizen's Committee for Historic Preservation the **Santa Fe Trail Interpretive Center** (116 Bridge St.; 505-425-8803) has historical displays, history-related brochures, vintage photographs of no-longer-extant Las Vegas buildings, and other archival resources.

The **City of Las Vegas Museum and Rough Rider Memorial Collection** (727 Grand Ave.; 505-426-3205) is in the old Municipal Building, a Pueblo-style Works Progress Administration structure built in 1940. As the museum advertises, it has more than seven thousand "answers to questions you haven't even asked yet." (As in interesting artifacts.) Exhibits cover all aspects of Las Vegas history, including its lawless era and the Rough Riders of Spanish-American War fame, who had their first reunion in Las Vegas.

Nothing Mysterious About Dave Mather in Las Vegas Days

The Wild West character later known as **Mysterious Dave Mather** came to Las Vegas from Dodge City in 1879 when the railroad arrived. He hired on as a San Miguel County sheriff's deputy, part of the Dodge City gang. (A cabal of shady sorts late of Kansas, including Wyatt Earp, Doc Holliday, Hoodoo Brown, and others who soon gained control of East Las Vegas.) Duly commissioned, Mather proceeded to kill two men in the line of duty in two separate incidents, wounded another, and is believed to have led a lynch mob that strung up three accused killers. His reputation as a gunfighter firmly established, he moved on in March 1880.

La Gavilla de Silva

Vicente Silva (1845–1894), with help from wife Telesfora and her brother Gabriel Sandoval, ran the Imperial Saloon on the south side of the town plaza. But the saloon was not Silva's only income source. Long before the term entered the vernacular, Silva was an organized crime boss. Of course, only his immediate family and gang members knew that. Most people viewed Silva and his family as pillars of the community, the couple usually walking hand-in-hand to mass at Our Lady of Sorrows.

Silva's gang—**La Gavilla de Silva**—rustled, robbed, and killed. In addition to the largest percentage of the take, Silva demanded absolute loyalty from his henchmen. When he suspected gang member Patricio Maes of betrayal, Silva gathered his associates at his saloon on the night of October 22, 1892, for a "trial" that resulted in Maes's conviction and summary hanging. (The hanging windmill on the plaza was long gone by this time; Maes ended up dangling from a nearby bridge.) The following year, Silva became disillusioned with his brother-in-law and, along with two of his men, ambushed and killed him near the intersection of South Gonzales and South Pacific Streets.

The murder of his wife's brother and the dumping of his body in an abandoned outhouse doubtless put a strain on the Silvas' marriage, but he was nothing if not a problem solver. By that time Silva had a mistress and, a divorce being out of the question, he decided to kill his wife and start a new life with his girlfriend. He stabbed Telesfora to death at his ranch on the Sapello River on May 19, 1893, but when he emerged from his ranch house, gang member Antonio Jose Valdez (better known as Patas de Rana, or Frog Legs) shot and killed him. Whether Frog Legs did it out of moral outrage or simply to steal all his boss's money remained a matter of speculation.

By the late 1890s, most of Silva's gang had been executed or imprisoned, but one former member lived on until 1940.

Silva is buried with his wife in **Campo de los Cadillos Cemetery** (5.1 miles east of State Highway 518 on County Road A6; GPS coordinates: N35° 44.02', W105° 09.06') north of Las Vegas on his former ranch, now the Ruby Ranch. Drive south on the county road and make two left turns. The cemetery is on the west side of the river.

Lincoln (Lincoln County)

Spanish-speaking New Mexicans settled La Placita del Rio Bonito (the place by the pretty river) in the 1850s. By the 1870s the village had become the seat of the territory's largest political subdivision, it, and the county, both named for the late President Abraham Lincoln. In 1878 the county saw the outbreak of what came to be called the **Lincoln County War**, a conflict born of greed and criminality, sustained by revenge. Before the war ended, more than two score men had been shot to death, many in Lincoln. After losing its status as county seat, and having no rail connection, Lincoln might have died as well except for one of the war's combatants—Billy the Kid.

In the Rio Bonito valley, fifty-seven miles west of Roswell on US 380, the entire town of Lincoln, including more than a dozen historic structures, is a state-managed historic site. The town's only modern building, the **Anderson-Freeman Visitor Center** (1027 Calle de La Placita; 575-653-4025), has interpretive exhibits documenting the pre–Lincoln County War history of the area, what led up to the war, and how the conflict played out. There's also a video on the conflict. All of Lincoln's structures are easy walking from the visitor center.

When Englishman **John H. Tunstall** (1853–1878) came to Lincoln County in 1877 to start a mercantile business, he acquired an 1850s adobe building, enlarged it, and opened a store and bank. The building also had an office for Tunstall's partner, lawyer Alexander McSween (1843–1878). When the **Tunstall Store** (US 380) began competing with the mercantile and ranching enterprises of Lawrence Murphy and James Dolan, a high-stakes business rivalry led to Tunstall's February 18, 1878, murder by gunmen hired by Murphy and Dolan.

That was the beginning of the Lincoln County War. The next event, the April 1, 1878, ambush and murder of Sheriff William J. Brady (1829–1878) and Deputy George Hindman by The Kid and other men working for McSween, took place behind the store.

Under several owners, the building continued in use as a store until 1957, when the state acquired it. It now houses one of the museums that are part of the state historic site.

The most intense clash between the pro-McSween Regulators, as they were called, and the Murphy-Dolan faction began July 14, 1878, and lasted five days. Essentially a standoff in which the Regulators were besieged by forces led by newly appointed Sheriff George Peppin, it ended July 19 with an intense gun battle that left five Regulators dead, including McSween. Two sheriff's deputies also were killed.

Deputy Robert Ameredith B. (Pecos Bob) Olinger (1850–1881) had just walked out of the Wortley Hotel, where he had taken several prisoners for their supper, when he heard shots in the courthouse. Running across the street, he was felled by a blast from a 10-gauge shotgun fired by The Kid, who had already killed Deputy James W. Bell. The original eight-room hotel was razed, but a new **Wortley Hotel** (585 Calle la Placita; 575-653-4300) was later rebuilt on the same site and still operates as a hotel.

Jose Montano and his wife Josefa ran the **Montano Store** (US 380), a long, one-story adobe structure built prior to 1868 that served as a store and boarding house. During the five-day battle, the store was occupied by some of the gunmen from the McSween faction, including Fernando Herrera who made a 440-yard shot from the adobe that mortally wounded Charlie Crawford, one of the Murphy-Dolan men. The state acquired the old store in 1966 and it now houses an exhibit on Lincoln's early days as a Hispanic settlement.

Though they were killed on opposite sides and on different days, Tunstall and McSween are buried next to each other just behind the Tunstall Store, their graves marked only by crosses. With McSween's death, the Lincoln County War was over.

El Torreon

Built in the 1850s, the two-story rock tower known as **El Torreon** (927 Billy the Kid Trail) was intended as a place of refuge and defense in the advent of an attack by Apaches. Women and children would be gathered behind a thick door on the ground floor while men with rifles stood behind the circular parapet on the open-topped second level. Nearly three decades after its construction, the tower, more European looking than western, would be used for observation and sniping during the Lincoln County War's climactic five-day battle. The tower was restored by the federal Works Progress Administration in the 1930s. A state historical marker stands nearby.

Old Lincoln County Courthouse

Scheduled to hang in only fifteen days for the murder of Sheriff William Brady three years earlier, Billy the Kid escaped from the Lincoln County Courthouse on April 28, 1881. In the process, he killed two more Lincoln County officers, Deputies James Bell and Bob Olinger.

Unlike most courthouses, this two-story, stucco-covered adobe building had not been built for government use. Constructed in 1873 and 1874, it had been a store owned by the L.G. Murphy Co. until the company went bankrupt in 1880. Lincoln County bought the building and it served as the courthouse until the county seat moved to Carrizozo in 1913. After seeing a variety of uses, the property was purchased by the state in 1938 and opened as a museum a year later. Outside the museum (US 380), memorial stones mark the site where each deputy shot by The Kid fell.

Lordsburg (Hidalgo County)

Lordsburg developed when the Southern Pacific Railroad cut through the territory in 1880. The town was probably named for Southern Pacific official Delbert Lord, but some sources suggest the honoree was Dr. Charles H. Lord, a prominent Tucson, Arizona, businessman.

Lordsburg-Hidalgo County Museum (710 East 2nd St.; 575-542-9086) tells the story of the town and area around it.

"O Fair New Mexico"

Pat Garrett rid New Mexico of Billy the Kid, and the lawman's blind daughter gave New Mexico its state song, "O Fair New Mexico." Elizabeth Garrett (1885–1947) was living in Lordsburg in 1915 when she wrote the piece. Governor Washington E. Lindsey signed the measure making it the official state song in 1917. Eleven years later, noted composer John Philip Sousa presented the people of New Mexico an arrangement of the song that conveyed in music the early history of the state.

MESCALERO (OTERO COUNTY)

First called Blazer's Mill, Mescalero saw one singular event, an April 4, 1878, Lincoln County War shoot-out known as the **Gunfight at Blazer's Mill**. On that day, only three days after Billy the Kid killed Lincoln County Sheriff William J. Brady, The Kid and fifteen other members of the Tunstall faction (the so-called Regulators) were having a meal at the combination store and sawmill when Andrew (Buckshot) Roberts showed up. Since he was believed to have had a hand in Tunstall's murder, the Regulators promptly started shooting at him. Wounded, Buckshot ran to an adobe building and held off the Tunstall men until he ran out of ammunition. He was fatally wounded shortly after that, but not before he had killed Regulator leader Dick Brewer. The Kid and several others suffered nonfatal wounds.

A historical marker on US 70 three miles west of Mescalero summarizes the battle. Roberts and Brewer were buried in the Blazer Family Cemetery (GPS coordinates: N33° 09.41', W105° 47.16').

RATON (COLFAX COUNTY)

Travelers along the mountain branch of the Santa Fe Trail, which cut through the Sangre de Cristo Mountains at Raton Pass, camped here for the good, cool water from Willow Springs and to recover from their arduous trek along the pass. US Army engineers improved the trail across the mountain range in 1846. Twenty years later "Uncle" Dick Wooten did additional work on the twenty-seven-mile stretch of road, including building a gate across the road, which allowed him to begin charging travelers a toll. Even with the improvements, it still took five days to navigate the pass. In 1878, the Atchison, Topeka, and

Santa Fe Railway purchased the toll road as a right of way for its soon-to-be-laid tracks. When the railroad reached the area in 1879, it built a depot. In 1880 it platted a townsite. Within a year this northeastern New Mexico town had three thousand residents and continued to grow as a railroad, mining, and ranching center.

Raton's downtown became a National Historic District in 1977. Bounded by Clark and Rio Grande Avenues and 1st and 3rd Streets, the district covers two hundred acres and contains ninety-five historic buildings. A self-guided walking tour is available from the **Raton Museum** (108 South 2nd St.; 575-445-8979). This museum began on a small scale in the early 1930s with an exhibit in Raton City Hall. As the collection grew, the museum moved from location to location to accommodate its holdings. In 2004 the Raton Archeological and Historical Society purchased a former bank built in 1906, remodeled it, and opened the museum there in 2008. Displays cover the full range of the area's history.

Alcohol Plus Gunpowder Equals Trouble

If **Gus Mentzer** had only stuck to what Bank Exchange Saloon owner William Burbridge paid him for, he and four other Raton men might have lived to old age. But Mentzer sampled too much of the product he dispensed and Burbridge fired him. The twenty-four-year-old left town, but on June 26, 1882, he returned—drunk and armed with a revolver. What unfolded that evening proved a tragic comedy of errors. Early on, Colfax County Deputy Sheriff Pete Dollman tried to disarm and arrest Mentzer, but that ended in an exchange of gunfire that left an innocent bystander wounded by one of the lawman's errant shots. Mentzer, meanwhile, ran into his former workplace and out the back door. When citizens S.H. Jackson and Hugh Eddleston confronted Mentzer at the rail yard, Mentzer shot and killed both.

Deputies Dollman and William Burgen finally corralled Mentzer and took him to another saloon where they locked him in a back room, guarded by Burgen. Shortly, Justice of the Peace Harvey Moulton showed up armed and attempted to seize Mentzer so he and other friends of Jackson and Eddleston could lynch him. In the process of trying to protect Mentzer, Deputy Burgen fired and mortally wounded the judge. Still, Moulton had enough time before he fell dead to inflict a mortal wound on the deputy. Meanwhile, Mentzer escaped again but was shortly recaptured. Before he had a chance to make another break, outraged townspeople decided enough was enough. They took control of the prisoner, put a rope around his neck, tossed the other end over a sign, considerately offered him a chance to pray, and then hoisted him up. All was going well for everyone but Mentzer until the sign broke and he fell, still alive. A young boy helpfully took the end of the rope and draped it over a sturdier sign and Mentzer again rose skyward. This time the sign held and soon Mentzer dangled permanently cured of overindulging in spiritous beverages.

Concerned that five violent deaths in one evening might tarnish Raton's image, a large number of citizens met a few days later and produced a written warning that all "professional gamblers, footpads, thieves, cappers, dance hall men, bunko men, and all . . . who have no means of visible support, as well as all dance hall girls and prostitutes" had until noon July 3 to vacate town. How long they stayed gone was not reported, but the town's saloon, gambling, and bawdy house district continued to flourish into the early twentieth century.

The Bank Exchange Saloon stood in the 100 block of 1st Street. It has not survived, but the two buildings (132 North 1st St.) that once accommodated the old Gem and Home Ranch saloons still exist. Mentzer was lynched at the corner of Clark Street and 1st Street.

Deputy Burgen lies in an unmarked grave in the Blossburg Cemetery. Blossburg is a ghost town five miles northwest of Raton. The remnants of this long-defunct coal mining town and the cemetery are on the Vermejo Park Ranch, owned by Ted Turner, and not open to the public. Burgen's name is etched into the National Law Enforcement Officers Memorial (panel: 40-W: 22) in Washington, DC.

Reserve (Catron County)

Someone impersonating a law enforcement officer almost always does so for a nefarious reason. In the fall of 1884, nineteen-year-old Socorro, New Mexico, store clerk **Elfego Baca** (1865–1945)—outraged at reports of Anglo cowboys abusing Hispanics—commissioned himself as a sheriff's deputy with the intention of doing something good. He claimed at the murder trial he soon faced that in trying to bring law and order to the village of Lower San Francisco Plaza he had operated under the color of the law. But most historians believe he just took it upon himself to single handedly undertake the taming of San Francisco (usually referred to as Frisco) and now known as Reserve.

Armed with two six-shooters and wearing a mail-order badge, Baca arrived in Frisco and began trying to police drunken cowboys on rancher John Slaughter's payroll. After Baca arrested and disarmed a drunken cowboy, the cowboy's friends intervened and Baca started shooting. One of Baca's bullets hit the Slaughter Ranch foreman's horse and when the animal toppled, its weight killed the rider. When the local justice of the peace sent a deputized citizen to bring Baca in for murder, he barricaded himself in a wooden and adobe jacal. When the man approached the small house, Baca shot through the door and fatally wounded him.

Scores of cowboys surrounded the structure and a gun battle ensued. Most of the bullets went into the adobe or through the wooden front door, though Baca fired back occasionally. The siege lasted twenty-four hours—by some accounts more than thirty hours—before Baca emerged—guns still in hand—after negotiating a surrender in which he had been assured protection from lynching-minded cowboys.

At his murder trial in Albuquerque, the jacal's bullet-riddled door was introduced into evidence to show the intensity of the siege. Baca was acquitted and went on to a long and celebrated career as a sure-enough sheriff, US deputy marshal, politician, and lawyer.

In 1958, thirteen years after Baca's death, Walt Disney produced a ten-part television series called *The Nine Lives of Elfego Baca*. The show was well-received and one of the first portrayals of a Hispanic as someone other than the era's stereotypical evil or lazy Mexican.

The standoff took place at what is now the **Lower Frisco Store** (State Highway 435) on the plaza. In 2007 *One Man, One War*, a life-size bronze statue of Baca standing in a door frame, pistol in hand, was dedicated on State Highway 435 across from the Catron County Courthouse (100 Main St.). Baca is buried in **Sunset Memorial Park** (924 Menaul Blvd., Albuquerque; block 11, plot 41, lot 1).

Roswell (Chaves County)

John S. Chisum, who came to be called the Cattle King of the Pecos, brought his first herd of longhorns to New Mexico Territory in 1867 along the newly blazed Goodnight-Loving Trail. Coping with unfriendly American Indians, rustlers, and the vagaries of weather, by the mid-1870s Chisum had become the largest cattle producer in the US, with some eighty thousand longhorn steers. He first located his ranch headquarters at **Bosque Grande** on the Pecos River between Roswell and Fort Sumner, but in 1875 moved his headquarters to the southern edge of the small community that grew into Roswell. Despite his friendship with John Tunstall, the first victim of the vicious Lincoln County War, and Alexander McSween, the final victim, he managed to stay on the periphery of the conflict. Even so, he befriended Billy the Kid only to later have a role in picking Pat Garrett as Lincoln County sheriff.

Chisum is memorialized in a larger-than-life statue (Pioneer Plaza, between 4th and 5th Streets and Main) placed in 2001. Executed by sculptor Robert Summers, the bronze depicts the mounted cattleman wrangling a cantankerous longhorn.

Goodnight-Loving Trail

The well-traveled **Goodnight-Loving cattle trail** extended from Texas through New Mexico to Colorado. Later the route expanded to Wyoming. A historical marker describing the trail stands at Mile Marker 167 on US 360 (GPS coordinates: N33° 24.32', W104° 18.65').

Pat Garrett in Roswell

Pat Garrett and family moved to the Roswell area in 1883. He ranched, farmed, invested in rental property, and envisioned building irrigation canals to divert water from the Pecos River, but none of those enterprises proved successful for him. With the organization of Chaves County, he ran for sheriff in 1890. Losing the election, he left Roswell in disgust in 1891 to ranch in Uvalde County, Texas.

One hundred twenty-one years later, a larger-than-life bronze statue of the famed lawman was erected across from the county courthouse (400 North Virginia Ave.; GPS coordinates: N33° 23.83', W104° 31.26'). Sculpted by Glen Rose, Texas, artist Robert Summers, the piece was funded by a $250,000 legislative appropriation.

A one-and-a-half-story adobe house (GPS coordinates: N33° 24.23', W104° 26.28') dating to the 1880s that Garrett and his family lived in still stands on Bosque Road, three miles north of Roswell. It was listed on the National Register of Historic Places in 1988.

Born blind, Sheriff Pat Garrett's daughter **Elizabeth Garrett** (1885–1947) learned music at the State School for the Blind in Austin, Texas, and had a noted career as a singer and song writer-composer. Among her numerous compositions was the New Mexico state song, "O Fair New Mexico." She was living in Roswell when on October 16, 1947, during a power blackout, she is believed to have tripped and fallen, hitting her head. She is buried in South Park Cemetery (3101 South Main St.; 575-624-6748).

Lincoln County War Vets

Three Lincoln County War participants are buried in **South Park Cemetery** (3101 South Main St.; 575-624-6748).

John William Poe (1850–1923) was Pat Garrett's deputy at the time Garrett killed Billy the Kid and succeeded him as Lincoln County sheriff. Later Poe defeated Garrett again when he ran for sheriff in Chaves County. Poe went on to become a prominent Roswell banker. His former residence still stands at 311 West 7th St.

Jacob Basil Matthews (1847–1904) took part in several Lincoln County War gun battles and later served as Roswell postmaster from 1898 until his death six years later.

Milo Lucius Pierce (1838–1919), a Murphy-Dolan partisan, was wounded in the 1879 Seven Rivers gunfight, later moved to Roswell and became a successful cattleman.

In a Southwest-style building constructed by the federal Works Progress Administration, the **Roswell Museum and Arts Center** (1011 North Richardson Ave.; 575-624-6744) opened in 1935. With an initial focus on art, the museum later began developing exhibits related to area history. Operated by the Chaves County Archaeological and Historical Society and the Roswell Friends of Art, the museum has expanded over the years to fifty thousand square feet accommodating twelve galleries.

Since 1976 the **Historical Society for Southeast New Mexico** has maintained a local and regional history museum (200 North Lea Ave.; 575-622-8333) in the two-story, tile-roofed, yellow brick house built in 1912 for pioneer cattleman James Phelps White (1856–1934) and his wife Lou. The nephew of famed Texas rancher George W. Littlefield, White came to New Mexico Territory in 1881 and established the LFD Ranch north of Roswell. By 1920 he was said to be the wealthiest rancher in the state.

Across the parking lot from the museum is another old two-story brick house that contains the society's archival collection of some twenty-five thousand documents and fourteen thousand photographs concerning the history of southeastern New Mexico.

White and his wife are buried in South Park Cemetery (3101 South Main St.; 575-624-6748).

Ruidoso (Lincoln County)

In 1869 former army captain **Paul Dowlin** homesteaded in the area that would become Ruidoso, hoping to make a living—not to enjoy the mountain scenery. Dowlin built a sawmill on the Rio Ruidoso (Spanish for "noisy river") to provide lumber for an expansion underway at nearby Fort Stanton, where he had been stationed. When a flood washed that mill away, he built another mill on higher ground, powering it with water that came down a three-mile wooden flume from the river. This time he used it for grinding grain and thrashing beans. Business was good and got a further boost in 1873 when the government opened a reservation nearby for the Mescalero Apaches. In 1877 Dowlin sold a half-interest in his mill to Frank Lesnett, also an ex-soldier. But on May 5 that year, a former mill worker named Jerry Dillon fatally shot Dowlin. Dillon fled to Texas and was never heard of again.

Meanwhile, a store and blacksmith shop opened near the mill. The small community was known as Dowlin's Mill, but when a post office opened there in 1891 it was renamed Ruidoso. Early on, the small town gained recognition as more than just a place to have grinding done or buy supplies. "Certain it is that the Ruidoso has already won rank as the most popular resort for camping out in all the country for 200 miles about El Paso," the *El Paso Times* observed in 1889, "a grassy mountain valley surmounted by a dense forest in which weary mortals from the city may hide themselves for a few weeks or rest and refreshment. . . . Before many years, summer hotels will abound in the locality." That is exactly what would happen.

The **Dowlin's Mill** (641 Sudderth Dr.) with a reconstructed water wheel still stands, but it was gutted by fire in 2017. The adobe building, listed on the National Register of Historic Places, was restored.

R.D. and Joan Dale Hubbard started a museum in 1989 to house their large art collection. The same year, Anne Stradling, another longtime collector of horse-related items and art donated her collection to the museum. The Hubbards purchased a former convention center in nearby Ruidoso Downs and converted it into a museum originally called the Hubbard Museum of the Horse, opened in 1992. Thirteen years later, the Hubbards donated the museum to the City of Ruidoso Downs and its name was changed to the **Hubbard Museum of the American West** (26301 US 70, Ruidoso Downs; 575-378-4142). In addition to its Western art, with wagons, carriages, saddles, firearms, and American Indian artifacts, the museum is focused on the Old West in general.

Santa Clara (Grant County)

The early years of the nation's longest-running armed conflict, the Apache Wars, led to the establishment of **Fort Bayard** in 1866. Three decades later, the surrender of Geronimo made the post strategically irrelevant. Notable figures stationed there during its active years include Gen. George Crook; Second Lt. John J. Pershing; and Medal of Honor recipient Cpl. Clinton Greaves, an African-American soldier with the famed Ninth Cavalry, one of the old army's two Buffalo Soldier regiments. When the military abandoned the fort in 1886, the installation was converted into an army tuberculosis hospital and later became a Veteran's Administration facility. In 1965 New Mexico took it over as a state hospital, but that closed in 2010.

The old fort is a half a mile north of the intersection of State Highway 152 and US 180. A monument commemorating the Buffalo Soldiers was erected on the old parade ground in 1993 and the site was named a National Historic Landmark in 2004. Adjacent to it lies the Fort Bayard National Cemetery (200 Cam De Paz; 505-988-6400).

The **Santa Clara-Fort Bayard Visitor Center** (US 180), with displays on the fort's history, opened in 2019 in the old national guard armory.

Santa Fe (Santa Fe County)

By the time the nation began the intense period of expansion that brought on the Wild West, Santa Fe was an old town. Lying at the base of the Sangre de Cristo Mountains, it began as a Spanish settlement thirteen years before the pilgrims arrived on the East Coast. When the first traders arrived from Missouri along the route that would soon be known as the Santa Fe Trail, Santa Fe was already more than two hundred years old. Unlike many old cities, Santa Fe never became a large metropolitan center, but it is the state capital and the historical and cultural heart of New Mexico. From remnants of its Pueblo culture to a wide range of historical sites and museums to its artistic community, Santa Fe lives up to its modern descriptor as "The City Different."

Spanish colonial towns were built around square plazas. The plaza in Santa Fe was laid out more than four hundred years ago and continues as the center of the city. Listed on the National Register of Historic Places, the Santa Fe Plaza has seen the entire history of the Old West, from Spanish and Mexican bullfights to heavily laden freight wagons arriving from St. Joseph, Missouri, to military clashes and gunfights to political events to American Indians selling tourists hand-crafted jewelry.

Explorations of Santa Fe are best started at the **Santa Fe Plaza Visitor Information Center** (66 East San Francisco St.; 800-777-24890). The plaza is framed by Lincoln, Palace, San Francisco, and Washington Streets.

The circa-1610 **Palace of the Governors** (105 West Palace Ave.; 515-476-5100) predates the Alamo by more than a century and is the oldest public building constructed by people of European descent still in use in the continental US. Built as the home of the first royal Spanish governor, the adobe palace has seen more than four hundred years of Southwestern history. During the **Pueblo Revolt** (1680–1693) the palace was occupied by the Pueblo people. The palace also served the governments of Mexico and the Confederate States of America. After the US took control of New Mexico in 1846, the palace was the territorial capitol until 1886 and remained the governor's residence until 1907.

The building was named a National Historic Landmark in 1960. From 1909 to 2008, the **New Mexico History Museum** occupied the old adobe building but moved to an adjoining building (113 Lincoln Ave.) in 2009. The palace and the museum both have exhibits.

The **Santa Fe National Cemetery** (501 North Guadalupe St.; 505-988-6400) is the final resting places of numerous notable figures, including Charles Bent (1799–1847), the slain first governor of New Mexico Territory (see Taos). Among numerous military graves are four recipients of the Indian Wars Congressional Medal of Honor and Capt. George Niles Bascom (1837–1862), whose handling of the kidnapping of a rancher's son in Arizona led to the twenty-year war with the Cochise Apaches.

On March 1, 1873, young Henry McCarty (known in Western history as outlaw Billy the Kid) and his brother attended the wedding of their mother Catherine McCarty to William Antrim at Santa Fe's **First Presbyterian Church** (208 Grant Ave.). The original 1867 church was replaced by the present sanctuary in 1937 and 1938. Years later, The Kid spent a little over two months in the county jail on the lower floor of the two-story **Cornell Building** (208 West San Francisco St.). A historical plaque was placed on the former jail building in 1944.

In addition to its exhibits and artifacts interpreting New Mexico's long history, the **New Mexico History Museum** (113 East Lincoln Ave.; 505-476-5200) has a pair of Billy the Kid's spurs and the letters he wrote from 1879 to 1881 to territorial governor Lew Wallace.

Three Out of Four's Not Bad

The flat granite stone over **Samuel W. Ketchum**'s grave notes he was "Cowboy, Husband, Father & Outlaw." The latter occupation is what got him into trouble. After he and Wild Bunch associates Kid Curry and Elzy Lay robbed a train at Folsom, New Mexico, on July 11, 1899, a posse trailed them to Turkey Creek Canyon near Cimarron. The shoot-out that followed left Sheriff Edward Farr dead and Ketchum mortally wounded. Taken to the New Mexico Territorial Prison in Santa Fe, the outlaw died that July 24. His younger brother Tom, while not involved in the Folsom robbery, continued his outlaw ways—but not for long (see Clayton). Sam Ketchum lies in **Odd Fellows Cemetery** (1125 Cerrillos Rd.; GPS coordinates: N35° 40.44', W105° 57.59').

The Other Judge Parker

Federal Judge Isaac Parker, the so-called "Hanging Judge," added to the lore of the Old West from his bench at Fort Smith, Arkansas. In New Mexico Territory, District Judge **Frank W. Parker** (1860–1932) could be called the Non-Hanging Judge in that his two most famous capital cases both ended in acquittals. While the jury made the final determination as to guilt or innocence, Judge Parker wielded the gavel.

The first well-known acquittal in Parker's court came in the 1899 murder trial of Oliver Lee and Jim Gilliland in the disappearance and presumed murder of Albert Jennings Fountain and his son Henry (see Las Cruces). The second trial saw the acquittal of Wayne Brazel, accused killer of Pat Garrett, in 1909.

Parker later served on the New Mexico Supreme Court. Judge Parker is buried in **Fairview Cemetery** (1134 Cerrillos Rd.; section B, plot 189).

Shakespeare (Hidalgo County)

Prospectors found rich silver ore in the hills around future Shakespeare in 1870. The discovery attracted California capital, and a town named for San Francisco bank president William Ralston soon developed. When the silver soon played out, word spread that diamonds had been found in the vicinity of the new town. That kept the economy going until it became apparent that no one was finding any diamonds—the report had been a hoax.

In 1879 William G. Boyle purchased promising gold and silver claims in the area and gave the town a new name honoring the world's best-known playwright, William Shakespeare. Boyle's Shakespeare Gold and Silver Mining Company enjoyed good profits as the town experienced its second boom.

Unlike many boomtowns, Shakespeare never had a tough, fearless lawman who became famous, but it did have a catchy local tradition: "If you kill a man, you dig his grave." Desert digging, as any miner would attest, was not easy. While the town never had its "Wyatt Earp," some of the West's better-known bad men did pass through, including Curly Bill Brocius, John Ringo, Billy the Kid, and Tom (Black Jack) Ketchum. Two criminally minded characters who came to Shakespeare and never left, at least not while drawing breath, were Sandy King and a want-to-be bravo from Russia known as Russian Bill. Both men were afforded a rare indoor lynching; someone with a sense of humor mixed with a tad of compassion later wrote Bill's mother in Europe that her son died of breathing difficulties due to high elevation.

But having a railroad connection was critical for any town hoping to last, and the Southern Pacific laid its tracks three miles from town. That marked the beginning of Lordsburg and the beginning of the end for Shakespeare. The Panic of 1893 was another major setback for the town. Fourteen years later, a copper mine opened a mile south of town and the figurative curtain went up on Shakespeare's final act as an active community. When that boom ended, no encore was forthcoming.

When Frank and Rita Hill bought ranch land in 1935, it included the old town. They watched over the place and let visitors walk around the property, which in 1970 was made a National Historic Site. A nonprofit foundation now works to preserve Shakespeare, which because of its protective owners over the years is considered one of the Old West's best preserved ghost towns.

Shakespeare is two and a half miles southwest of Lordsburg on State Highway 494. The lynching of Russian Bill and Sandy King occurred inside the Grant House Dining Room on November 9, 1881. The building still stands. The two men are buried in Shakespeare Cemetery (section 2, lot 43). A substantial granite stone placed by an area rancher marks their two graves.

Silver City (Grant County)

The shortest version of Silver City's history is its name. Though gold mining had been going on around Pinos Altos since 1859, another decade passed before brothers John and James Bullard discovered a rich vein of silver-bearing ore where Silver City soon took shape. The mining district that developed around Silver City went on to produce millions of dollars in precious metal, but John Bullard did not live to enjoy prosperity. During a clash with Apaches in 1871, Bullard took a bullet through the heart.

As the new town of Silver City filled with the standard traveling troupe of boomtown players, from sellers of booze to renters of female bodies, the fast-growing town kept the journalists employed by its six competing newspapers busy covering all the winging and killing. Pointing out that Silver City preceded such famous places as Dodge City, Deadwood, and Tombstone, writer Bob Alexander wrote: "Historically cataloging all of the six-shooter dustups taking place on Silver City streets or in her rowdy and jam-packed saloons during the early 1870s is virtually an unworkable undertaking." The town later calmed with a decline in silver mining, but agriculture and copper mining kept it going. A self-guided walking tour of the historic downtown is available at the **Silver City Visitor Center** (201 North Hudson St.; 575-538-5555).

Billy's Mama

Despite years of research, no one has ever determined who Henry McCarty's (aka Billy the Kid) father was. But none have questioned that his mother was **Catherine McCarty**, even though no one knows for sure if McCarty was her maiden name or that of her first husband. Catherine and her second husband, William Antrim, moved to Silver City in the spring of 1873. And here Billy's mama stayed, dying of tuberculosis in her early to mid-forties in 1874. Less than a year after losing his mother, young Henry was arrested for theft. The case never went before a judge because Henry escaped from the Grant County Jail, the beginning of his six-year outlaw career. A reproduction of the log cabin where Catherine and her family lived stands outside the Silver City Visitor Center (201 North Hudson St.; 575-538-5555). Catherine is buried in Memory Lane Cemetery (2000 Memory Ln.; plot D-E27-14).

Opened in 1967 and operated by the Town of Silver City, the **Silver City Museum** (310 West Broadway St.; 575-538-5921) occupies a building that looks like it ought to be a museum, the 1881 **H.B. Allman House**. Built of locally made bricks and lumber milled from timber felled in nearby forestland, the house was a private residence for twenty years before becoming a boarding house. That usage lasted for a quarter century. After that, the house served for a time as city hall, followed by thirty-five years as a fire station. As the museum's website notes, the house is the museum's largest artifact. There are another fifty thousand artifacts and documents in the museum's collection.

Taos (Taos County)

As the website maintained by Taos's tourism office points out, it can take a while to explore a millennium's worth of history. Taos began as a large, multistory adobe pueblo that still exists, the only living American Indian community that is a United Nations World Heritage Site and a National Historic Landmark. Since early Pueblo people settled here around 1000 AD, Taos has indeed seen a lot of history.

Taos Visitor Center (1139 Paseo del Pueblo Sur; 575-758-3873) has a self-guided walking tour with information on twenty-two downtown historic sites along with material on other historic sites and attractions.

Kit Carson

By the time mountain man and scout **Kit Carson** and his new wife Josefa moved into an adobe house here in 1843, Taos was a well-established waypoint on the Santa Fe Trail. Though under Mexican control since that country gained its independence from Spain's colonial empire in 1821, the Republic of Texas had an audacious, paper-only claim on eastern New Mexico and Taos. But war between the US and Mexico would bring Taos and all of New Mexico under American control in 1848. Carson spent much time afield in military service, but always came home to Taos.

The one-story, four-room adobe house the Carsons lived in until 1867 was built around 1825. Its two-foot-thick walls house a museum that interprets Carson's life with exhibits and artifacts. A National Historic Landmark, the **Kit Carson House and Museum** (113 Kit Carson Rd.; 575-758-4082) is owned by Taos's Masonic Lodge.

Carson died in 1868, and he and other noted Taoseños are buried in **Kit Carson Cemetery** (211 Paseo Pueblo del Norte, one and a half blocks north of the plaza).

A Governor Assassinated

Charles Bent (1789–1847) had gone from mountain man, fur trapper, and trader to the presidentially appointed governor of New Mexico. His ascension to political office came in 1846 during the Mexican War, when the US invaded Mexico and seized much of the Southwest, including New Mexico. But Bent's time as governor was not long. In the early morning hours of January 19, 1847, he was killed in his residence by a mob bent on forcing the US out of New Mexico. As his wife (Kit Carson's sister) and children looked on, the wounded governor was scalped alive. He later died, along with Sheriff Stephen Lee and four others, including Mrs. Bent's brother. US troops arrived from Santa Fe a few days later to assure American control over the area.

The governor's body was taken to Santa Fe for burial. Originally laid to rest in Santa Fe's old Masonic and Odd Fellows Cemetery (last used in 1895), Bent's remains were reburied in the **Santa Fe National Cemetery** (501 North Guadalupe St., Santa Fe; 505-988-6400).

Bent's former residence, **Governor Bent House and Museum** (117 Bent St.; 505-758-2376) houses a privately operated museum.

Long John Dunn

John Dunn stood only six feet, but his lanky frame was tall enough to earn him his nickname of Long John. Having escaped from prison in Texas, his "appeal" of a life sentence for murder that to his mind was nothing more than a necessary killing, Dunn arrived in Taos in 1889 and stayed the rest of his life. He ran saloons and a gambling place, but also had a livery stable and later operated a couple of private toll bridges. All that made him a venerated Taos character, but his pre-Taos years amounted to a history of the Wild West. He had lived through (and participated in) the peak of the gun-fighting era, the trail-driving days, and more than half-way into the twentieth century, dying at ninety in 1955. Fortunately for posterity, noted New Mexican writer Max Evans spent time interviewing Dunn and told his story in his 1959 book, *Long John Dunn of Taos: From Texas Outlaw to New Mexico Hero.*

Dunn's renovated former residence (120 Bent St.) is leased to a group of shop owners. Dunn is buried in Kit Carson Cemetery (211 Paseo Pueblo del Norte).

Tucumcari (Quay County)

Tucumcari began as a railroad construction camp when the Chicago, Rock Island, and Pacific Railroad cut into eastern New Mexico in 1901. First called Ragtown because it consisted of tents, its next name was Six-Shooter Switch in recognition of its rowdy character. Then it became Douglas before it gained its fourth and final name after nearby Tucumcari Mountain.

Mass Murder at the Legal Tender

After the railroad arrived, bad blood developed between area cowboys and railroad men working on the line's extension. First, Wild Jack Donavan gunned down a railroad worker in the middle of Main Street. Donavan took a fast horse out of town and things quieted down until later that month when a fight between railroaders and cowboys in the **Legal Tender Saloon** derailed into a general shooting. When the smoke cleared, thirteen dead gandy dancers lay on the sawdust-covered wooden floor. With the sheriff out of town and the marshal otherwise occupied, the cowboys sobered enough to collect the bodies, toss them in a wagon, sweep up the bloody sawdust, and roll out of town with the evidence as fast as the driver could whip the team. Once the cowboys made it to a remote location, they buried the bodies in a mass grave, and no one was ever the wiser. At least that's the story told by Tucumcari old-timer Jess Price in the April-May 1963 issue of *Frontier Times* magazine. The article's headline called the cowboy cover-up the "Best Kept Secret of the West!" It must have been, because contemporary newspapers and other sources offer no evidence any such thing ever occurred in Tucumcari. The story seems to be conflated from something that did happen—the killing of three rustlers by a posse in February 1902, the same month and year the mass murder was said to have happened.

The **Tucumcari Heritage Museum** (416 South Adams; 575-461-4201) fills all three floors of a 1903-vintage schoolhouse. The museum's website reflects something of the attitude that must have led to such a wild story about Tucumcari's early days: "A lot of big city museums are antiseptic and sterile. This museum is different. It's like one giant attic of old stuff . . . about anything goes."

White Oaks (Lincoln County)

Gold discoveries generally meant big money, but not always for the finder. The rich gold ore vein found in 1879 in the mountains of Lincoln County brought about the mining boomtown of White Oaks. Of the four men involved—Jack Winters, John Baxter, John Wilson, and George Wilson (no relation to John)—only Winters made any big money. And he died of pneumonia aggravated by overuse of whiskey in 1881 before he was able to enjoy his wealth. At least Baxter got a mountain named after him. That mountain is where the men staked their claims and where a half dozen mines produced millions in gold ore before the vein petered out. Beneath that mountain, the town of White Oaks sprouted and grew rapidly. The town still had a chance at survival by securing a railroad connection, but when property owners asked too much for the right-of-way the railroad needed, it bypassed White Oaks and the town wilted. Listed on the National Register of Historic Places in 1970, White Oaks (twelve miles northwest of Carrizozo off State Highway 349) is often referred to as a ghost town, but it still has a few score residents. One original commercial building, a couple of two-story Victorian houses, and the former White Oaks school are the primary remnants of the old town. The school is the only publicly owned building. Built in 1892 at a cost of $10,000 on a hill overlooking town, the two-story, four-room brick former schoolhouse accommodates a museum. The building is owned by the state while the museum is operated by the local historical society.

Cedarvale Cemetery

The **Cedarvale Cemetery** (one mile west of White Oaks on County Road A044), listed on the National Register of Historic Places, was originally known simply as White Oaks Cemetery. In the 1930s, residents decided to hold a contest to come up with a more pleasing name and the winning suggestion was Cedarvale.

The cemetery may possibly be the final resting place of **James W. Bell** (1853–1881), one of two deputies Billy the Kid killed in his escape from the Lincoln County jail in 1881 (see Lincoln). Bell's grave had been lost until a researcher concluded that the lawman was buried in White Oaks. Based on that, in 2003 a substantial gravestone was placed at the supposed location of his grave. Seven years later, another researcher cast doubt on that earlier determination. Wherever Bell lies, he did finally get a lasting memorial.

Long-standing custom in the nineteenth century was to bury people facing east. All the graves in the Cedarvale Cemetery lie west to east except for the final resting place of prospector **Jack Winters**, one of the men who triggered the White Oaks boom. At his request, he was buried north to south so he could "face his strike on Baxter Mountain forever."

The Cattle Queen of New Mexico

Also buried in Cedarvale Cemetery is **Susan Homer McSween Barber** (1845–1931), the "Cattle Queen of New Mexico," the widow of Alexander McSween, killed in the Lincoln County War in 1878. Two years later, she married George Barber. While George practiced law in Lincoln and White Oaks, Susan ran their Three Rivers Land and Cattle Co. They divorced in 1892, but she held the ranch another decade before moving to White Oaks.

N
NEW MEXICO
OKLAHOMA
ARKANSAS
LOUISIANA
TEXAS
MEXICO
GULF OF MEXICO
Adobe Walls
Jacksboro
Fort Worth
Dallas
Waco
Round Rock
Austin
Houston
Galveston
San Antonio
Indianola
Kingsville
Brownsville
El Paso
Fort Davis
Langtry
SIERRA DIABLO
DAVIS MOUNTAINS
SIERRA VIEJA
Rio Grande
Canadian River
Red River
Lake Texoma
Arkansas River
Sulphur River
Sabine River
Brazos River
Lake Whitney
Colorado River
Pecos River
San Saba River
Llano River
Lake Travis
Neches River
Lake Livingston
Guadalupe River
Medina River
Frio River
San Antonio River
Nueces River
Laguna Madre
Rio Conchos
0 100 200 kilometers
0 100 200 miles

TEXAS

Abilene (Taylor, Jones Counties)

Abilene—named for the Kansas cattle town—began as a frontier tent town when the Texas and Pacific tracks reached what is now Taylor County in 1881. The community grew as the principal city in what would come to be called the Big Country. Thirty years before settlement began in the area, the military established one of the Old West's most evocatively named outposts.

Fort Phantom Hill

The army designated this fort as Post on the Clear Fork of the Brazos, even though it was on Elm Creek. Everyone else called it **Fort Phantom Hill**.

Established in 1851, it stood on high ground known as Phantom Hill. One version of how the hill got its name is that from a distance it looked higher than it did close-up. As riders got closer, the hill appeared to disappear, a phantom hill. The other legend is that a jumpy soldier on night guard duty shot at what he thought was a foe sneaking up on the fort. When no one found any trace of an intruder, someone opined that the sentry must have fired on a phantom. The fort proved almost as ethereal as its name. Abandoned in 1854, its buildings soon were destroyed by fire. No one knows for sure how that happened either.

The ruins of the old fort (10818 Farm to Market Road 600) are fourteen miles north of Abilene in Jones County. Until 1997 the site was on private property, but that year the owners donated thirty-eight acres to the nonprofit **Fort Phantom Hill Foundation** (325-667-1309). The foundation placed interpretive signs marking points of interest among the ruins and oversaw construction of restroom facilities. A state historical marker also stands at the site.

.45 Caliber New Year's

City marshal **John J. Clinton** (1848–1922) fought Yankees in the Civil War and American Indians on the Great Plains, but as a peace officer he would not shoot someone unless he had to. However, he was not reluctant to use his six-shooter as a communication device.

Newly founded, Abilene's city ordinances called for the rowdy railroad town's numerous saloons to close at midnight, and there was no exception for New Year's Eve. Folks inclined to celebrate the changing of the calendar needed to do so prior to midnight or spend part of the first day of the new year in the clink.

Not having enough deputies to go from saloon to saloon to remind celebrants and bartenders of the midnight curfew, Marshal Clinton passed word that he would signal last call by discharging his pistol into the air from the corner of South 1st and Chestnut Streets.

The marshal was an old-school lawman, not a scientist. But he readily understood that when he pointed his .45 to the sky and pulled the trigger, the discharge would be loud enough to be heard in every watering hole within his jurisdiction. Accordingly, on December 31, 1884, Abilene's top cop emptied his handgun into the night sky to let it be known to all revelers that the party was over.

Abilene's saloons closed for good during World War I, but by then, the chief's New Year's Eve pistol shooting had become a holiday tradition, a Wild West–style "Auld Lang Syne." So, every December 31, when both hands of his watch overlapped on twelve, Clinton pulled his six-shooter and rang in the new year with orange muzzle blasts and flying lead. The marshal stayed in office for the rest of his life, continuing the tradition until his death in 1922.

A state historical marker commemorating the chief and his six-shooter salutes stands at South 1st and Chestnut Streets. Clinton is buried beneath a flat gray granite marker in the Masonic section of Abilene's **Municipal Cemetery** (1133 Cottonwood St.).

Frontier Texas (625 North 1st St.; 325-437-2800) is a multimedia center dedicated to the history of West Texas from the days Plains Indians held sway over the region to the arrival of the first railroad and the final taming of the Texas frontier.

The **Grace Museum** (102 Cypress St.; 325-673-4587) in the old Grace Hotel, focuses on art and local history.

Albany (Shackleford County)

Albany was founded in 1874 as a more respectable alternative to the boisterous town of Fort Griffin adjacent to the nearby military post of the same name. Even so, murder and cattle theft continued at a worrisome level.

When rancher John Larn was elected Shackelford County sheriff, the citizenry believed he would settle things down. Larn hired John Selman as his deputy, but crime, particularly cattle theft, continued to run rampant. Eventually, community leaders figured out that the sheriff and his deputy were behind much of the lawlessness. On June 22, 1878, a vigilante group seized Larn, locked him in his own jail, and shot him to death. Selman made it out of town, but he would be heard from again (see El Paso). Albany finally quieted down and after the railroad arrived, it developed as a ranching trade center.

Albany Visitor Center (2 Railroad St.; 325-762-2525) offers a self-guided walking tour that includes twenty-four historic buildings or sites. Built in 1877 and 1878, the **old Shackleford County jail** held problematic buffalo hunters, soldiers, cowboys, and outlaws until the county built a more modern lockup. The sturdy stone jail was the town's first public building, pre-dating the courthouse by five-plus years. Following renovation, the former hoosegow was opened as the **Old Jail Art Center** (201 South 2nd St.; 325-762-2269) in 2000. The art center also has local history exhibits.

Fort Griffin State Historic Site

First called Camp Wilson but soon renamed **Fort Griffin**, this post was established in 1867 on a hill overlooking the Clear Fork of the Brazos River. The fort saw its highest level of activity during the 1874 Red River War, the military campaign that drove the last of the Comanches and Kiowa from Texas and onto reservations near Fort Sill, Oklahoma. Famed American Indian fighter Col. Ranald S. Mackenzie maintained his headquarters at the post during the conflict.

Between the fort and the river lay the town of Fort Griffin, more commonly known as The Flat or Hide Town. Not only did the town have saloons, gambling places, and bawdy houses catering to the soldiers, the streets were filled with buffalo hunters, Tonkawa Indian scouts, cowboys, outlaws, and other Wild West types. Wide open and isolated, the town attracted some of the West's more famous characters, including Doc Holliday and Wyatt Earp. The Texas Historical Commission maintains that during Fort Griffin's heyday, it ranked among the Old West's five wildest towns.

By 1881 the buffalo were gone, the American Indians were gone, and soon, so was Fort Griffin. The army marched away that spring, leaving the post to fall to ruin. The state acquired the site in 1938 and developed it as **Fort Griffin State Historic Site** (1701 North US 283, fifteen miles north of Albany; 325-762-3592). Today it is managed by the Texas Historical Commission. A portion of the official State of Texas Longhorn Herd is also maintained at the site.

Alpine (Brewster County)

A railroad stop called Murphyville was established in 1883 when the Texas and Pacific Railway arrived, but the town was later renamed Alpine because it is surrounded by mountains. Alpine became the seat of Brewster County, the largest of the state's 254 counties. A ranching trade center and gateway to Big Bend National Park, it is the largest community between Fort Stockton and El Paso.

The state opened Sul Ross College in Alpine in 1920. Now Sul Ross University, since 1937 the school has maintained the **Museum of the Big Bend** (follow signs from Entrance 4 at Sul Ross University; 432-837-8730), a large museum dedicated to the long history of the sprawling region. Named because it lies in an exceptionally big bend of the Rio Grande, the culture and history of this area began when a people called the Jumanos settled along the Rio Grande before recorded history. They were followed by Spanish explorers and missionaries, Mexican ranchers, the American military, cattle ranchers, the arrival of the railroad, the Mexican Revolution, and the development of Big Bend National Park, the nation's largest national park.

Amarillo (Potter, Randall Counties)

By the mid-1880s the Texas Panhandle was blanketed with large cattle ranches covering so much land they were described by the number of sections (640 square acres) they included, not their acreage. The rest of the state was crisscrossed by rail lines, but ranchers in the sparsely settled Panhandle had to travel several hundred miles to catch a train or ship their cattle. That changed in 1887 when the Fort Worth and Denver Railway cut through the Panhandle on its way to Colorado. First called Ragtown, then Oneida, and finally Amarillo, the town out-maneuvered and out-lasted a couple of rivals and became a major cattle shipping point and later a regional trade and agricultural center.

Amarillo has three museums of interest to Old West history buffs, the **Kwahadi Museum of the American Indian** (9151 I-40 East; 806-335-3175), the **Amarillo Historical Museum** (1620 Johnson St.; 806-206-3926), and the **American Quarter Horse Hall of Fame and Museum** (1600 Quarter Horse Dr.; 806-376-5181).

Descended from horses brought to the Southwest by Spanish explorers, the American quarter horse helped win the West twice. No matter their fine horses, Spain's colonial presence in the West did not last, but when Plains Indians learned to tame the wild horses sired by escaped or abandoned Spanish horses, it enabled them to dominate their homelands until they were ultimately overwhelmed by Euro-Americans who also relied on the quarter horse, from the US cavalry to cowboys. The quarter horse museum has a timeline on the history of this most American of breeds along with a hall of fame recognizing notable quarter horses and horsemen and women.

AUSTIN (TRAVIS COUNTY)

Prior to his inauguration as the second president of the Republic of Texas, Mirabeau B. Lamar joined friends on a buffalo hunt in the Colorado River valley thirty miles upstream from Bastrop. Lamar liked what he saw, observing that it would be "the future seat of empire." After taking office, he appointed three commissioners to select a site for the republic's capital and they agreed with Lamar. By the summer of 1839, a log- and wood-frame town named in honor of Texas colonizer Stephen F. Austin was under construction. Beyond the western frontier of the republic, the new capital lost several of its earliest residents to incursions by unwelcoming Indians. Texas statehood came in 1845 and Austin remained the capital. In the 1870s, with its first rail connection, the town enjoyed a growth spurt, but even after the University of Texas opened in 1883, Austin remained a relatively small city until well into the twentieth century.

Driskill Hotel

Col. Jesse Lincoln Driskill, like many Texans of his day, learned most of what he knew from cattle. He came to Texas in 1849 from Missouri and got into the cattle business by selling beef to the Confederacy. After the war, he made a fortune in trailing longhorns to Kansas railheads. In 1884 he diversified his business pursuits and invested $400,000 into building and furnishing a first-class hotel for Austin. The four-story property, billed as "the finest hotel south of St. Louis," opened in 1886. Three years after the colonel's death in 1890, his estate sold the property, but the 189-room accommodation is still doing business as the **Driskill Hotel** (604 Brazos St.; 512-439-1234).

Established in 1839, **Oakwood Cemetery** (1601 Navasota St.) is the capital city's oldest cemetery and, with more than twenty-three thousand graves, is the final resting place of numerous notable people. The oldest known graves belong to two men killed by American Indians in 1842. The other burials represent the city's history and diversity, graves ranging from African-American slaves to those who fought on both sides during the Civil War to statesmen and civic leaders to lawmen, outlaws, and prostitutes. A newer but still old addition to the cemetery is located at 1601 Comal Street. Both are just east of I-35 in downtown Austin.

One of Oakwood Cemetery's residents is one of the Old West's better-known gunmen, **Ben Thompson** (1843–1884). The British-born Thompson came to Austin in 1851. He had a couple of nonfatal shooting scrapes as a teenager and then joined the Confederate army at nineteen. Back in the capital city after the Civil War, he was arrested by occupying Union troops for another shooting. He learned the printer's trade but soon found professional gambling more to his liking. A skillful gambler and good with a gun, Thompson developed a reputation of being an affable man, loyal to family and friends. But he drank too much and got mean when he did. Even so, he served two terms as Austin's city marshal and was praised for reducing crime. He resigned after killing Jack Harris in Harris's San Antonio saloon and theater on July 11, 1882. Acquitted in that killing, Thompson didn't quite make it two years before getting shot to death in the same Alamo City establishment (see San Antonio). A modern monument and a historical marker summarizing his career stand near Thompson's original gravestone (section 1, lot 340).

Several former Texas rangers are buried in Oakwood Cemetery as well, including **John B. Jones** (1834–1881), who as commander of the Frontier Battalion successfully presided over the transition of the Texas Rangers from fighters of American Indians to legendary state lawmen. Short and slight but smart and battle-tested during the Civil War, Jones was no deskbound administrator. He spent much of his time in the field, traveling from trouble spot to trouble spot by buggy or horse with a small escort. He took part in the Lost Valley Indian Fight in the summer of 1875 and the shoot-out with outlaw Sam Bass in 1878 (see Round Rock). In addition to the actual fighting in which he took part, the major also sparred with a penurious legislature, always eager to cut Ranger appropriations if not abolish them altogether. Though a strict disciplinarian, Jones had the respect of his men. In 1879 Jones gained promotion to adjutant general, but he continued to have operational control of the Rangers. Only forty-six, he died in Austin on July 19, 1881, of complications following surgery.

Lizzie Johnson: Schoolteacher, Cattle Dealer, and Investor

Elizabeth Ellen Johnson Williams (1840–1924) started out as a teacher in the Austin area but came to see more financial potential in herding cattle than children. Well educated, she sold articles to *Frank Leslie's Illustrated News* and other publications to supplement her earnings as a teacher. She also worked as a bookkeeper for several cattlemen, which is how she learned that business.

With her earnings, in the early 1870s she acquired land for a ranch, registered her brand, and took up cattle raising. When her herd was ready to market, she hired cowboys to help her and became the first woman to drive her own herd up the Chisholm Trail. She made the risky and rigorous trip more than once. Before she married Hezekiah G. Williams in 1879, she had him sign a prenuptial agreement that would keep her money separate from his. Lizzie, as she was best known, proved much more astute in business than her husband and had to bail him out financially on several occasions. Even so, they stayed married until his death in 1914. After that, Lizzie became an eccentric, miserly recluse. When she died a decade later, people assumed she was destitute. But when her estate was settled, it was found she had accumulated $250,000. Adjusted for inflation, that amount in today's dollars would be $3.6 million.

Texas State Cemetery

Edward Burleson served the Republic of Texas as a Texas ranger, soldier, and statesman. When the former vice president of the republic died December 26, 1851, he was buried on a tract of land in East Austin that had been donated to the state. Burleson's grave was the first in the **Texas State Cemetery**—Texas's "Arlington"—a cemetery that now holds more than three thousand graves of noted Texans, from unknown Civil War veterans to legendary peace officers to writer-historians to governors and empire builders.

In the latter category is Texas colonizer **Stephen F. Austin**, whose remains were relocated to the cemetery in 1910. Counting Austin, considered the father of the Texas Rangers, twenty-four rangers who served in the nineteenth century or early twentieth century are buried here.

In the mid-1990s, then Lieutenant Governor **Robert (Bob) Bullock** was the prime mover in a major renovation of the eighteen-acre cemetery and construction of a visitor center (909 Navasota St.; 512-463-0605), which interprets the cemetery's history.

When an accidental fire in the fall of 1881 gutted the 1853 limestone state capitol building (destroying, among other things, a small museum's worth of American Indian cultural material collected over the years by Texas rangers), the state soon began construction of the red granite **Texas Capitol** (1100 Congress Ave. at 11th St.) still in use today. From the capitol's opening in 1887 until the mid-1930s, the adjutant general's department had its offices there. Rangers were in and out all the time, and old rangers often worked as assistant sergeants at arms for the house and senate.

Life-size marble statues of Stephen F. Austin and Sam Houston stand inside the south foyer of the capitol. The two pieces by sculptress

Elisabet Ney (1833–1907) were dedicated on January 19, 1903. A bronze statue by sculptors Terry and Cindy Burleson of a high-booted ranger holding a lever-action rifle was dedicated on the second floor of the capitol on March 1, 1986, during the Texas sesquicentennial celebration.

On capitol grounds, the **Texas Peace Officer Memorial**, dedicated in 1999, lists all rangers and other law enforcement officers killed in the line of duty in Texas since August 5, 1823.

Across from the capitol stands an even more historic structure, the 1853 **Governor's Mansion** (1010 Colorado St.; 512-305-8524). Guided tours are available by reservation.

Just north of the state capitol, the **Bullock Texas State History Museum** (1800 North Congress Ave.; 512-936-3746) has three floors of exhibits with an extensive collection of artifacts and multimedia presentations. Opened in 2001 and since expanded, the museum covers four thousand years of history, telling the story of Texas from before the arrival of European explorers to the 1970s. The museum is named for the man who, while serving as the state's thirty-eighth lieutenant governor, pushed through the legislation that made it possible, Robert (Bob) Bullock (1929–1999).

Designed in 1854 by a German immigrant and reminiscent of a European castle, the limestone **Old Land Office** building (southeast corner of the capitol grounds; 512-305-8400) was constructed in 1856 and 1857 and opened in 1858 to hold the land records and maps of the Texas General Land Office. In 1883 William S. Porter, who later became far better known as the short story writer O. Henry, began a three-year career as a land office draftsman. He drew maps and inspiration for two of his short stories in the building. The land office moved to another state building in 1918 and from then until 1989 the Old Land Office was used as a museum by the Daughters of the Republic of Texas and Daughters of Confederate Veterans. The building was restored in the mid-1990s and opened as the **Texas Capitol Visitor Center** (112 East 11th St.; 512-305-8400).

Austin Author, O. Henry

O. Henry (1862–1910), whose real name was William S. Porter, lived for a time on a South Texas ranch managed by former Texas Ranger Lee (Red) Hall. He based several of his short stories on tales he heard from Hall or his brother Richard. In all, O. Henry wrote more than forty Western stories, including the classic "Ransom of Red Chief." O. Henry's life is the focus of the **O. Henry Museum** (409 East 5th St.; 512-974-1398), located in a restored one-story frame house once occupied by the writer and his wife when they lived in Austin.

Adjacent to the O. Henry house is the restored **Susanna Dickinson House**, built in 1869 by Joseph Hannig, who was married to Alamo survivor Susanna Dickinson. Her previous husband died in the 1836 siege of the Alamo, but Gen. Antonio Lopez de Santa Anna used Susanna to spread the word of his victory.

Camp Mabry and Texas Military Forces Museum

Established in 1892 as a training encampment for the state militia, predecessor of the Texas National Guard, **Camp Mabry** (35th Street and MoPac Boulevard) was named for Adjutant Gen. W.H. Mabry, who died of illness in Cuba during the Spanish-American War. Two historical markers inside the camp's old main entrance honor important figures in Texas Ranger history, former Adjutant Gen. John B. Jones and Adjutant Gen. William Steele, and a third marker explains the role of the state adjutant general, a gubernatorially appointed officer who from 1874 to 1935 oversaw the Texas Rangers.

The **Texas Military Forces Museum** (2200 West 35th St.; 512-782-5659) tells the story of Texas fighting men—and women—from the Texas Revolution through all the nation's wars.

BANDERA (BANDERA COUNTY)

The first settlers of what would become Bandera arrived in 1852 and set up a camp along the Medina River where they cut cypress trees and converted them to roofing shingles. A year later, Charles de Montel acquired land in the area and had a townsite laid out. Blazed in 1874, the Great Western Cattle Trail extended from South Texas through Bandera and northward to Kansas. Today, Bandera bills itself as the Cowboy Capital of the World. While several other western towns would debate that, it is true that Bandera has had an inordinate number of world champion rodeo performers as residents and puts on numerous rodeos every year. Adding to the claim is the prevalence of dude ranches in the area.

A state historical marker (State Highway 16 and Hackberry Street) in **Western Trail Heritage Park** summarizes the Great Western Trail.

The 1881 **Old Bandera County Jail** (12th Street), used for thirty-eight years, still stands one block off State Highway 16.

J. Marvin Hunter, an itinerant job printer and newspaper editor-publisher, finally decided to settle in Bandera, where, in 1923, he founded *Frontier Times* magazine. A decade later, he established the **Frontier Times Museum** (510 13th St.; 830-796-3864). One of the state's oldest museums, and definitely the most eclectic, it may be unique in how its construction was partially funded.

Hunter reprinted an early book on the notorious outlaw Sam Bass, *The Authentic History of Sam Bass and his Gang*, and sold copies for a dollar each. The Great Depression slowed sales, but income from the book and magazine subscriptions finally enabled him to get the museum built. Reprinting another classic work of Texana helped Hunter pay for a later expansion of the museum, which following his death in 1957 was purchased by a local family who created a nonprofit foundation to keep it operating. In 1972 the family transferred ownership to Bandera County. With more than eleven thousand artifacts, from antique firearms and American Indian lithic tools and projectile points to a two-headed goat and a shrunken head, the museum continues to intrigue visitors.

Blessing (Matagorda County)

Most men are content to let their accomplishments in life be their monument in death, but not **Abel Head (Shanghai) Pierce** (1834–1900). Born in Rhode Island, Pierce arrived at the port of Indianola in 1852 when he was nineteen. He got a job working on a ranch and within twenty years, partnering with his brother Jonathan, had built a ranching empire on Texas's coastal plains. Pierce did not have much formal education, but he came to know a lot about the four-legged animals that made him rich. Once, when checking into a hotel, the clerk asked for his name. He is said to have replied, "I am Shanghai Pierce, Webster on cattle, by God, Sir."

In his sixties, sensing his mortality, Pierce commissioned a life-size statue of himself to be placed over his grave when the time came. When someone asked him why he'd have a monument made of himself, the crusty cattleman replied, "Sir, if I don't do it myself, they will forget Old Shang." Pierce died at sixty-six years old the day after Christmas in 1900, and as soon as the tombstone maker completed his work, "Old Shang" stood in carved stone above a tall gray granite pillar marking his grave. Pierce is buried beneath his towering statue in **Hawley Cemetery** (off State Highway 71, three miles northeast of Blessing).

Belton (Bell County)

In 1850, only five years after Texas became a state, the legislature created Bell County. The county seat was Nolanville, later renamed Belton. The Chisholm Trail went through Belton and it grew as a trade center.

The **Bell County Museum** (201 North Main St.; 254-933-5243), located in the 1904 Carnegie Library, covers the history of the city and county.

Mass Murder in the Jail

Vigilantes usually strung up folks they deemed not worthy of their community—or life. But there were exceptions. On May 26, 1874, a mob surrounded the **Bell County Jail** (201 North Pearl St.), broke in, overpowered the lone deputy inside, and singled out eight accused horse thieves and a ninth man awaiting trial for killing his wife. Rather than hang the nine men, the citizens summarily shot them to death.

Later that day, the bodies were removed from the jail and laid out behind the lockup. A coroner's jury concluded the men had been shot to death by parties unknown. That legality out of the way, the victims were buried in a common grave. Meanwhile, county commissioners met and approved the expenditure of $9.90 to clean up the jail and repair the damage caused when the vigilantes forced their way inside.

Ironically, William L. Coleman, the man accused of murdering his wife, had been transferred to Belton from nearby Coryell County in the interest of his safety. Citizens of *that* county had been planning to remove him from jail, tie him to a tree, and burn him alive.

The two-story, cut limestone jail was used until 1884 when a larger jail replaced it. Later covered with stucco, the old jail is now a private residence. A state historical marker relates the structure's history.

The shooting victims were buried in the **South Belton Cemetery** (South Penelope Street and East Avenue E). Their common gravestone lists only the last names of the slain prisoners beneath a terse and incorrect inscription reading "Bell County Jail Prisoners Died May 25, 1874." (The killings occurred after midnight, making the date May 26.)

Borger (Hutchinson County)

Borger wasn't founded until 1926 when the discovery of oil turned it into an overnight boomtown, but it acted like a Wild West town until

Texas rangers tamed it. And one of the West's most storied American Indian fights took place not far from the future community.

Adobe Walls

Buffalo hunter Billy Dixon found himself in a mighty bad fix on June 27, 1874, when an estimated three hundred or so Comanche, Kiowa, and Southern Cheyenne Indians (some accounts have this number double) led by Isa-tai and Quanah Parker attacked the only Anglo enclave in the grassy vastness of the Panhandle in what is now Hutchinson County.

An array of warriors sat on their horses along a mesa nearly a mile to the east, readying for one more charge toward the twenty-eight hunters, traders, a bartender—and one woman—who constituted the residents of a scattering of dried-mud structures known as **Adobe Walls**.

With a borrowed .50-90 Sharps rifle he braced on a wall, windowsill, or barrel (accounts vary) Dixon raised his peep sight and mentally calculated distance, trajectory, and windage. A twenty-four-year-old Virginian, he knew nothing of ballistics, but he had killed hundreds if not thousands of buffalo.

Dixon pulled the set trigger (which releases some of the tension on the firing mechanism, but not all) and then squeezed off a shot. As the rifle kicked his shoulder, a conical lead bullet weighing nearly an ounce spun through the heavy octagonal barrel followed by a cloud of white smoke. Before the targeted warrior even heard the shot, he toppled from his horse, dead or dying.

At that, the others kicked their mounts and galloped for cover or at least to put more distance between them and whoever had fired that shot. The buffalo hunters, outnumbered but better armed, had killed fifteen to thirty of their attackers (some accounts have this number much higher) while losing only three of their own. After Dixon's near miraculous shot, the American Indians gave up and rode away. Among the survivors at the settlement was a young man who would become much better known, Bat Masterson.

Four historical markers at a roadside park (State Highway 207; GPS coordinates: N35° 44.63, W101° 25.06) six miles north of Borger, summarize the 1874 battle and an earlier 1864 engagement in the same area that pitted a regiment of New Mexico volunteer cavalry led by the legendary Kit Carson against a large contingent of Plains Indians.

Another site that has a monument, dedicated on the fiftieth anniversary of the second fight, is owned by the Panhandle Plains Historical Society. Eleven miles north of Stinnet on State Highway 207, turn right on County Road 23 and follow for seventeen miles to the remote site, which is surrounded by the sprawling Turkey Track Ranch. The ranch allows access but has signs warning visitors not to leave the roadway.

In addition to displays on the history of Borger and Hutchinson County, the **Hutchinson County Museum** (618 North Main St., Borger; 806-273-0130) has an exhibit on both Adobe Walls fights.

Brownsville (Cameron County)

Texas won its independence from Mexico in 1836, but ten years later, with Texas just having joined the Union, the US and Mexico went to war over whether the Rio Grande or the Nueces River was the boundary between the two nations. The 1846 to 1848 conflict, which resulted in US acquisition of the Southwest and California, began at the far southern tip of Texas in and around future Brownsville. After the war, founded by pioneer businessman and rancher Charles Stillman, Brownsville grew in the shadow of the fort as an international market center.

Historic Brownsville Museum (641 East Madison St.; 956-548-1313) interprets the city's long history and includes the restored **Stillman House** (1325 East Washington St.), where Stillman lived from 1850 to 1866.

The restored circa-1850 **Laureles Ranch House** (1501 East 7th St.) was moved to Brownsville from the ranch once owned by Stillman.

Fort Brown

Originally Fort Texas, the fort began as a star-shaped, earthen-walled cantonment across the Rio Grande from Matamoras, Mexico. In the first artillery exchange of the Mexican War, the fort was shelled by Mexican forces on May 3, 1846. Major Jacob Brown, the ranking officer, died in the action and the fort was named in his honor. The post remained active for a century, abandoned in 1946. The old post hospital, cavalry barracks, guardhouse, and morgue still stand, now used by Texas Southmost College (International Boulevard at May Street).

Palo Alto and Resaca de la Palma

On May 8, 1846, at a point called Palo Alto in present Cameron County, 2,300 US troops and a small ranger company battled 4,000 Mexican soldiers. The next day, the two armies met again at Resaca de la Palma. The Americans prevailed in both engagements and the US Army soon crossed into Mexico. **Palo Alto Battlefield National Historic Park** (7200 Paredes Line Rd. and Farm to Market Road 511/550; 956-541-2785) is on the north side of Brownsville. Exhibits and artifacts in the site's visitor center interpret the two battles.

Juan Cortina

Juan Nepomuceno Cortina rode into Brownsville on July 13, 1859, to eat with friends at Castel's Saloon. As Cortina sat with his friends, he heard a commotion. Walking outside, he found Marshal Robert Shears beating a Mexican man who had worked on Cortina's family ranch, Rancho del Carmen. Incensed, Cortina intervened and ended up shooting the city officer. Then he galloped out of town with the beaten vaquero on the back of his horse.

The lawman recovered, but Cortina soon faced charges. He tried to buy his way out of it, but when that didn't work, he moved across the river to Mexico. The next time he went to Brownsville, he did so at the head of a small army of seventy well-armed and mounted men. By the time he left, two men lay dead, and three others wounded. Some accounts reported five deaths. While the governments of Texas and the US saw Cortina's September 28 incursion as an invasion, to Cortina's mind he had merely settled a grievance.

When word of the raid reached San Antonio, former city marshal William Tobin decided to raise his own company of volunteers and ride to the aid of the terrified valley community. On his way, Tobin sent a letter to Governor E.M. Pease, offering his services as a ranger captain. The governor soon gave him an official commission.

Not long after Tobin reached Brownsville, the situation worsened. A party of vigilantes—likely some of Tobin's men—lynched a captured Cortinista. Enraged, Cortina threatened to burn the town. Brownsville survived, but it took another company of rangers under John S. (Rip) Ford, plus elements of the US Army, to squelch Cortina's mini war on South Texas. Despite all the fighting, Cortina survived and died of old age in Mexico in 1894.

Built in the 1850s, the **Neale House** (230 Neale Rd.) is the city's oldest frame residence and in poor repair. Its first residents were English-born Brownsville mayor William Neale (1807–1896) and his family. When Cortina staged his raid, his men torched a store Neale owned and fired on this house, killing Neale's son. Donated by family descendants to the Brownsville Art League in 1950, the house is now owned by the City of Brownsville. Though not currently open to the public, there are plans to relocate and restore the structure.

Old City Cemetery Center

Established in 1853, the **Old City Cemetery** (Madison and East 5th Streets) tells the story of Brownsville in stone. Graves of Brownsville and Rio Grande Valley pioneers include those of people who died of tropical diseases, in gunfights, and in war.

The **Old City Cemetery Center** (1004 East 6th St.; 956-541-1167), housed in the former baggage room of the old Southern Pacific Railroad depot, has interpretive exhibits on the cemetery.

Brownwood (Brown County)

Settled in the mid-1850s along Pecan Bayou, a tributary of the Colorado River, Brownwood and Brown County were named for Texas Revolution hero Capt. Henry S. Brown. The county was organized in 1857 and Brownwood grew as a ranching and trade center.

Barbed wire is as ubiquitous in Texas as prickly pear cactus, but some Texans didn't cotton to it at first. Big ranchers liked barbed wire because it kept other people's cattle—and to some extent other people—off their land. Small-time cattlemen did not like seeing the open range crisscrossed with wire. To underscore their point, in the mid-1880s some of them began cutting other people's fences, usually at night. That set off the so-called **Fence Cutter War** of 1883 to 1888. As wars go, it didn't claim many lives, but two of the fatalities occurred in Brown County.

The **Brown County Museum of History** (209 North Broadway; 325-641-1926) focuses on the area's history, including the Fence Cutter War.

Across from the museum is the castle-like former **Brown County Jail** (212 North Broadway), built in 1902. An annex to the museum, this building houses exhibits that focus on the history of law enforcement in the county.

The **Martin and Frances Lehnis Railroad Museum** (700 East Adams St.; 325-643-6376) stands across from the 1910 Santa Fe

Railroad depot and the 1914 **Harvey House**, one of the trackside eateries established on the Santa Fe system by food service and hospitality industry pioneer Fred Harvey.

Buffalo Gap (Taylor County)

Buffalo Gap is exactly that—a gap in a range of hills known as the Callahan Divide through which buffalo passed to the south in the fall and to the north in the spring. Buffalo hunters hunted and made their camps in the vicinity and later, with the buffalo and the Comanches gone from West Texas, the gap saw cattle herds headed to connect with the Western Cattle Trail.

A settlement developed at the gap and in 1878 became the seat of Taylor County. But when the Texas and Pacific Railway crossed the county farther to the north, Buffalo Gap lost its status as county capital to newly founded Abilene.

The **Taylor County History Center** (133 North Williams St.; 325-572-3365) consists of a collection of restored vintage Buffalo Gap structures, including the original two-story, stone county courthouse.

Canyon (Randall County)

In 1888, a dozen miles west of Palo Duro Canyon, cattle rancher Lincoln Guy Conner bought land from the state for $3 an acre and laid out a townsite. Envisioning a law-abiding, religious town, he opened a general store and provided space for a post office. As people began taking the free lots Conner offered (providing they constructed a house or building on their lot), they wanted to name the new town in his honor, but he said he preferred Canyon City for the nearby canyon. When Randall County was organized in 1889, Canyon City became county seat. Following the arrival of the Pecos and Northern Texas Railway in 1898, Canyon (it would drop the "City") became a busy cattle shipping point. In 1910 West Texas State Normal College was established there, now West Texas A&M University.

One of Texas's oldest museums, the **Panhandle Plains Historical Museum** (2503 4th Ave.; 806-651-2244) opened in 1933 and has a vast collection of artifacts related to the small-state-size Panhandle of Texas. Enlarged and remodeled three times since its dedication, the museum has 285,000 square feet of space and two million artifacts, including famed Comanche chief Quanah Parker's headdress, lance, and other possessions and noted rancher Charles Goodnight's silver-studded saddle.

Called the Grand Canyon of Texas, **Palo Duro Canyon** is the nation's second-largest canyon, stretching 120 miles long with an average width of six miles. Human occupation of the canyon goes back more than ten thousand years, and in the 1500s Spanish conquistadors passed through. US Army Capt. Randolph B. Marcy led an expedition through the canyon to map it in 1852, but it remained the domain of the Comanches, Kiowa, and Cheyenne until the Red River War more than twenty years later.

On September 28, 1874, after finding a trail that enabled his Fourth Cavalry troopers to ride down to the canyon floor seven hundred feet below the rim, Gen. Ranald S. Mackenzie attacked a large American Indian village. While casualties were minimal, the soldiers destroyed the village and rounded up more than one thousand of the village's ponies and destroyed them. The people who escaped spent a harsh winter with only a meager food supply. On June 2, 1875, they surrendered at Fort Sill. They were the last of the Plains Indians to be vanquished from Texas. In 1876, Charles Goodnight pushed 1,800 head of cattle into the canyon and, with John Adair, established the JA Ranch. Before their partnership ended in 1887, the ranch supported one hundred thousand head.

A large portion of the canyon became **Palo Duro Canyon State Park** (11450 Park Road 5; 806-488-2227) in 1934. Additional acreage has been added since then along with a visitor center that offers interpretive exhibits on the canyon's geology and history.

Center Point (Kerr County)

No one knows why the small cemetery in the hill country community of Center Point came to be the final resting place of so many Texas rangers, but with thirty-seven ranger tombstones, the cemetery has more ranger burials than anyplace in the state, including the Texas State Cemetery in Austin.

The three best known nineteenth-century rangers lying in the cemetery are **Andrew Jackson Sowell, Jr**. (1848–1921), **Neal Coldwell** (1844–1925), and **Nelson Orcelus Reynolds** (1846–1922). All just happened to spend their final days in Center Point.

Born in Seguin in 1848, Sowell joined the Rangers in 1870. Soon after, he participated in the force's 1870–1871 campaign against the Wichita Indians. After his ranger service, he wrote three classics of Texas history: *Early Settlers of Southwest Texas* (1880), *Rangers and Pioneers of Texas* (1884), and *The Life of Big Foot Wallace* (1899).

When the Frontier Battalion organized in the spring of 1874, Coldwell became captain of Company F. He continued as a company commander until 1879, when he was promoted to ranger quartermaster, a job he held until 1883.

Reynolds joined the Rangers in May 1874, serving first under Company D Capt. Rufe Perry and later as a lieutenant under Captain Coldwell in Company E. As a Frontier Battalion lawman, Reynolds was involved in mitigating the deadly Horrell-Higgins feud in Lampasas and the 1878 breakup of the Sam Bass gang in Round Rock. After rangers returned killer John Wesley (Wes) Hardin to Texas, Reynolds guarded the notorious gunman during his trial and then escorted him to prison at Huntsville. The lieutenant resigned from the Rangers in 1879 and later settled in Center Point.

Center Point is on State Highway 27 between Kerrville and Comfort. The cemetery is off Farm to Market Road 480, half a mile from town. A historical marker placed in 1986 lists the ranger burials.

The two-story **Woolls Building** (318 San Antonio St.), is one of the community's oldest buildings. Built in 1873 through 1875, it served as the meeting place of the local Rising Star Masonic Lodge. Many of the former rangers buried at Center Point belonged to this lodge.

Nelson Orcelus Reynolds's residence from 1918 to 1922, a native limestone house, is across from the cemetery at Farm to

Market Road 480 and Elm Pass Road. A 2001 historical marker stands outside the house.

Colorado City (Mitchell County)

When the westbound tracks of the Texas and Pacific Railway crossed the upper Colorado River in 1881, a town called Colorado City was founded and grew fast. Within two years it had a population of five thousand. For a time, the nearest rail connection to the Panhandle, Colorado City was the largest city between Fort Worth and El Paso.

The **Heart of West Texas Museum** (340 East 3rd St.; 325-728-8285) focuses on the history of the once wild cow town.

Nip and Tuck at the Nip and Tuck

To provide security a company of rangers had been shadowing the Texas and Pacific track-laying crews as they moved across West Texas. In fast-growing Colorado City, using a dugout for an office, rangers collected pistols from visitors and held their hardware until they left town.

One of those rangers was R.C. (Dick) Ware (1851–1902), the officer who had killed Seaborn Barnes during the rangers' 1878 shoot-out with the Sam Bass gang in Round Rock. But with the organization of Mitchell County, he quit and successfully ran for sheriff. He defeated W.P. Patterson, a rancher with an interest in the new town's newspaper. Described as a man of "fine intellect, great willpower and good literary talent," Patterson's willpower often weakened when it came to whiskey.

On the night of May 17, 1882, rangers heard gunfire at the **Nip and Tuck Saloon** (1st and Elm Streets). Rushing to the scene, three rangers saw Patterson was on another drunk. Suspecting him as the shooter, they asked him to hand over his pistol for inspection. Instead, he took a shot at one of the rangers. He missed, but Patterson got no second chance. Ranger Jeff Milton dropped him dead with one bullet. Adrenaline surging, another ranger put a second bullet in Patterson after he fell.

Patterson had many friends, and Milton ended up having to level his Winchester at bystanders to hold back a potential lynch mob. The rangers surrendered to Sheriff Ware, their former colleague. All were indicted for murder, but when the case came to trial in Abilene in November 1883, a jury acquitted them. By that time, after three years of service, Milton had left the Rangers. The incident in Colorado City, however, wouldn't be his last shooting.

Ware is buried in **Colorado City Cemetery** (State Highway 208 at I-20 Business), just east of town. The Nip and Tuck Saloon no longer stands.

COMANCHE (COMANCHE COUNTY)

Despite the long-standing enmity between Texans and Comanches, early Anglo settlers named this West Texas county for the fierce tribe. Founded in 1858, Cora was the first seat of Comanche County, but a year later the new town of Comanche was made county seat and Cora quickly withered. At the time, Comanches remained a serious threat along the frontier, but for the next couple of decades after its founding, Comanche the town was dangerous enough in its own right. Being on the edge of settlement, Comanche's saloons catered to buffalo hunters, soldiers, trail drivers, and bad men. One of them was a preacher's son named John Wesley (Wes) Hardin.

A Day at the Races

One of Texas's deadliest gunfighters, **John Wesley (Wes) Hardin** came to Comanche to visit family after being involved in several killings in and around Cuero, Texas, during the ongoing Sutton-Taylor feud. On May 26, 1874, Hardin made $3,000 or so in a day of horse racing and gambling. That night, if not earlier, he started drinking. Inside a saloon run by Jack Wright, Hardin got into a disagreement with Charles Webb (1848–1874), a sheriff's deputy from nearby Brown County. The lawman was not in town in his official capacity—technically he had no jurisdiction—but he was armed, and so was Hardin. When hard words escalated to violence, both men went for their guns. Webb grazed Hardin but Hardin put a bullet in the deputy's head. Texas rangers under Capt. John R. Waller were already in the area, and the following day they set out after Hardin. The rangers found Hardin and several of his associates on May 30, but they escaped in an exchange of gunfire.

On June 1, a delegation of Comanche County residents removed Hardin's brother Joe and two Hardin cousins from jail and hanged them. Captain Waller, still hunting Wes Hardin, did not even consider the matter worthy of inclusion in his report to headquarters. Three years passed before rangers caught up with Hardin again.

Deputy Webb died near the east door of **Jack Wright's Saloon** (northeast corner of West Grand and North Page Streets). A nearby historical marker details the shooting. Webb is buried in **Greenleaf Cemetery** (2615 US 377, Brownwood; 325-646-6919). A historical marker stands near the grave.

The **Comanche County Historical Museum** (402 Moorman Rd.; 325-356-5115), along with other exhibits and artifacts, has a replica of the saloon.

After Comanche became county seat the old log cabin courthouse at Cora fell to ruin. Later, preservationists moved the structure to the courthouse square in Comanche and restored it. The cabin (US 377 at North Houston Street) is Texas's oldest surviving one-time courthouse.

Corpus Christi (Nueces County)

Founded in 1838 by Henry Lawrence Kinney, Corpus Christi began as a remote frontier trading post on the mid-Texas coast. The place emerged from obscurity in 1845, when Gen. Zachary Taylor established a large camp here for some three thousand troops who would take part in his 1846 campaign against Mexico.

Hurricanes and progress erased any trace of the military encampment and most of the city's earliest structures, but the 1849 **Britton-Evans House** (411 North Upper Broadway; 361-882-8691)—made of crushed shells and concrete—still stands. Its history is essentially the story of Corpus Christi. Forbes Britton, a partner in a shipping company that ran a freight line between the new settlement and Galveston, built this two-story, Greek Revival–style house in 1849. He sold it in 1861, and a year later the Confederate army took it over for use as a hospital. When federal forces occupied the city for a time following the Civil War, they continued to use the house as a hospital and also as a mess hall for officers. In 1880, George F. Evans purchased the property and it remained in his family until 1936. The Corpus Christi Area Heritage Society acquired it in 1964 and opened it to the public.

The **Corpus Christi Museum of Science and History** (1900 North Chaparral St.; 361-826-4667) interprets five hundred years of South Texas history. With nearly one hundred thousand square feet, the museum documents the 1686 wreck in Matagorda Bay of Sieur de La Salle's ship *La Belle*, two Spanish shipwrecks off the shore of Padre Island in 1554, the history of Corpus Christi, early ranch life in the region, and other topics.

After the Civil War, the nearby Arkansas County community of Rockport became a coastal cow town. Texas cattlemen drove their stock to Rockport where so-called hide and tallow plants converted hides to leather, extracted tallow for candle-making and other uses, and produced salted, pickled beef for shipment by steamboat to New Orleans. While nothing remains of these early enterprises, the **Fulton Mansion State Historic Site** (317 South Fulton Beach Rd.; 361-729-0386) preserves the 1877 mansion built by rancher-inventor-entrepreneur George Fulton. He was the prime mover in developing Rockport as a meatpacking center.

The **Texas Maritime Museum** (1202 Navigation Circle, Rockport; 361-729-1271) focuses on all aspects of the state's coastal history, including early French and Spanish exploration of Texas.

Cuero (DeWitt County)

The Chisholm Trail passed through DeWitt County and its county seat of Clinton, which soon lost out to a new town called Cuero, Spanish for "cowhide." Cowboys made things lively in Cuero, but the real trouble came from local and area residents in a mini-war known as the Sutton-Taylor feud. The state sent a company of Texas rangers to DeWitt County to suppress the violence, but it did not subside until the principal participants had killed each other off.

Cuero has fifty-plus structures on the National Register of Historic Places and a self-guided walking tour is available at the **Chamber of Commerce and Visitor Center** (124 East Church St.; 361-275-2112). Two museums focus on the history of the South Texas town and county, the **Cuero Heritage Museum** (124 East Church St.; 361-485-8090), inside the 1915 former federal building, and the **DeWitt County Museum** (312 East Broadway; 361-275-6322). The DeWitt Museum is in a two-story wood-frame Victorian house partially built with lumber salvaged following the devastating 1886 Indianola, Texas, hurricane (see Indianola). A third museum, the **Chisholm Trail Heritage Museum** (302 North Esplanade; 361-277-2866), focuses on Cuero's trail-driving days.

Sutton-Taylor Feud

A feud pits one faction against another, and well more than a century after the last death connected to the Sutton-Taylor imbroglio, Wild West historians have two distinct views of the violence. The most common narrative is that the feud was between two strong-willed families, their grievances both personal and political. The other, revisionist view is that the violence was associated with a large, if loose-knit, criminal enterprise. The only undisputed fact is that beginning during Reconstruction and continuing into the 1890s, a lot of people ended up dead as a result of whatever it was. Cemeteries in Aransas, Brown, Comanche, DeWitt, El Paso, Gonzales, Victoria, and Wilson Counties have graves of Sutton-Taylor participants. Findagrave.com has a virtual cemetery of twenty-eight feud victims.

Dalhart (Dallam, Hartley Counties)

In 1901 the Chicago, Rock Island, and Pacific Railroad intersected the Fort Worth and Denver Railway at a point in the upper northwest corner of the Panhandle. First called Twist, then Twist Junction, then Denrock, the town that developed at the crossroads got its permanent name when someone suggested combining the first three letters of Dallam County with the first four letters of Hartley County.

The headquarters of the giant **XIT Ranch** was at Channing, twenty-nine miles southeast of Dalhart, but Dalhart figured prominently in the final decades of the ranch's existence, and in 1937 became home of the annual reunion of XIT cowboys. All the old XIT cowboys are gone, but the event, now called the XIT Rodeo and Reunion, continues. Part of the celebration is a no-cost barbeque for all comers, billed as the world's largest free barbeque.

XIT Ranch

Throughout the nineteenth century, the state never had an abundance of money in the treasury, but it had a whole lot of unassigned land. In 1882, the state offered three million acres in the Panhandle to any entity willing to build a large new capitol in Austin in exchange for the land. A consortium of investors in Chicago decided to go for the deal.

In 1885 the newly organized **Capitol Freehold Land and Investment Company** began its effort to make money off the Panhandle land. They would transform it into what would become the world's largest cattle ranch, but first they needed cattle.

In the early summer that year, **Abner Pickens Blocker** started for the new ranch with 2,500 head of cows and calves from his brother's ranch in Tom Green County. **B.H. (Barbecue) Campbell**, a Kansas cattleman imported by the syndicate to manage the new ranch, met the herd when Blocker arrived that July. The cattle needed branding, but the new ranch did not yet have a brand.

"Barbecue wanted to use three letters and he wanted a brand a rustler couldn't blot," Blocker recalled. "He had drawn a lot of designs with his boot in the dust. I started drawing in the dust with my boot heel. For some reason I happened to draw XIT.

"'How's that, Barbecue?' I asked, and he said, 'Get to branding them cows.'"

As for the soon-to-be-famous brand, Blocker continued: "There was absolutely no reason for my drawing an XIT. . . . It was just a brand that could be put on with an iron that had only one bar. The brand could be blotted out, of course. So could any brand that was ever created."

Since the ranch, which extended more than two hundred miles north to south and roughly thirty miles wide, covered parts of ten Panhandle counties, the legend arose that XIT stood for "Ten in Texas." But Blocker scoffed at that. "It didn't mean [that] or anything else."

At its peak, enclosed by six thousand miles of fence, the giant ranch had 150,000 head of cattle, 1,500 horses, and 150 cowboys. But the XIT was never financially successful, and the Chicagoans only profited from their investment when they started selling off the ranch in parcels in 1912.

The **XIT Historical Museum** (108 East 5th St.; 806-244-5390) tells the story of the once giant spread.

Built in 1898 and 1899, the brick, Victorian-style **XIT General Office** (517 Railroad Ave., Channing) is a recorded Texas Historic Landmark.

Sculpted by artist Bobby Dycke, a statue dedicated in 1940 that depicts an empty saddle (off US 87, just north of underpass) honors XIT cowboys and area pioneers.

Dallas (Dallas County)

Dallas began as a trading post in 1841 when John Neely Bryan built a log cabin near the only ford of the Trinity River for miles around. Neely's trading post stood at the intersection of two well-worn animal and American Indian trails that became major transportation routes. By 1844, a half-mile-square townsite had been surveyed and staked out.

Dallas has the distinction of being one of the few, if not the only, major America cities with an uncertain pedigree. No one knows for sure if Dallas was named for the man who served as vice president of the US from 1845 to 1849 (George Mifflin Dallas), Dallas's brother, Naval Commodore Alexander J. Dallas, or one of the area's early settlers, Joseph Dallas.

When Dallas County was organized in 1846, Dallas became the temporary county seat. Two other communities, long since absorbed by Dallas, rivaled it for a time. But in 1850, voters picked Dallas as the permanent county capital. Six years later, the Texas legislature granted it a town charter.

Slow growth marked Dallas's first thirty years. By 1870, it had only three thousand people. Twenty years later, thanks to the convergence of two railroad lines Dallas was a city of more than thirty-eight thousand and continued to grow as a major business, marketing, and manufacturing center.

Old Red Museum of Dallas County History and Culture (100 South Houston St.; 214-757-1914) is housed in the 1892-vintage former county courthouse, locally known as Old Red for the red sandstone used in its construction.

A replica of **John Neely Bryan's log cabin** (214-327-8263) stands on Main Street at Market Street, just across the street from the old courthouse. The **Hall of State** (3939 Grand Ave.; 214-413-3947), located on the grounds of the State Fair of Texas, is an Art Deco building dating to the 1936 Texas Centennial. The Dallas Historical Society maintains its exhibits, which are related to Texas's history. **Dallas Heritage Village** at Old City Park (1515 South Harwood St.; 214-421-5141) features restored nineteenth-century houses and commercial buildings from the greater Dallas area.

Making the Scene in Scyene

Founded in 1854, Scyene was a small but lively town ten miles southeast of Dallas. Financially devastated by the Civil War, a Missouri farmer named John Shirley moved there and bought an eight-hundred-acre farm. In the late 1860s, some of Shirley's Show Me State acquaintances hung out for a while in Scyene, including, at various times, former Missouri guerrilla fighters Cole, Jim, John, and Bob Younger. Soon they would be better known as the Younger gang. Their friends Frank and Jesse James also spent some time in Scyene.

Another Scyene hardcase was Shirley's son-in-law Jim Reed, an on-the-dodge cattle thief and stagecoach robber. Not long after a Collin County sheriff's deputy shot and killed Reed near Paris, Texas, in 1874, Reed's widow and two young children left Dallas County for Indian Territory. There Myra Maybelle Shirley Reed would marry Sam Starr and gain the name she's remembered by—Belle Starr.

Friday the Thirteenth

An old man named Russell walked into the Dallas County Sheriff's Office on a winter weekend in 1871 to report an assault. In one of Scyene's half a dozen saloons on Friday night, January 13, a man named John Younger forced him to sit still while he drunkenly tried to shoot a pipe out of his mouth. Younger missed the pipe but several of his shots came perilously close to Russell's head.

Another version of the incident has Younger shooting off the man's nose. Sheriff Jerimiah (Jerry) Brown secured a warrant for Younger's arrest and on Monday, January 16, deputy sheriff Charles H. Nichols (1841–1871) rode to Scyene to take Younger into custody. When he got to town, he deputized James McMahan (1844–1871), a local blacksmith, as a backup. Younger told the men he'd accompany Nichols to Dallas but asked if he could eat breakfast first. The deputy said that would be okay and went with McMahan to a nearby store to keep warm.

Younger and another Missouri outlaw named Thompson McDaniels had no intention of eating breakfast, at least not then. However, when they slipped off to get their horses, they found the deputy had posted several civilians to watch the corral. Incensed that Nichols apparently didn't trust him, Younger stormed to the store, barged inside, and immediately started shooting. The blacksmith was killed outright, the deputy mortally wounded. That done, Younger and McDaniels returned to the corral, fetched their horses (the volunteer guards had disappeared when the shooting started), and galloped out of town. Nichols's January 20 death made him the first peace officer killed in the line of duty in Dallas County. Younger was shot to death in Missouri by a Pinkerton operative three years later.

Nichols is buried in **Pioneer Cemetery** (1201 Marilla St.) adjacent to the Dallas Convention Center. His tombstone condenses the story to eight words, "Shot and killed in the line of duty." McMahan is also buried here.

Scyene declined after 1872 when Dallas got railroad service and it didn't. Eventually the fast-growing county seat absorbed the smaller town. The only reminders of the old town are Scyene Road and a pair of state historical markers (9500 block of Scyene Road at Belle Starr Drive) summarizing the road and town's history.

Sam Bass Returns to Texas

Outlaw Sam Bass and gang members Seaborn Barnes, Frank Jackson, Arkansas Johnson, and Henry Underwood robbed a Texas and Pacific train on February 22, 1878, at the Allen Depot near Dallas, the first train robbery in Texas history. The gang held up three other trains and two stagecoaches—all in the Dallas area—before riding south to hit a bank in the small central Texas town of Round Rock. That turned out to be a very bad idea (see Round Rock).

The **Allen Heritage Depot Museum** (100 Main St., Allen; 972-396-8546) features a documentary video on the Bass gang.

A historical marker placed in 1968 at **Heritage Plaza** (200 block of West Main, McKinney) details the Bass gang's April 10, 1878, train robbery at McKinney, thirty-three miles north of Dallas. The outlaws missed a hidden shipment of $30,000, netting only $152.

Cattle King of Texas

Born in 1837 in Sabine County, **Christopher Columbus Slaughter** (1837–1919) worked with his father and brothers on a ranch the family established in Palo Pinto County in 1857. Slaughter served for a time as a Texas ranger and in the military during the Civil War. After the war, he pushed cattle up the Chisholm Trail. Making good money at that, he started his own ranching enterprise in 1873. By 1905, he owned forty thousand cattle and controlled over one million acres. Known as the Cattle King of Texas, he was cofounder of the Texas and Southwestern Cattle Raisers Association in 1877. Later he founded a Dallas bank and in 1904, Baylor Hospital. Slaughter died in 1919 and is buried in Greenwood Cemetery (3020 Oak Grove Ave.; block 22, lot 6).

Moving Along the Dogies

The Chisholm Trail went through Fort Worth, not Dallas, but Dallas's **Pioneer Plaza** (Young and Griffin Streets) features the world's largest bronze monument—a herd of life-size longhorns and the cowboys forever pushing them north. The series of detail sculptures was done by Glen Rose artist Robert Summers. The plaza, which adjoins Pioneer Cemetery (1201 Marilla St.), is the largest open space in downtown Big D.

"Got Wes Hardin"

In 1877 former Dallas police officer **John Riley Duncan** (1850–1911) went to work as a Texas ranger operative and posed as an itinerant farmhand in Gonzales County hoping to gain insight into where wanted killer John Wesley (Wes) Hardin was hiding. He learned that Hardin was living in Alabama under an assumed name. Based on Duncan's information, Ranger John B. Armstrong nabbed Hardin in Florida. The outlaw might have dodged the law even longer, or possibly forever, had it not been for Duncan's undercover work. In 1990, the National Association for Outlaw and Lawman History (now the Wild West History Association) placed a new marker on Duncan's grave noting that he "Got Wes Hardin."

Later, a Dallas prostitute nearly got Duncan, shooting him in the chest at her workplace. The one-time Texas ranger undercover man recovered, later dying in a decidedly modern way—an automobile accident. Duncan is buried in **Greenwood Cemetery** (3020 Oak Grove Ave.; block 24, lot 26, space 11).

Del Rio (Val Verde County)

Del Rio developed along the Rio Grande across from an older community in what is now Mexico that dated back to the Spanish colonial era. A small settlement grew near a prolific spring on the north side of the river, known as San Felipe del Rio. That gave the Texas town its name, though postal authorities dropped "San Felipe" since the state already had a town by that name. The community grew as a border crossing and trade center.

The **Whitehead Memorial Museum** (1308 South Main St.; 830-774-7568) is devoted to this border town's history.

The Last of the Dalton Gang

Born in Xenia, Kansas, **Oscar Latta** (1868–1954) came to Texas with his parents in 1874 as a six-year-old and grew up in West Texas. He married in 1890, and a year later, had a son. But the marriage soon soured, and Mrs. Latta filed for divorce. What role her parents had in the breakup is not known, but any chance of reconciliation ended when Latta shot and killed his father-in-law. A jury found he acted in self-defense and acquitted him. After that, he turned to law enforcement, hiring on as a deputy sheriff in Kimble County.

On February 6, 1897, riding in a posse led by Sheriff John L. Jones, Latta and the other lawmen encountered three suspected cattle rustlers on a ranch near the Kimble-Menard County line. The outlaws opted to take their chances on gunplay, which proved a matter of faulty judgment. After the final hammer fell, Jourd Nite and Jim Crane had been lastingly rehabilitated. The wounded survivor, Jourd's brother Jim turned out to be wanted for the violent robbery of the First National Bank of Longview on May 23, 1894.

Not long after arresting Nite, Latta became a Texas ranger, serving with Company F in Duval County in South Texas. After leaving the state force, he worked for a time in Brady as a deputy city marshal. In 1932, after the Rangers had evolved from horseback lawmen to state cops with cars, Latta again pinned on a ranger badge for a time. He always played down his role in capturing the last member of the Dalton gang. Latta is buried in **Westlawn Cemetery** (1200 West 2nd St.).

Denison (Grayson County)

Late in the evening on December 25, 1872, a Missouri, Kansas, and Texas Railroad steam locomotive pulling three coaches and a Pullman car arrived at the new town of Denison. The first train to enter Texas, it pulled into the depot with its whistle blowing. Some one hundred passengers, many of them dignitaries, alighted from the train for a boozy wild game banquet to celebrate Texas's first interstate rail connection. Named for railroad official George Denison, the North Texas town was only a scattering of tents and wooden false-front buildings surrounded by a short thicket of wooden stakes marking newly surveyed lots, but that quickly changed.

Only one hundred days after its founding, Denison had a population of three thousand and, within five years, twice that. Slated wooden stockcars carried thousands of head of cattle to market north through Denison while thousands of people coming from the other direction arrived in Texas in somewhat more comfortable frame passenger coaches.

Lee (Red) Hall, who went on to become one of Texas's most noted ranger captains, cut his law enforcement teeth as a sheriff's deputy in Denison. Known as Red Hall for his flaming red hair, he had his hands full in the wild railroad boomtown, but he established a reputation as an effective lawman. A Denison newspaper editor later called him "the gamest man in Texas."

Located in the 1917 Missouri, Kansas, and Texas Railroad depot, the **Red River Railroad Museum** (101 East Main St.; 903-463-5289) has exhibits and archival records related to the railroad as well as a collection of vintage rolling stock.

The **Grayson County Frontier Village** (US 75 at Loy Lake Rd.; 903-463-2487) has a local history museum and preserves an assortment of vintage structure.

Denton (Denton County)

Settled in 1857, Denton was named for the victim of a fight with American Indians, **John B. Denton**. The North Texas town grew as the county seat and the home of two colleges that later became universities.

A minister, lawyer, and ranger captain, John Denton died in what became known as the Battle of Village Creek, six miles east of Fort Worth. On May 25, 1841, the day after the battle, rangers buried Denton under a tree near Olive Creek about twenty-five miles from where he died. The grave was forgotten, but fifteen years later, some boys playing on the creek found it. Rancher John Chisum remembered hearing about Denton's burial from his father and exhumed the remains. Chisum found someone who had been in the fight, and he identified the remnants of the blanket that Denton had been wrapped in. The rancher put the bones in a box, hoping he could find someone related to Denton so he could have a more proper final resting place. Unsuccessful, the rancher reburied the bones on his property. At the turn of the twentieth century, Denton's bones made one more trip—the county Old Settler's Association had him reinterred on the courthouse square. Denton's grave, marked with a 1901-vintage stone and a 1936 state historical marker, is the only courthouse burial in Texas.

Denton County Courthouse-On-The-Square Museum (110 West Hickory St.; 940-349-2850) documents the history of the county and city.

Denton County Historical Park (317 West Mulberry St.; 940-349-2865) maintains interpretive exhibits in two old homes, the 1904-vintage Bayless-Selby House and the Quakertown House. The latter, also built in 1904, focuses on the community's African-American heritage.

El Paso (El Paso County)

The Rio Grande—Great River—created a valley between the foothills of the Rocky Mountains to the north and another chain of mountains rising from the desert just south of the river. It was this natural gap in North America's high backbone that gave El Paso its name when Spanish explorers first came to the area in the late 1500s. They called it El Paso del Rio del Norte—the Pass of the River of the North.

The first settlement here developed along the river's southern bank, in present Mexico. At the time, the river was merely a water source, not a national border. Spain held the land along both sides of the stream, and far beyond it, until Mexico became an independent republic in 1821. Settlement finally began on the north side of the river, still part of Mexico, in the mid-1820s when three Mexican families began ranching across from the village of El Paso del Norte.

After the Mexican War of 1846 to 1848, the north side of the Rio Grande became part of the US—attached to New Mexico Territory. Late in 1846, Benjamin Franklin Coons leased ranch land across the river from El Paso del Norte and gave the new settlement that developed there his middle name. The California gold rush and the establishment of Fort Bliss helped the settlement of Franklin grow, and the following year it became part of Texas. In 1859, a year after the Butterfield Overland Mail Company built a stagecoach stop at Franklin, newly arrived developer Anson Mills acquired land around the village, surveyed a townsite, and renamed it El Paso. (El Paso del Norte, Mexico, eventually became Juarez.)

When the first southern transcontinental railroad went through El Paso in 1882, its future was assured and the town grew quickly into a city. The railroad, and El Paso's proximity to another country, made it particularly attractive to the rougher elements of society. The wide-open, fast-growing community soon had a nickname, "Hell Paso."

The **El Paso Visitor Center** (400 West San Antonio Ave.; 915-534-0658) offers a self-guided walking tour of downtown historic sites.

Magoffin Home State Historic Site (1120 Magoffin Ave.; 915-533-5147) is an example of Territorial style architecture and offers exhibits about the multicultural family of Joseph Magoffin (1837–1923). The Magoffins were active in US expansion and settlement, military service, trade on the Santa Fe–Chihuahua Trail, Civil War turmoil, and US-Mexico relations.

El Paso Museum of History (510 North Santa Fe St.; 915-351-3588) focuses on the city's colorful story.

Fort Bliss

El Paso has been an army town since 1848. For decades its soldiers shouldered the dual task of dealing with American Indians and keeping a watchful eye on Mexico, especially during the Mexican Revolution, when bullets sometimes flew into El Paso as fighting raged in Juarez. Gen. John J. (Black Jack) Pershing and future Gen. George S. Patton spent time at the fort along with other notable military figures. The day of the horse soldier ended with World War II, but the sprawling post, which has artillery ranges extending into New Mexico, remains an active installation. Learn about the post at the **Fort Bliss and Old Ironsides Museum** (Building 1735, Marshall Rd.; 915-568-5412).

Four Dead in Five Seconds

Gus Krempkau's command of Spanish apparently wasn't as good as he thought. His questionable translation of Spanish-language testimony in the inquest following the killing of two young Mexican ranchers by cattle thief Johnny Hale led to a particularly sanguinary gun battle.

The April 14, 1881, legal proceedings in recess, an infuriated and still-armed Hale shot and killed Krempkau. Seeing this, city marshal Dallas Stoudenmire drew his six-shooter and fired at Hale. That shot missed Hale, accidentally killing an innocent passerby. The marshal's next shot took out Hale. When former city marshal George Campbell, a friend of Hale's, drew his pistol, Stoudenmire's fourth and final shot dropped him. An estimated five ticks of the clock had passed, and four men lay dead on El Paso's dusty street.

Before his forced resignation, Stoudenmire had killed six people as city marshal. A running feud fueled by too much booze, and aggravated by a bad temper, ended on September 18, 1882, when he was killed in a gunfight with brothers Doc, James, and

Frank Manning. A historical marker detailing the fight is at the southwest corner of South El Paso and West San Antonio Streets.

Murder on Pirate's Island

On June 29, 1893, thirty-six-year-old ranger captain **Frank Jones** and four rangers, accompanied by an El Paso County deputy sheriff, left Ysleta headed for an area about thirty miles downriver known as Pirate's Island. Back in the 1850s, the Rio Grande had changed course, leaving an international no-man's-land. The rangers carried arrest warrants for Jesus and Serverino Olguin, well-known cattle thieves. They also hoped to recapture brother Antonio Olguin, a prison escapee.

Finding only the Olguins' blind father at the family residence, the rangers pulled back and made camp for the night. The next morning, the state officers saw two suspicious looking riders who galloped off when the rangers approached. The rangers started on their trail, riding straight into an ambush. When the intense firefight ended, Captain Jones lay dead. Substantially outnumbered, the rangers withdrew, leaving Jones's body behind. Later, authorities discovered the incident had happened in Mexico, which complicated the return of Jones's body and personal effects. (The captain's pistol and handcuffs were never found.)

Fact or folklore, no one will ever know, but several writers have noted over the years that Capt. John R. Hughes—Jones's friend and successor—kept a list of twenty-one Mexican citizens and that, in time, he drew a line through eighteen of their names.

The Rio Grande has continued to alter the area's geography over the years, so the exact spot of the fight is no longer known. A historical marker placed in 1937 stands at 8461 Alameda Avenue in Ysleta. Jones's grave there has been lost, his remains believed to have been swept away at some point when the Rio Grande changed course. The house in Ysleta where Jones lived, which for years had been used as Ranger headquarters for the El Paso area, was torn down in 1974.

Adios, John Wesley Hardin

John Wesley (Wes) Hardin didn't shoot the forty-one men some writers have credited him with killing, but he certainly stands as one of the Wild West's more prolific killers. He made his reputation in east and south Texas and along the cattle trail to Kansas before receiving a long prison sentence for killing a deputy sheriff in Comanche, Texas, in 1874. Prison didn't rehabilitate him, but it did allow him plenty of time to read the law. After his release he passed the bar examination and soon headed west to El Paso to practice his new profession. Unfortunately, he still drank too much and gambled.

On August 19, 1895, while drinking whiskey and rolling dice in the Acme Saloon, Hardin went down with three .45 slugs in him or having passed through him. Sore over the way Hardin had treated his son, El Paso constable John Selman, no deacon himself, did the honors. If Selman enjoyed any notoriety for killing Hardin, it didn't last long. Less than a year later, on April 6, 1896, US Marshal George Scarborough ended Selman's career in gun smoke.

The Acme Saloon stood at 227 East San Antonio Avenue. A historical marker placed in 1966 marks the site. Hardin is buried in Concordia Cemetery (3700 East Yandell Dr.). A century after his death, descendants tried to get Hardin's remains reburied at Nixon in South Texas, but a district court's permanent injunction ended that. For years, Hardin had only a flat granite marker. Today, to prevent vandalism or worse, the grave is protected by a stone and metal-barred enclosure appropriately reminiscent of a jail cell. A historical marker in the cemetery tells the story of Hardin's El Paso days.

Concordia Cemetery

Considered one of the more historic graveyards in the West, **Concordia Cemetery** (3700 East Yandell Dr.; 915-842-8200) covers fifty-four acres and has more than sixty-five thousand burials. It is the final resting place for both the respected and disreputable, rich and poor of all ethnicities.

A trapper turned trader, Kentucky-born Hugh Stephenson and his wife Juana Maria began ranching in the area in 1842. Twelve years later, he built a chapel named San Jose de Concordia el Alto for his family and others in the community.

On February 6, 1856, a pet deer fatally gored Mrs. Stephenson. The distraught rancher buried her near the Concordia chapel, the cemetery's first grave. When Stephenson lost his land following the Civil War, his son-in-law bought it at a forced sale in 1867 and in turn sold Stephenson's heirs equal portions for $1 each.

In 1881 the city purchased some of the Stephenson land for a pauper's cemetery. Over the next decade, various groups acquired sections to serve as their cemeteries. Today, African-Americans, Chinese, Euro-Americans, and Hispanics share the cemetery. Its various sections include those set aside for Catholics, Jews, Mormons, and Protestants as well as assorted fraternal organizations and military veterans.

Evergreen Cemetery (4301 Alameda Ave.), while not as old or large as Concordia, also has some notable burials, including longtime El Paso attorney Thomas C. Lea, Jr. (1877–1945) and his son, writer and artist Tom Lea III (1907–2001). Another grave (section K, lot 211) is that of Albert B. Fall (1861–1944), the New Mexican attorney who successfully defended Wayne Brazel, accused killer of Pat Garrett. Victoriano Huerta (1854–1916), a Mexican general and dictator who figured in the Mexican Revolution, also is buried here.

The Only Jail Billy the Kid Ever Broke Into

While surely apocryphal, legend has it that **Billy the Kid** pulled off a jail delivery (as nineteenth-century newspapers sometimes labeled jail breaks) at the El Paso County Jail in 1876. Supposedly The Kid freed his friend Melquiades Segura from the lockup at gunpoint, then returned to New Mexico Territory. The story is shaky but the legend persists.

The old jail still stands in what was El Paso County's first county seat, the city of San Elizario, just downstream from El Paso and since absorbed by the larger town. Next to the small, white-washed adobe building is a statue of The Kid sculpted by Guadalupe Jacquez Calderon. Operated by the San Elizario Genealogy and Historical Society, the **Old El Paso Jail Museum** (1551 Main St., San Elizario; 915- 830-2563) interprets the multi-cultural history of the San Elizario area, which dates to the establishment of a Spanish presidio there in 1680.

San Elizario has seventeen historic structures in its National Historic District. Housed in an adobe building dating to the 1850s, the **Los Portales Museum** (1521 San Elizario Rd.; 915-851-1682) explores the history of the early Spanish colonial efforts in the El Paso Valley, which included missions at the nearby communities of Ysleta and Socorro and the presidio at San Elizario.

Eagle Pass (Maverick County)

A centuries-old Rio Grande crossing, Eagle Pass was developed as a town by John Twohig following the establishment of nearby Fort Duncan in 1849. Thirteen years before, Gen. Antonio Lopez de Santa Anna forded the river just below what would become Eagle Pass on his way to San Antonio. The town grew as a busy border crossing and market center.

Though periodically left unoccupied, Fort Duncan continued to be used by the military until after World War I. Seven of its original buildings still stand in Fort Duncan Park. The history of the old border post is interpreted at the **Fort Duncan Museum** (310 Bliss St.; 830-773-4343).

Frontier CSI

With most Wild West killings, the perpetrator was readily apparent or easily determined. Mysterious murders were not unknown, but certainly not common. One whodunit came to light in February 1889, when within a few days the bodies of three women and one man were pulled from the Rio Grande above Eagle Pass. Someone had tied heavy rocks to the corpses and thrown them in the river. What the slayer had not realized was that the decomposition process would cause the corpses to eventually float to the surface. Local officers had no idea who they were, much less who killed them. Soon, Texas rangers took on the case, and their detective work solved the quadruple homicide.

Pioneer forensic work on the part of **Ranger Sergeant Ira Aten** and **Private John R. Hughes**, including the nation's first known use of dental records to confirm the identity of a dead person, led to the eventual indictment of **Richard H. (Dick) Duncan**.

When the case went to trial in December 1889, evidence showed that the San Saba man had killed four members of a Central Texas family on their way to Mexico after he bought their San Saba County farm. A jury found the defendant guilty, and after the case went all the way to the US Supreme Court, the conviction was upheld. Duncan was hanged in the county jail, then part of the courthouse, on September 18, 1891.

Built in 1884 and 1885, the two-story brick and stone **Maverick County Courthouse** (501 Main St.) where the trial and execution occurred was used until 1979, when a new courthouse was completed. After standing vacant for years, the old courthouse, listed on the National Register of Historic Places, was restored in 2005 and is open to the public for tours. A historical marker (Jefferson Street at Quarry Street) mentioning the murder case was dedicated in 1971 in downtown Eagle Pass.

Fort Davis (Jeff Davis County)

Traveling through the Southwest toward the California goldfields was a dangerous undertaking, but a remote military post in far western Texas made the journey somewhat safer. For nearly four decades troops stationed at Fort Davis—named for Jefferson Davis when he was US secretary of war—protected emigrants, prospectors, freight haulers, stagecoach travelers, and others along the trail from San Antonio to El Paso and points west.

Established in 1854, the post stood east of the Davis Mountains in a rocky box canyon along Limpia Creek within sight of the busy Overland Trail. The army vacated Fort Davis and its other Texas garrisons at the start of the Civil War but reoccupied the post in 1867. And, despite Jefferson Davis's recent effort as president of the Confederacy to tear the nation apart, the government did not change the fort's name. The army did, however, change the location of the fort, building a larger, more substantial post just east of the original site.

By the 1880s, the fort consisted of around a hundred buildings and accommodated more than four hundred troops. Soldiers from the fort played a major role in the army's 1880 campaign against the Apache leader Victorio, having several engagements with the American Indians. Under Col. Benjamin Grierson, troops finally forced Victorio into Mexico where he and most of his band were slain by Mexican soldiers. That operation ended the Indian Wars in Texas and the army closed the fort in 1891. The town that had developed adjacent to the post and taken its name continued as a ranching community and seat of Jeff Davis County. The fort returned to federal control seventy years later, in 1961, when it was designated as **Fort Davis National Historic Site**.

Located on the northern edge of the town at State Highways 17 and 118, Fort Davis's visitor center and museum (101 Lt. Flipper Dr., No. 1379; 432-426-3224) interprets the history of the fort.

Operated by the Fort Davis Historical Society, the **Overland Trail Museum** (510 North Fort St.; 432-242-3663) focuses on the history of the town and county. The museum is housed in the former residence and office of one of the area's more colorful characters, justice of the peace (and former Texas ranger) Nick Mersfelter.

FORT MCKAVETT (MENARD COUNTY)

Established in 1851 near the San Saba River, Fort McKavett was mainly garrisoned by infantry, no match for Comanche warriors on horseback. Fortunately for the soldiers at the post, no significant clashes occurred before the army abandoned the fort in 1859. When the post was reoccupied in 1866 after the Civil War, it was with a mixture of infantry and cavalry. Troops stationed at the fort saw action during the Red River War of 1874 to 1875, but after that garrison life became routine. The post was abandoned in 1883.

Fort McKavett State Historic Site (7066 Farm to Market Road 864; 325-396-2358) is twenty-three miles southwest of Menard off US 190.

Shoot-out in Scabtown

An inelegant name, Scabtown was not an inappropriate way to refer to the collection of saloons, gambling dens, and bawdy houses across the San Saba River from Fort McKavett.

On New Year's Eve, 1877, five Texas rangers under Lt. Nelson Orcelus Reynolds made camp near the post. If the rangers did anything special to celebrate the new year, they did so in camp. But the squad's African-American cook, along with the teamster, walked to Miller's Dance Hall in Scabtown to kick up their heels.

The pair found the dance hall crowded with drunk ex–Buffalo Soldiers, some of them not having much use for other African-Americans who worked for white lawmen. Owner Charles Miller, with help from some of his customers, disarmed the new arrivals, roughed them up, and tossed them out.

When the pair sheepishly returned to camp to report what had happened, Reynolds and his men went to the dance hall to retrieve the state-issued firearms. As Mrs. Ida Miller cooperatively handed one of the handguns to the rangers, an inebriated celebrant grabbed it and snapped off a shot at Ranger Tim McCarty. The round missed, but when the ranger shot back, as was later reported, shooting "became general on both sides."

Ranger McCarty fell with a bullet in his chest, and soon Charles Miller, his young daughter, and two customers lay dead. McCarty died the next day. The Menard County sheriff investigated the incident, and a coroner's jury soon ruled that the four African-Americans "came to their death while resisting officers in the discharge of their duties."

After the army abandoned Fort McKavett, Scabtown's denizens left for greener pastures.

Fort Stockton (Pecos County)

Fort Stockton the town developed adjacent to Fort Stockton the military post. Established in 1858 near a prolific spring on the Comanche War Trail, Fort Stockton remained an active garrison until 1886. Losing the soldiers was a blow to its economy, but the town survived as a ranching center and county seat.

Occupying an old hotel and stagecoach stop, the **Annie Riggs Museum** (301 South Main St.; 432-336-2167) interprets the history of the town and Pecos County.

Historic Fort Stockton Museum (Barracks Number 1, Old Fort Stockton, 301 East 3rd St.; 432-336-2167) focuses on the history of the old fort.

Who Shot A.J.?

Pecos County Sheriff **A.J. Royal** (1855–1894) was not popular, either among his constituents or the Texas rangers who dealt with him. When he sought reelection in 1894, feelings ran so strong that five rangers came to town to assure honest, violence-free voting. The balloting proceeded without incident and Royal was voted out of office. But on November 21, 1894, two weeks after he lost the election, and with three rangers still in town, someone shotgunned the lame duck sheriff as he sat at his courthouse desk. Officers never figured out who did it.

Folklore has a group of civic leaders drawing straws to determine who would kill the former sheriff. Some even speculated the killer wore a ranger's badge.

The killing occurred inside the sheriff's office in the **Pecos County Courthouse** (400 South Nelson St.). Built in 1883, the three-story building, extensively remodeled, remains in use.

Royal was buried in what is now known as the **Old Fort Stockton Cemetery** (8th and North Water Streets).

"Bud" and the "Deacon" Didn't Get Along

A Fort Stockton native, **George Alexander (Bud) Frazer** (1864–1896) served two terms as Reeves County sheriff from 1890 to 1894. During that time, James (Deacon Jim) Miller worked for him as a deputy. (Miller came by his nickname because he didn't drink or smoke, but he seemed to have believed he was exempt from the sixth commandment, the one about not killing people.) For a variety of reasons, rather than bonding in a mutual dedication to law and order the two men came to loathe each other. On April 12, 1894, six months after being voted out of office, Frazer confronted Miller in Pecos. Correctly calling him out as a cow thief and murderer, Frazer shot Miller in the arm and then put a well-grouped pattern in Miller's chest. When his enemy went down, Frazer assumed him dead and walked off. Unknown to Frazer, the Deacon wore metal body armor under his shirt. The .45 slugs had bruised him badly, but he got over it, at least physically.

Encountering Miller again eight months later, Frazer shot him in the arm and leg and put a couple of rounds about where his heart should have been beating its last. Apparently, no one had ever told Frazer that Miller wore body armor. Frazer fled.

On September 13, 1896, Miller found Frazer in a saloon at Toyah in Reeves County and permanently settled the score with his favorite weapon, a double-barreled shotgun. A jury acquitted Miller, but in a few years a lynch mob in Ada, Oklahoma, would refer his case to a higher court.

Frazer is buried in **East Hill Cemetery** (GPS coordinates: N30° 52.51', W102° 50.72'), one mile south of Fort Stockton. Take US 285 to Parkview and then a half mile east.

Fort Worth (Tarrant County)

Major Ripley A. Arnold of the US Second Dragoons established Fort Worth on a bluff overlooking the Trinity River in 1849. When the army left in 1853, the small settlement that had developed in view of the fort's flag remained.

The first seat of Tarrant County, organized in 1850, was Birdville. By 1855, despite the departure of the military two years earlier, townspeople in Fort Worth moved to usurp Birdville as county seat. In an election in which the Democratic process was liberally fostered with free whiskey and voters imported especially for the occasion, Fort Worth won.

But Fort Worth's exposed position on the frontier, which left the county vulnerable to American Indian raids, kept the town small. At one point after the Civil War, the population was only 175.

Prosperity finally came in the early 1870s along with the dust kicked up by longhorn cattle being driven up the Chisholm Trail to the railhead in Kansas. Fort Worth became a wild and wooly cow town—a place to lay in supplies and enjoy a little recreation before resuming a long, hard trek north.

By 1875 a revived Fort Worth had incorporated as a city. In the summer of 1876, the Texas and Pacific Railway reached the city, further stimulating its economy. Within a twenty-four-year period, eight additional railroads converged on the city, adding to its growth and importance.

In the early 1900s, cattle brought about a second boom as Fort Worth grew into a beef processing center. Sprawling stockyards developed adjacent to the railroad lines and soon served three large packing plants operated by Swift, Armour, and McNeill & Libby. The stockyard area is now a National Historic District, no longer in operation, but Fort Worth still claims to be "Where the West Begins."

A bronze plaque on a large rock (200 West Belknap St.) marks the site of the old military post. Fort Worth had no role in the Civil War, but the conflict certainly influenced Old West history. For one thing, it produced a notorious crop of Western outlaws. The calamity that nearly ripped the nation apart is interpreted at the **Texas Civil War Museum** (760 Jim Wright Freeway North; 817-246-2323). It is the largest Civil War museum west of the Mississippi.

Founded by the Texas and Southwestern Cattle Raisers Association, the **Cattle Raisers Museum** occupies the second floor of the **Fort Worth Museum of Science and History** (1600 Gendy St.; 817-255-9300).

The **Amon Carter Museum** (3501 Camp Bowie Blvd.; 817-738-1933) has one of the nation's largest collections of Western art, including many works by Frederick Remington and Charles Russell, and has exhibits on the trail-driving era.

The **Sid Richardson Museum** (309 Main St.; 817-332-6554) also has numerous original paintings by Remington and Russell.

Quanah Parker's Fort Worth

Fort Worth was the nearest large city to the Comanche reservation outside Fort Sill, Oklahoma, and their chief Quanah Parker visited periodically. His first trip here, however, was nearly his last. That was in 1885 when Parker and another chief named Yellow

Bear shared a room at the Pickwick Hotel. Their room had state-of-the-art amenities, including gas lighting. When Parker and Yellow Bear went to bed that night, one of them did not properly extinguish the lamp. That caused the room to fill with gas, killing Yellow Bear and almost claiming Parker's life. A state historical marker is located near the site (115 West 3rd St.).

Twenty-five years earlier, the chief's mother, Cynthia Ann Parker, had stayed for a time at her uncle Isaac Parker's log cabin not far from Fort Worth in Birdville. That was in 1861, shortly after Texas rangers repatriated the former Comanche captive in a fight with her adopted people on Pease River.

Issac Parker's cabin was moved from Birdville to Fort Worth in 1929. It now is one of several historic structures preserved in **Log Cabin Village** (2100 Log Cabin Village Ln.; 817-392-5881). Still standing at the original site of Parker's cabin, adjacent to the Parker Cemetery, are several old trees known as the **Parker Oaks** (Cardinal Road, east of Loop 820, Hurst).

In the 1890s and early 1900s, Quanah sometimes came to Fort Worth to see his friend, legendary rancher Burk Burnett, who leased three hundred thousand acres of grazing land on the Kiowa and Comanche reservations in Oklahoma. Parker had brokered the deal.

Hell's Half Acre

As Fort Worth grew, the need arose for a venue where all the buffalo hunters, cowboys, drummers, freighters, gamblers, outlaws, and railroad men descending on the city could let off a little steam. A fifteen-block red-light district with saloons, gambling halls, and bordellos soon developed. Folks called it Hell's Half Acre.

During the vice district's heyday, Old West characters like Bat Masterson, Doc Holliday, Wyatt Earp, "Longhair" Jim Courtright, Luke Short, Butch Cassidy, and lesser lights all contributed to the local economy.

According to the November 29, 1878, *Fort Worth Democrat*, Hell's Half Acre's denizens included "lewd women of all ages 16 to 40 . . the most respectable of citizens, the experienced thief . . . the ordinary murderer, the average cowboy and the ordinary young man about town."

Hell's Half Acre remained a popular Fort Worth destination until the commander of the army's Camp Bowie pressed city officials to shut it down during World War I. The area was cleared in the 1960s to make room for a convention center.

White Elephant Saloon

The elephant in the room at the **White Elephant Saloon** that day was **"Longhair" Jim Courtright** (1848–1887), so named because he wore his hair long. Courtright had been Fort Worth's first city marshal, serving from 1876 to 1879. Now it was February 8, 1887, and Courtright owned the T.I.C. Detective Agency, the initials representing his full name—Timothy Isaiah Courtright. But Courtright was more shakedown artist than sleuth.

What brought him to the town's best watering hole and gambling venue was a prospective business deal. If owners Jake Johnson and Luke Short would be willing to pay for it, he would protect their business. As with all "protection" racketeers, the inference was that the saloon proprietors would be paying to keep their business protected from Courtright.

Johnson, Short, and Courtright emerged from the saloon deep in discussion. They stopped a short distance from the White Elephant and were standing—appropriately enough—in front of Ella Blackwell's shooting gallery. When Courtright perceived that Short was going for a gun, the former marshal said, "You needn't be getting out your gun." Short assured him he wasn't heeled. But when Courtright went for his revolver, it turned out that Short *was* armed. Unfortunately for the one-time lawman, his gun jammed. Short's six-shooter worked just fine, and he sent five bullets into Courtright, permanently putting the T.I.C. Detective Agency and its owner out of business. Courtright received a nice funeral and Short got off scot free in the killing.

The shooting occurred in the 300 block of Main Street near the original White Elephant, which opened in 1884. That building no longer stands, but the building the saloon occupied in the mid-1890s is still there at 608-610 Main Street.

Founded in 1879 by Fort Worth pioneer John Peter Smith, the sixty-two-acre **Oakwood Cemetery** (701 Grand Ave.; 817-624-3531) has more than fourteen thousand burials representing a cross section of Fort Worth and Texas history. Three of those graves belong to notorious gunmen: "Longhair" Jim Courtright (1848–1887), Luke Lamar Short (1854–1893), and James Brown "Deacon Jim" Miller (1861–1909; block 101, lot 14, space 1).

Among the noted ranchers or ranch family member buried in Oakwood are Four Sixes Ranch founder Samuel Burk Burnett (1849–1922), W.T. (Tom) Waggoner (1852–1934), ranching heiress Electra Waggoner (1882–1925), and her brother Guy Waggoner (1883–1950).

Thistle Hill House

In 1903 cattle baron **W.T. (Tom) Waggoner** built a red brick, two-story, Georgian Revival–style mansion for his daughter Electra as a wedding present. The eccentric Electra went through two husbands and a lot of money (having once spent $20,000 in one day at Dallas's tony Neiman Marcus department store) before she died at forty-three in 1925. By then, the eighteen-room, eleven-thousand-square-foot house had been sold to Winfield Scott, who remodeled it to its current appearance. The restored mansion (1509 Pennsylvania Ave.; 817-332-5875) is open for tours when not rented for weddings or other special events.

The cattle are gone except for the longhorn herd paraded down Exchange Street every day in the heart of the district, but cowboys and want-to-be cowboys keep the Stockyard District a busy place. The 1902 **Livestock Exchange Building**, the centerpiece of the district, was the Wall Street of the West.

The **Stockyards Museum** (131 East Exchange Ave.; 817-625-9715) is in the old Stockyards Exchange Building. Two other museums are devoted to cowboys and cowgirls, the **Texas Cowboy Hall of Fame** (2515 Rodeo Plaza; 817-626-7131) and the **National Cowgirl Museum and Hall of Fame** (1720 Gendy St.; 817-336-4475).

Cowtown Coliseum

Pecos, Texas, and several other Western communities claim to have staged the nation's first rodeo. Fort Worth has never asserted that, but as part of its annual Fat Stock Show and Livestock Exhibition, it did have the first indoor rodeo, the first nighttime rodeo, and numerous other "firsts." Those events took place in the nation's first indoor coliseum, an engineering marvel of its day where the Old West and New West would overlap. Construction began in 1907, and at a cost of $250,000 the facility was completed in 1908. The following year, Chief Quanah Parker and thirty-six other Comanches appeared in the newly built coliseum. In 1911, Quanah's friend President Theodore Roosevelt spoke at the venue, followed over the years by a veritable Who's Who of entertainers, from Bob Wills to Elvis Presley. The historic **Cowtown Coliseum** (121 East Exchange Ave.; 888-COWTOWN [269-8696]) was extensively renovated in 1986, including installation of an air-conditioning and heating system, and is still booking events.

FREDERICKSBURG (GILLESPIE COUNTY)

When German immigrants settled Fredericksburg in 1846, nothing lay beyond the new community but hundreds of miles of open terrain—and the Comanche, Kiowa, and Apache people. To protect the settlement, the army established Fort Martin Scott on the wagon road just to the east of town. But to protect themselves, two years prior to the building of the fort, a delegation of Germans led by town founder John O. Meusbach negotiated a peace treaty with the Comanche people that both sides honored—a rarity in the Old West. For the most part, the treaty held, though Gillespie County residents were not immune to American Indian raids during the 1860s, especially during the Civil War. The town grew slowly as a county seat, trade, and agricultural center, but the pace picked up considerably in the 1970s with increased tourist traffic and development of its wine-making industry.

The town has more than seven hundred historically significant structures. A self-guided downtown walking tour featuring thirty of those sites is available at the **Fredericksburg Visitor Information Center** (302 East Austin St.; 830-997-6523).

Pioneer Museum (325 West Main St.; 830-997-2835) features exhibits and restored vintage structures depicting the history of this German settlement.

The army established Fort Martin Scott in 1848, the first post established on Texas's western frontier after statehood. In addition to the fort's normal compliment of around a hundred soldiers, at various times Texas rangers camped adjacent to the post. That continued occasionally after the army left in 1853. During the Civil War, Confederate troops also used the fort at times. A Gillespie County pioneer later purchased the property and farmed on it for decades. Heirs of the original owners sold the land to the City of Fredericksburg in 1949. One surviving original building has been restored, and three other fort buildings have been reconstructed to original specifications. **Historic Fort Martin Scott** (1606 East Main St./US 290; 830-307-8715) is open for self-guided tours during the day.

Texas Rangers Heritage Center

In 1897, aging former Texas Ranger John S. (Rip) Ford, who, as a newspaper editor, American Indian fighter, soldier, and politician made his share of Texas history, began to realize that if a society is to learn from the past, it must know what that past involved. In addition to writing a memoir and helping organize the Texas State Historical Association, Ford formed the forerunner of the Former Texas Rangers Association.

More than a century later, the nonprofit Former Texas Rangers Foundation (the fundraising arm of the Former Texas Rangers Association) began planning for a heritage center dedicated not only to ranger history and all the rangers who have died in the line of duty since 1823, but also as a place where the character traits that helped the lawmen build their legend could be instilled in young people.

The first phase of the **Texas Rangers Heritage Center** (1618 East Main St.; 830-990-1192) opened in 2015. Situated on twelve acres adjacent to old Fort Martin Scott, the complex includes a limestone campanili that rises fifty feet and at night is bathed in blue light and a Ranger Ring of Honor built around a twenty-ton, five-point concrete replica of a ranger badge that's thirty feet in diameter. The Texas-size monument features plaques listing the names of all known rangers killed in the line of duty. Carved along the circumference of the badge are five ranger-defining character traits: courage, determination, dedication, respect, and integrity. The center also has an outdoor pavilion, an amphitheater, and a historical reenactment area. The heritage center's second phase includes a 7,600-square-foot building with five galleries for interactive museum displays as well as a Ranger library and archive.

Sculpted by Richard O. Cook and dedicated in 1983, a two-thirds-size bronze statue of a ranger leading a pack mule was moved from San Antonio and placed outside the heritage center's pavilion in 2015. Standing nearby is a two-thirds-size bronze by Erik Christianson of an 1850s ranger holding a Sharps rifle. The largest sculpture at the center is artist Dustin Payne's *The*

Legend, The Lore, The Law, a life-size bronze showing four rangers, each representative of an era of ranger history, from their earliest days to the twentieth century. The statue was dedicated in 2016.

The facility is open during daylight hours, and the pavilion is available for private events. The FTRA offices are at 103 Industrial Loop, Suite 700, in Fredericksburg.

Galveston (Galveston County)

Until Texas got its first interstate rail connection in the early 1870s, the island city of Galveston was the state's primary gateway for people and goods. The largest of only two natural deep-water ports, Galveston was founded in 1837 when Texas was a republic and soon grew into its largest city. For decades, rivaled only by San Antonio, Galveston's status as the state's most populated city held until a devastating hurricane struck it in 1900, killing thousands in what still stands as the nation's worst natural disaster. Despite the catastrophic storm, numerous nineteenth-century houses and commercial buildings still stand on the island.

Jesse James's Honeymoon

Even the most notorious Wild West outlaws needed the occasional break from robbing and killing. In late spring 1874, the newly married Jesse James took his wife (and first cousin) Zerelda to Galveston for their honeymoon. With its prevailing Gulf breeze and wide beaches, Galveston was a popular resort as well as a busy center of commerce and transportation. This was not James's first visit to Texas, but it was his first as a married man. James surely tried to keep a low profile, but someone from Missouri recognized him. On top of that, the man sent a letter to the

St. Louis Dispatch disclosing James's presence in the Oleander City. Since the Pinkertons were looking for him, James told the man he and his wife would be taking a ship to Vera Cruz, Mexico, and that he intended to take up farming there. But when their honeymoon ended, the couple returned to Missouri.

Where the Jameses stayed in Galveston is not known, but the best accommodation in town was the **Tremont House**. Built in 1872, the four-story hotel was razed in 1928. But in 1985 an 1879-vintage building near the site of the earlier hotel was remodeled and opened as a hotel called the Tremont House. That hotel (2300 Ship Mechanics Row St.; 409-763-0300) remains in business.

Located in a two-story brick orphanage built in 1894 and 1895 that was significantly damaged by the 1900 Galveston storm, the **Bryan Museum** (1315 21st St.; 409-632-7685) focuses on the history of Texas and the West. Twenty thousand square feet of space accommodates the thousands of artifacts, papers, and books collected by Houston attorney J.P. Bryan, a descendant of Texas colonizer Stephen F. Austin. Bryan acquired the historic building in 2013, renovated it, and opened the museum in 2015.

Opened in 1983, the **Galveston Railroad Museum** (2602 Santa Fe Place; 409-765-5700) is housed in the old Santa Fe Railroad depot and features vintage rolling stock, exhibits, and statuary of railroad workers and passengers as they would have appeared in the heyday of the station.

Giddings (Lee County)

Giddings dates to 1871 when the Houston and Texas Central Railway came through the area. When Lee County was established in 1874, Giddings became county seat.

The **Lee County Museum** (183 East Hempstead St.; 979-542-3455) shares space with the chamber of commerce in the two-story, Greek Revival-style **Schubert-Fletcher House**. Giddings merchant

August W. Schubert built the house in 1879. Fifteen years later he sold it to the Missouri Synod of the Lutheran Church, and it became the first home of Concordia Lutheran College. In 1900, Baylis John Fletcher (1859–1912) bought the house from the church and it stayed in his family for most of the rest of the twentieth century. As a young man, Fletcher had taken part in a cattle drive from Texas to Wyoming up the Chisholm Trail. His recollections of that experience were published posthumously in 1968 as *Up the Trail in '79*, a range classic.

The **Giddings Public Library and Cultural Center** (276 North Orange St.; 979-542-2716) has Texas's largest permanent display of American Indian artifacts, the Arnold Smith Collection.

Bill Longley

Led up the steps of the gallows, the handcuffed man stood patiently as the noose was placed around his neck and a black hood pulled over his head. Moments later the trapdoor sprang, and the hooded man dropped eight feet. A hundred onlookers stood silently as the man dangled before them.

"I'm alive," he finally said, and the crowd cheered.

It was September 20, 1987, and a sixty-seven-year-old, semi-retired magician named Woodrow T. Wilson (1919–1998) had just had himself hanged to prove a point: It was possible to fake a hanging. Under his shirt Wilson wore a customized brace that kept his neck from breaking. All he had were rope burns, and those would heal. The show hanging took place on a gallows Wilson had built outside his flea market on US 290 at the western edge of Giddings.

The reason Wilson went to such an extreme was his firm belief that his distant relative **Bill Longley** (1851–1878), an outlaw some claimed killed thirty-two people, had survived his October 11, 1878, execution because a family member had paid off the sheriff to make it only look as if the death sentence had been carried out. However, all but the most conspiracy-minded believe that Longley was quite dead when loaded into his coffin and taken to the Giddings cemetery for burial. What was in doubt until late in the twentieth century was just where in the cemetery his grave happened to be. An attempt had been made in 1986 to find his unmarked grave, but a skeleton exhumed in 1998 was identified by DNA analysis in 2001 as most likely Longley's. Unlike Woodrow Wilson, the outlaw had not escaped death at the gallows.

William Preston Longley was indeed buried in Giddings City Cemetery (US 290 and South Dallas St.). A sign in the cemetery points to the outlaw's grave, which has a state historical marker.

Woodrow T. Wilson is buried in the same cemetery.

Goliad (Goliad County)

In 1749, Spain established a mission on the San Antonio River downstream from the missions at San Antonio de Bexar. Across from the mission they built a presidio, or fortress, to protect the missionaries and their charges. The Spanish, in addition to their effort to convert American Indians to Christianity maintained large herds of longhorn cattle on ranches along the river, the beginning of ranching in Texas. The village that grew up in the vicinity after Mexico won its independence from Spain in 1821 was called La Bahia, but in 1829 the town—one of the three oldest in Texas—was renamed Goliad. The community declined after the Texas Revolution, but revived with the arrival of a rail connection in 1885.

The reconstructed **Presidio La Bahia** (217 Loop 71; 361-645-3752) is the most complete Spanish presidio in Texas. During the Texas Revolution, Col. James Fannin and his men occupied the fort until they were captured in the Battle of Coleto Creek on March 20, 1836. Mexican soldiers held them at La Bahia a week before they were marched off and most of them executed on Palm Sunday, March 27, 1836. A few men managed to escape, but Fannin and 341 Texans were killed. The massacre was the largest single loss the Texans experienced during the revolution, giving rise to the battle cry, "Remember

Goliad!" soldiers yelled at the Battle of San Jacinto (see Houston) along with "Remember the Alamo!"

A stone obelisk (734 Farm to Market Road 2506) stands at the site of the Battle of Coleto Creek. A monument two miles south of Goliad off US 183 marks the site where Fannin and his men were buried following their execution.

The restored **Mission Espiritu Santo** (108 Park Road 6; 361-645-3405) is a state park and historic site, one mile south of Goliad off US 183.

Gonzales (Gonzales County)

Settled in 1825 by people brought to Texas by colonizer Green DeWitt, Gonzales is one of Texas's earliest Euro-American towns. The first shot of the Texas Revolution was fired by some of its citizens in 1835 when a detachment of Mexican soldiers attempted to take a small cannon earlier located there for frontier defense. Less than a year later, Gonzales sent thirty-two volunteers to help defend the Alamo. All died in the final assault on the old mission. Sam Houston was in Gonzales when he learned of the Alamo's fall, and realizing that Gen. Antonio Lopez de Santa Anna's army would be marching in his direction, Houston ordered the town evacuated and torched. Gonzales was rebuilt after Texas won its independence from Mexico and continued to develop as a ranching and trade center.

Opened during the 1936 Texas Centennial celebration, the Art Deco–style **Gonzales Memorial Museum** (414 Smith St.; 830-672-6350), with its adjacent monument and reflecting pool, focuses on Gonzales's part in the revolution against Mexico.

Old Jail Museum

Built in 1887, the old **Gonzales County Jail** continued in use until 1975. In addition to prisoners, the three-story brick jail housed the sheriff's office as well as a residence for the sheriff and his family. The hoosegow also featured built-in gallows where, between 1891 and 1921, three men dropped through the trap on their way to eternity.

Sheriff Richard Glover, his wife, and six children lived in the jail when, on June 14, 1901, the sheriff led a posse in search of Gregorio Cortez, who two days before had shot and killed the sheriff of nearby Karnes County. In the shoot-out that erupted when they found Cortez, Glover died. The incident happened on the ranch of Henry J. Schnabel, who also was killed, probably by a stray bullet from one of the posse members.

Cortez was held in the Gonzales jail in 1904 during his trial for Sheriff Glover's murder. Convicted and sentenced to life in prison, he was transferred from Gonzales to Huntsville on New Year's Day 1905. He was later pardoned. Listed in the National Register of Historic Places, the jail now accommodates the **Gonzales County Jail Museum** (414 St. Lawrence St.; 830-263-4663).

Goodnight (Armstrong County)

Named for pioneer cattleman Charles Goodnight, the town was founded in 1887 when the Fort Worth and Denver Railway cut across the Texas Panhandle. Born in Illinois in 1836, Goodnight came to Texas with his family when he was nine. He later served with a volunteer ranger company in the upper Brazos River valley and at twenty-four worked as a ranger scout. It was Goodnight who put Capt. Sul Ross's rangers on the trail that led to a Comanche village on the Pease River where they "rescued" Cynthia Ann Parker in 1860 (see Groesbeck). During the Civil War, Goodnight signed up with a ranger company operating out of Fort Belknap in Young County.

Goodnight eventually settled in Palo Duro Canyon and ran the famous JA Ranch. Earlier, he had pioneered the trail-driving era in developing the Goodnight-Loving Trail with his friend Oliver Loving. A trailblazer both literally and figuratively, Goodnight did everything from inventing the mobile cowboy kitchen known as the chuckwagon to producing a silent Western film using real American Indians. He also helped save the American bison from extinction.

Goodnight's 1877 house has been restored, now part of the **Charles Goodnight Historical Center and J. Evetts Haley Visitor Center** (4901 County Rd. 25; 806-226-2187).

Goodnight died in 1929 at the age of ninety-three and he and his wife Mary Ann are buried in the **Goodnight Cemetery** (County Road 26, Clarendon; GPS coordinates: N35° 02.78', W101° 10.42') still surrounded by prairie. Years ago, some cowboy tied his bandana to the fence around Goodnight's grave to show his respect, and the tradition has continued.

In nearby Claude, the **Armstrong County Museum** (120 North Trice St.; 806-226-2187) documents Goodnight's storied life and the history of the area.

GRAHAM (YOUNG COUNTY)

E.S. Graham and his brother G.A. came to what is now Young County in 1872 to operate a salt works. They built a frame house, drilled a well, and installed boilers to distill salt from the well's sodium chloride–laden water. Next, they set about starting a town.

The brothers had a townsite surveyed on their land and to attract settlers, they offered free lots to anyone who would "build upon them good frame, stone or brick buildings and business houses, and will have them occupied and in use." Particularly sought were druggists, millers, blacksmiths, tanners, tinners, shoemakers, "or any other branch deemed desirable to a town, gambling and drinking houses excepted." In planning their town, the Graham brothers thought big. Their surveyor laid out wide streets and a large public square, seven-eighths of a mile across. Because of that, Graham claims the largest courthouse square in America, 670 feet by 890 feet.

The **Old Post Office Museum and Art Center** (510 3rd St.; 940-549-1470) occupies the Depression-era former post office, used until 1993. The local history museum opened in 2002.

Fort Belknap

Established in 1851, **Fort Belknap** was part of a line of forts built along the Texas frontier from the Red River to the Rio Grande to protect settlers from American Indians. In 1854, when the government established two American Indian reservations near the fort, the post's focus changed to protecting the reservation Indians from tribal enemies or Indian-hating whites. By 1859, following several instances of bloodshed, it became evident that having Indian reservations in Texas was a bad idea and the American Indians were relocated to what is now Oklahoma. Fort Belknap was abandoned soon after, though the fort saw some use by state forces during the Civil War. In 1867 the US Army briefly reoccupied the post, but lack of water led to its permanent closure. Eleven miles northwest of Graham, the old fort (5385 Farm to Market Road 61; 940-846-3222) is owned and managed by Young County. The fort's former commissary houses the Fort Belknap Museum, which has an exhibit that details a bloody episode that would become the basis of a Hollywood film.

The Sons of William Marlow

The 1965 John Wayne Western movie, *The Sons of Katie Elder,* is loosely based on what really happened to the sons of Dr. William Marlow.

In 1888, four of Marlow's five boys were charged in federal court with horse theft. Charley, Alfred (Alf), Boone, and Lewellyn (Epp) were arrested and taken to Graham for trial. The fifth brother, George, traveled to Graham with his mother to get them cleared but he, too, was arrested.

The brothers made bail and got jobs on an area ranch while awaiting trial. Meanwhile, Young County Sheriff Marion Wallace came to their cabin to arrest Boone on a state murder charge filed in Wilbarger County, Texas. During the arrest attempt, deputy

Tom Collier fired a shot at Boone. Boone grabbed a rifle and fired twice at the deputy. Both shots missed Collier, but one round hit and mortally wounded the sheriff. At that, Boone fled while Epp rode to town for a doctor. (Boone was later killed by bounty hunters in Indian Territory.)

Epp was promptly arrested, and a posse rode to the Marlow cabin to round up the other brothers, even though George and Alf hadn't been present when the shooting happened.

Sentiment ran strong against the boys in Graham. Fearing mob action, they broke jail but were soon captured. Then a mob did try to lynch them, but the brothers succeeded in defending themselves and the crowd dispersed. Believing the mob would try again, Deputy US Marshal Edwin Johnson left on January 19, 1889, to take the four brothers and two other federal prisoners to the Parker County jail in Weatherford, Texas. The prisoners, guards, and a supply of rifles and ammunition filled three wagons. With Charlie chained to Alfred and George to Lewellyn, the party made it to Dry Creek where they were ambushed.

The brothers managed to get to the rifles and started fighting back. Alfred and Lewellyn were killed, and George and Charles were seriously wounded. Three of the attackers also died in the shoot-out. After the ambushers fled, despite their wounds, George and Charles found knives and cut off the feet of their dead brothers to escape.

They made it back to the family cabin and later held off a posse until they finally surrendered to federal officers. George and Charles were tried and acquitted in the killing of the sheriff and the horse theft. Both moved to Colorado, became respected citizens, and lived long lives.

Groesbeck (Limestone County)

One of the classic dramas of the Old West, the capture and subsequent rescue of Cynthia Ann Parker, began just north of future Groesbeck at a cedar-log stockade built in 1833 and 1834 by the family and followers of Elder John Parker.

On the morning of May 19, 1836, less than a month after Texas gained its independence from Mexico at the Battle of San Jacinto, several hundred Comanche and Kiowa warriors attacked the fort. Most of the settlers who lived in and around the stockade were working their fields at the time. Five men died in the attack, including family patriarch John Parker and two of his sons, Benjamin and Silas. The warriors kidnapped five women and children, including Rachel Plummer and nine-year-old Cynthia Ann. The others managed to escape.

Reconstructed in 1936 by the Civilian Conservation Corps, **Fort Parker** (866 Park Road 35; 254-729-5263) was part of Fort Parker State Park when it opened in 1941. By 1965 the fort badly needed renovation, which the state oversaw. In 1992 the Texas Parks and Wildlife Department deeded the reconstructed fort to the city of Groesbeck, which continues to operate it. The Fort Parker site has exhibits and signage interpreting the attack and its aftermath. The state park remains a separate attraction.

A year to the day after the attack, James Parker led an armed group to the abandoned fort and collected the animal-gnawed bones of the victims. They buried five sets of remains in a common grave, the beginning of a cemetery first called Union Burial Ground, then Lewisville Cemetery, then Glenwood Cemetery and, finally, **Fort Parker Memorial Park** (two miles north of Groesbeck on Farm to Market Road 1245). A concrete slab marks the grave. A large monument was dedicated at the site in 1932.

HELENA (KARNES COUNTY)

Founded in 1852 by Thomas Ruckman and Dr. Lewis S. Owings, Helena was named for Owings's wife, Helen. Being on a busy trade route, the new community grew rapidly. Ruckman and Owings successfully lobbied for the creation of a new county and Helena became county seat.

When armed Anglos in 1857 began waylaying Mexican *carteros* (ox cart drivers who hauled freight) along the road from San Antonio to the port of Indianola, Governor E.M. Pease called for a ranger company to end the violence. A series of robberies and killings born of racial prejudice and market competition, the trouble became known as the Cart War. A state historical marker with more details on the war stands near the old Karnes County courthouse in Helena. Nearby two state historical markers tell Helena's story.

Built in 1873 and used until the county seat moved, the former courthouse houses the **Karnes County Museum** (8167 North Farm to Market Road 81; 830-780-3210). Maintained by the Karnes County Historical Society, the old courthouse museum complex includes Thomas Ruckman's two-story, 1878-vintage house and Helena's old Masonic Lodge.

"Helena Killed My Son, I'll Kill Helena"

The day after Christmas 1884, twenty-year-old **Emmet W. Butler** (1864–1884) and a friend were enjoying an afternoon of drinking in one of Helena's numerous saloons. When they became, as one newspaper put it, "quarrelsome," **Sheriff Edgar Leary** (1849–1884) arrived to prevent any serious trouble. When arresting them seemed the only option, they resisted. As the county lawman struggled to subdue them, Butler pulled a concealed handgun and shot the sheriff in the heart. With Leary dead on the saloon floor, Butler ran outside to his horse and galloped off. (Butler's buddy wisely stayed put.) But even the best horse can't outrun a bullet, or, in this case, a flurry of bullets. Townspeople began firing on the fleeing killer and he fell off his horse mortally wounded. Butler's father, **William G. Butler** (1834–1912), was one of the area's wealthiest ranchers. Leading twenty-five armed cowboys, he came to town to claim his son's body and to deal with whomever had killed him. Learning that his son's death had been a community project, he supposedly declared: "Helena killed my son, I'll kill Helena."

While historians don't think Butler really said that, the fact he was a prominent, influential man is not contested. The following year, as the San Antonio and Aransas Pass Railway laid tracks toward the coast, the company chose to bypass Helena. The community could not survive that severe of an economic blow. In 1894, the county seat was moved to Karnes City, and Helena became a ghost town.

Sheriff Leary was buried in the Helena Cemetery (Farm to Market Road 1 just outside of town). Emmet Butler and his father are buried in the Butler Family Cemetery (601 Farm to Market Road 719, Kenedy).

William T. (Brack) Morris

On June 12, 1901, Sheriff **William T. (Brack) Morris** (1860–1901) rode from his office in the county jail at Karnes City to a ranch outside of town to question **Romaldo Cortez** about a stolen horse. Cortez's younger brother **Gregorio** worked with him on the same ranch. With a deputy serving as translator, Morris and the two Cortez brothers misunderstood each other. A struggle ensued and Morris shot and wounded Romaldo. Gregorio then shot and killed the sheriff. The shooting, soon followed by Gregorio killing the sheriff of nearby Gonzales County, marked the beginning of an epic pursuit by several hundred posse members and rangers that ended in Cortez's capture. The distance he covered and the number of officers it took to finally track him down made him an enduring South Texas folk figure. The slain sheriff is buried in the **Runge City Cemetery** (1300 Helena St.), sixteen miles from Karnes City.

Hico (Hamilton County)

Settled in the mid-1850s, Hico was named by town founder Dr. John Alford for his old Kentucky home. The town opened a post office in 1860 but had only a few businesses until the Texas Central Railway approached in 1880. To be on the tracks, Hico moved a little over two miles to its present location and continued as an agricultural shipping point and trade center.

North central Texas is the last place a visitor would expect to see a museum dedicated to Billy the Kid, but this **Billy the Kid Museum** (114 North Pecan St.; 254-796-2523) is more about a character named **Brushy Bill Roberts** (1879–1950), who, beginning in the 1940s, claimed to be Billy the Kid. He said Pat Garrett did not kill him in 1881. Roberts made the assertion as an old man, and while newspapers made much of it, no historian took it seriously. Oliver Pleasant (Ollie) Roberts, aka Billy the Kid, is buried in **Oakwood Cemetery** (off US 281 just north of town) in the county seat of Hamilton.

Houston (Harris County)

In the spring of 1837, a visitor found a newly surveyed town on Buffalo Bayou particularly impressive: "Upwards of 100 houses finished and going up rapidly (some of them fine frame buildings) and 1500 people, all actively engaged in their respective pursuits." Only three months earlier, he wrote, "a small log cabin & 12 persons were all that distinguished it from the adjacent forests. . . ." As president of the newly created Republic of Texas, the author of those observations—Sam Houston—would do all he could to support the growth of the new town. After all, it was named in his honor.

It all started in the summer of 1836 when brothers John K. and Augustus C. Allen paid $5,000 for a 6,642-acre townsite on the west bank of Buffalo Bayou, a winding stream navigable to Trinity Bay and on to Galveston. From 1837 to 1839, Houston was capital of the young republic, but after the election of Mirabeau B. Lamar as Sam Houston's successor, the seat of government was moved to Austin.

Though it lost its role as a government center, Houston's geography could not be changed by political whim. Though Houston lay fifty miles inland from the Gulf of Mexico, a cotton grower could move his crop by water from the fertile Brazos River valley to the marketplace of the world. Beginning in 1853, Houston developed as the railroad center of antebellum Texas. By the outbreak of the Civil War, five railroads converged on the city. None of the lines extended beyond the state's borders, but Houston was connected to Galveston and its port.

The development of the Spindletop oil field near Beaumont in 1901 began a growth surge that continued in Houston for most of the rest of the century. When army engineers dredged the bayou to accommodate seafaring vessels, the Bayou City soon eclipsed Galveston as a port and as a city. As oil grew more and more vital to the American economy, the ship channel became lined with refineries and Houston became one of the nation's largest cities.

Battle of San Jacinto

On April 21, 1836, a volunteer army under Sam Houston defeated Gen. Antonio Lopez de Santa Anna, the self-styled "Napoleon of the West," in the **Battle of San Jacinto**. Screaming "Remember the Alamo!" and "Remember Goliad!" the Texans killed some 630 Mexican soldiers while losing only nine of their own. In the process, they captured Santa Anna and won independence for Texas. That independence would be tenuous, but it held for nearly a decade.

The **Republic of Texas** was born that day, but the battle meant much more than that. It lit the fuse leading to the 1846–1848 US war with Mexico that came after Texas statehood. Prevailing in that war, in turn, the US gained sovereignty over a third of the land area of today's lower forty-eight states, including Texas, New Mexico, Arizona, California, Nevada, and Utah along with portions of Colorado, Kansas, Oklahoma, and Wyoming.

The state began acquiring land at the battle site in the 1880s and designated it a state park in 1907. The 570-foot **San Jacinto Monument**, built during the Texas Centennial, is the centerpiece of what is now **San Jacinto Battleground State Historic Site** (3523 Independence Parkway South; 281-479-2431). Since 1960 it has also been a National Historic Landmark.

In the base of the monument the **San Jacinto Museum of History** (One Monument Circle; 281-479-2421) interprets this history-changing battle.

Due to subsidence caused by drilling for oil and water, more than one hundred acres of the battlefield are now under water.

Given Houston's tremendous growth, skyscrapers and other modern buildings have long since replaced almost all of old Houston. But ten early-day Houston or Harris County structures have been relocated to **Sam Houston Park** and restored. The **Heritage Society Museum** (1100 Bagby St.; 713-655-1912) at the park is dedicated to the city's history.

The **Buffalo Soldiers National Museum** (3816 Caroline St.; 713-942-8920) is the only museum in the nation dedicated solely to telling the story of African-Americans who have fought for the US since Congress first created all-black military units in 1866. Buffalo Soldiers were given their name by the Cheyenne, who started calling black soldiers that because of their hair and fierce fighting skills. The museum opened in 2001, and in 2012 moved into the old Houston Light Guard Armory. With twenty-three thousand square feet of space, the museum is the largest repository of African-American military artifacts and memorabilia in the world.

Huntsville (Walker County)

Incarcerating convicted felons was the responsibility of the individual counties during Texas's time as an independent republic. But in 1848, three years after Texas statehood, the legislature voted to build a state prison. However, lawmakers did not stipulate where such a facility should be located. Governor George T. Wood appointed a three-member committee to select a location, and after due deliberation the group picked Huntsville. Why the small town on the edge of the East Texas piney woods was chosen has never been determined. Possibly it was only a coincidence that one of the decision makers just happened to be from Walker County. Also, Sam Houston lived in Huntsville. In fairness, the community had agreed to save the state money by donating the construction material.

The prison committee soon purchased 4.8 acres (total cost: $22) for the prison, plus an additional 94 acres ($470) to allow for future growth. In 1849, with construction of a castle-like, three-story brick lockup under way, a temporary prison built of heavy logs went up to house any prisoners arriving before completion of the more secure facility. That October, the man with the dubious honor of being the first state prison inmate was William G. Sansom, a convicted cattle rustler. (Five years later, Elizabeth Huffman, convicted of killing her infant, became the first female inmate.)

The **Texas Prison Museum** (491 Highway 75 North; 936-295-2155) displays everything from old ball and chains to "Old Sparky," the electric chair used from 1924 to 1964.

Occupying the 1862 Gibbs-Powell House, the **Walker County Museum** (1228 11th St.; 936-435-2497) tells the story of Huntsville and the county. The house was built by Thomas Gibbs, a friend of Sam Houston.

Sam Houston

Sam Houston (1793–1863), or, as he never minded being referred to, the Hero of San Jacinto, moved back to Huntsville after resigning as governor in opposition of Texas's secession on the eve of the Civil War. He died there on July 26, 1863, during the Civil War he had warned strongly against.

Dedicated October 22, 1994, a towering sixty-seven-foot statue of Houston (7600 State Highway 75 South, Huntsville) stands on a ten-foot base visible to all who travel busy I-45 between Dallas and Houston. A visitor center tells the story of the statue and the man it honors.

Houston is buried in Oakwood Cemetery (9th Street and Avenue J).

Sam Houston State University maintains the **Sam Houston Memorial Museum** (1836 Sam Houston Memorial Dr.; 936-294-1832).

Satanta and Big Tree

The Kiowa chiefs Satanta and Big Tree had been sentenced to death in Jack County for their role in the 1871 Warren Wagon Train attack, but giving in to pressure from humanitarian groups, Governor E.J. Davis commuted their sentences to life in prison at Huntsville. Another reason for his decision was his concern that their hanging would spark a more widespread Indian War.

Two years later, Davis softened even more, paroling the two headmen. Most white Texans were outraged by the governor's action, as was the hawkish Gen. William T. Sherman. "I believe Satanta and Big Tree will have their revenge, if they have not already had it, and if they are to take scalps, I hope that yours is the first that will be taken," Sherman wrote the governor.

Davis hoped the two chiefs would go in peace, but they went back on the warpath. Hounded relentlessly by the military, Satanta and Big Tree surrendered in September 1874. Satanta's parole was revoked, and he was returned to Huntsville while Big Tree was confined at Fort Sill, Oklahoma. Satanta committed suicide on October 11, 1878, by jumping from the second-story window of the prison hospital. He was buried in the prison cemetery, colloquially known as Peckerwood Hill, formally called the **Joe Byrd Cemetery** (380-398 Bowers Blvd.) In 1963, the chief's grandson had his remains exhumed and reburied at Fort Sill.

As for Big Tree, he remained in custody only a short time before converting to Christianity and assimilating. He died on the Oklahoma Kiowa reservation in 1929.

Indianola (Calhoun County)

Texas is dotted with ghost towns, but Indianola is a ghost city. For more than forty years, from the early days of the Republic of Texas through the mid-1880s, the Calhoun County city was second only to Galveston as the state's busiest seaport. "The Queen City of the West," some called it.

Thousands of German immigrants passed through Indianola in the mid-1840s before trekking to what was then Texas's western frontier to found New Braunfels, Fredericksburg, and other communities. A wave of gold seekers followed beginning in 1849. The camels the army imported as part of its experiment in using the African animals in the desert Southwest arrived at the port in 1856.

Indianola continued to prosper until 1875, when a hurricane heavily damaged the city and claimed 175 lives. In 1886, a second storm not only killed more people, but also killed the city. Port Lavaca, fifteen miles up the bay, became the county seat and by 1887 the Indianola post office had closed.

Double Murder on Deck

Few if any Wild West–era shootings took place on an oceangoing vessel, but on March 11, 1874, William Sutton and Gabriel Slaughter were gunned down aboard the steamer *Clinton* as it swayed on its lines at the Indianola wharf. Sutton's pregnant wife witnessed the murders and readily identified the killers as James and Bill Taylor. This was not the first violence connected to what came to be called the Sutton-Taylor feud, but it marked the beginning of the feud's most intense phase.

All that remains of old Indianola today is a concrete cistern and a couple of cemeteries. Two state historical markers dating from 1936 and 1963 stand at the former townsite (GPS coordinates: N28° 31.64', W96° 30.48'), at the end of State Highway 316.

A twenty-two-foot granite monument to French explorer René-Robert Cavalier, Sieur de La Salle is just off the highway.

The **Calhoun County Museum** (301 South Ann, Port Lavaca; 361-553-4689) has exhibits and artifacts related to Indianola.

The **Museum of the Coastal Bend** (2200 East Red River St., Victoria; 361-582-2511) documents the area's history.

Jacksboro (Jack County)

Settlers began farming along Lost Creek in what would become Jack County in the mid-1850s, and within a few years there were enough houses and business to consider it a community. First called Mesquiteville, with the creation of Jack County in 1858, the town became county seat and changed its name to Jacksborough. Later that got shortened to Jacksboro. The same year it received a new name, the frontier town became a stop on the newly begun Butterfield Overland Mail route.

Jack County Historical Museum (241 West Belknap St.; 940-567-5410) occupies the town's oldest house and tells the county's story.

Fort Richardson

Excepting distant El Paso, in the 1860s no town in Texas lay farther west than Jacksboro. To protect Jack County residents and settlers moving west, the army established **Fort Richardson** just outside town in 1868. Only seventy miles south of Indian Territory, the post was the most important garrison in the state for its first five years. And, in 1872, with more than 650 troops stationed there, Fort Richardson had more soldiers than any other post in the nation. From then until the end of the 1874–1875 Red River War, the final chapter of the Indian Wars in Texas, soldiers from the fort were almost constantly out on patrol or actively engaged in campaigns. With the American Indian threat ended in West Texas, the fort was abandoned in 1878.

Fort Richardson State Park and Historic Site (228 State Park Rd.; 940-567-3506) preserves several of the fort's original buildings, including the post hospital, officer's quarters, and barracks.

Close Calls and Bloodshed

On May 2, 1871, Gen. William T. Sherman, the army's highest-ranking officer, left San Antonio on an inspection tour of Texas forts. Traveling with only a small escort, the general and Maj. Randolph B. Marcy saw no American Indians nor any sign of them. Sherman was convinced that the army had the Comanche and Kiowa people well contained on their reservations in Oklahoma, and that Texas complaints of American Indian depredations were unfounded.

On May 17, 1871, Sherman's entourage was about twenty miles west of Fort Richardson when, unknown to them, some one hundred warriors who had slipped off their reservation a few days before watched from concealment as Sherman's party passed by. Though the warriors could have annihilated the entire command, including the commander of the US Army, they chose not to attack. But the next group of travelers were not so lucky. When a train of freight wagons came into view, the warriors swept down on the teamsters. The wagon train put up a good fight, killing one warrior and wounding five others, but seven of the teamsters were killed. Three escaped, making it back to Fort Richardson to report the ambush. Meanwhile, the warriors returned to the reservation. Their leaders were three Kiowas—Satank, Satanta, and Big Tree.

Four years later, on July 11, 1875, Frontier Battalion Commander Maj. John B. Jones and thirty-five of his Texas rangers found themselves facing more than one hundred well-armed Kiowa warriors.

Earlier that morning, two of Jones's men discovered American Indian signs. The rangers took up a trail that led them to a rugged expanse in Jack County known as Lost Valley. Unknown to the rangers, in following the Indian's pony tracks, they rode straight into a trap set by Chief Lone Wolf, a savvy headman eager to avenge his son's death at the hands of cavalry troopers the year before.

Suddenly, warriors attacked the surprised rangers. Overconfident, Jones rallied his men and ordered a charge. But as the rangers galloped toward the Indians, the Kiowas shot thirteen of their horses. While seeking cover, Ranger William A. (Billy) Glass collected five bullets and fell dead. Pulling back to a wooded draw, the rangers formed a line and began firing. Bravely but foolishly, Jones stood exposed above his men, directing their aim as Indian bullets clipped tree branches above his head.

As the fight settled into a standoff, each side taking an occasional shot, the summer sun bore down. Thirst overpowering good sense, Ranger Dave Bailey collected everyone's canteen and said he would fill them at a nearby water hole. Reluctantly, Jones let Bailey and another ranger go. That was another mistake. Some of the Indians swooped in on the two rangers. One escaped, Bailey did not.

At about four o'clock, Lone Wolf decided he had extracted his pound of flesh and left. Jones dispatched a rider to nearby Fort Richardson, and soon, one hundred cavalrymen rode in pursuit of the Kiowas, but they got away.

A historical marker stands at a roadside park with a view of Lost Valley (twelve miles north of Jacksboro on US 281; GPS coordinates: N33° 18.66', W098° 19.99').

Three of the Marlow Brothers

Alfred and Lewellyn Marlow (see Graham) were buried in Finis Cemetery (GPS coordinates: N33° 01.97', W98° 24.80') near the small Jack County community of Bryson. After bounty hunters poisoned brother Boone Marlow in Oklahoma, his body was taken to Texas and buried next to his brothers. A modern granite monument marks their grave site.

Jefferson (Marion County)

Jefferson is in the piney woods of deep East Texas, but from antebellum days until the 1870s, it was a Wild West riverboat town. Founded in 1842, Jefferson could be reached by steamboats coming up Cypress

Bayou, which connected to the Red River system and eventually, the Mississippi. Until the expansion of railroads sank the necessity of river navigation, Jefferson was Texas's largest and busiest inland port.

Jefferson Historical Society Museum (223 West Austin St.; 903-665-2775) covers the history of the once bustling riverport.

RIP, Bessie

It seemed too good to be true and it was. When a beautiful young woman with dark hair, creamy skin, and blue eyes met the handsome, wealthy gentlemen in Hot Springs, Arkansas, she surely thought her life had taken a wonderful turn. They traveled the riverboat towns together, from Cincinnati, Ohio, to New Orleans and then on to booming Jefferson. Arriving by train on Friday January 19, 1877, her well-dressed consort registered them at a nice hotel as "A. Monroe and wife" and they proceeded to take in the city. The lady's elegant attire and abundance of diamond jewelry sparked people's attention, even in a town that saw a lot of travelers. Dining and drinking at the best of places, Monroe spent lavishly. That Sunday, they appeared at a local restaurant where Monroe ordered lunch for two to go, saying he and his lady were going on a picnic.

The following day, Monroe was seen alone. When someone asked where the missus was, he said she was visiting friends but would be back in time for them to leave as planned on Tuesday. But when Monroe arrived at the depot, he boarded the eastbound train alone even though he was carrying both of their bags.

A norther blew in a short time later and left the area covered in snow. On February 5, 1877, someone gathering firewood found the body of a young woman in a park-like area on Big Cypress Bayou. It was Mr. Monroe's companion, minus her jewelry. She had been shot in the temple. Nearby lay an empty bottle, wrapping paper, and some chicken remnants.

Local lawmen were able to identify the missing man as **Abraham Rothschild**, son of a wealthy Cincinnati jeweler. The woman, who locals had taken to calling Diamond Bessie, was identified as eighteen-year-old **Annie Stone Morgan**, a prostitute. A murder warrant was issued for Rothschild's arrest, and he was soon picked up in Cincinnati and taken back to Jefferson by the Marion County sheriff.

The Rothschilds hired big-name defense lawyers and the legal maneuvering began. The case became a newspaper sensation and received national attention, Texas's nineteenth-century "Trial of the Century." Finally brought to trial in December 1878, despite the best efforts of his high-priced attorneys, Rothschild was found guilty and sentenced to hang. But his legal team appealed and won a reversal. The state tried him again in December 1880. This time the jury found him not guilty.

People in Jefferson had collected $150 to pay for Bessie's funeral, but that didn't include a tombstone. In 1941, thinking it wrong that she lay in an unmarked grave, a local resident put up a tombstone. Later, the local garden club installed an iron fence around her grave. A state historical marker stands at the site of the 1872 two-story **Brooks House** (GPS coordinates: N32° 45.442, W94° 20.784), the Victorian-style hotel where the couple stayed, a structure destroyed by fire in 1969. Every year since 1955, the Jesse Allen Wise Garden Club's Jefferson Historical Pilgrimage has presented a play based on the murder, *The Diamond Bessie Murder Trial.*

Kingsville (Kleberg County)

When the St. Louis, Brownsville, and Mexico Railway began laying tracks across South Texas toward the Rio Grande Valley and its fertile agricultural land, the King Ranch, in 1904, donated land for a new town on the rail line. Not surprisingly, the community would be known as Kingsville. When Kleberg County was created in 1913, Kingsville became county seat.

The restored original railway depot houses the **Kingsville Train Depot Museum** (102 East Kleberg Ave.; 361-592-8516) with exhibits and artifacts related to the role of the railroad in the development of the area.

The **John E. Conner Museum** (905 West Santa Gertrudis Ave.; 361-593-2810) covers the history and multiple cultures of lower South Texas, an area once known as the Wild Horse Desert. One of the museum's more unusual artifacts is the high-powered search light installed at the King Ranch headquarters during the Mexican Revolution to forestall nighttime bandit raids.

King Ranch

But for a Texas ranger's weakness for pretty women, the storied **King Ranch**, a state-size spread that once covered more than a million acres in South Texas, probably would be known as the King-Lewis Ranch.

When former Rio Grande steamboat pilot **Richard King** (1825–1885) first began acquiring land along Santa Gertrudis Creek, he partnered with Ranger **Gideon K. (Legs) Lewis**. Unfortunately for Lewis, he had an eye for the ladies, and it cost him what would become a ranching empire.

When a Corpus Christi doctor discovered Lewis's ongoing affair with his wife, the physician prescribed a couple of loads of buckshot. And the good doctor did nothing to treat his "patient" when he went down. Lewis having no heirs, his share of what would become the largest ranch in the world sold at auction on the courthouse steps in Corpus Christi. King's bid came in highest. King ran the ranch with an iron hand until his death in 1885. Through successive generations of descendants and in-laws, the ranch continues in operation, still one of the world's largest.

The entrance to the famed King Ranch (State Highway 141; 361-592-8055), where guided tours are available, is just west of Kingsville.

Located in a remodeled former ice plant, the **King Ranch Museum** (405 North 6th St.; 361-595-1881) tells the story of the ranch with artifacts and photographs.

For years the King Ranch was almost totally self-sufficient, including having a shop that made the saddles, tack, and other leather goods used by the ranch's cowboys. The **King Ranch Saddle Shop** (201 East Kleberg; 361-595-1424) continues in operation.

Richard King is buried in the **Chamberlain Cemetery** (southwest corner of South Armstrong Street and Caesar Avenue, section B, lot 1).

At Sarita, twenty-two miles south of Kingsville on US 77, the **Kenedy Ranch Museum of South Texas** (200 East La Parra Ave.; 361-294-5751) explores the history of another giant South Texas spread, the Mifflin Kenedy Ranch.

Lampasas (Lampasas County)

Twenty years after its 1856 founding, Lampasas still lay at the edge of Texas's western frontier. The county had a duly elected sheriff but he could not hope to consistently keep the peace in a community full of men inclined to settle things their way.

In 1876, cattleman **John Pinckney Calhoun Higgins**, better known as Pink, began losing calves, and he rightly suspected the brothers Horrell—Martin, Merritt, Sam, and Thomas. Because he suspected him particularly, Higgins filed charges against Merritt for cattle theft. A jury acquitted him.

On January 22, 1877, Higgins confronted Merritt in the Gem Saloon. "Mr. Horrell," he said almost politely, "this is to settle some cattle business." He then proceeded to "Winchester" Merritt, irrevocably breaking him of rustling. While Lampasas County had one less cattle thief, the shooting led to further violence.

Two months later, on March 26, 1877, someone ambushed Thomas and Martin Horrell as they rode toward town. They shot back and survived, though one was wounded. Soon, Higgins and his brother-in-law Bob Mitchell were named in arrest warrants. The two eventually turned themselves in and were freed on bail. Before the case could go to trial, on June 4, someone broke into the county courthouse and destroyed all the district court records having to do with their case.

Three days later the two men rode into town with some of their friends to make new bonds, but the Horrells and their supporters stood waiting. On the courthouse square, lead soon started flying. The June 7 gunfight lasted two hours with scores of rounds fired. Higgins and Mitchell and the Horrells all survived, but one man from each faction died. Likely more would have ended up in the cemetery had it not been for the armed intervention of local officers and deputized citizens.

A week later, Frontier Battalion Commander Maj. John B. Jones led fifteen rangers into town. He stayed until tensions eased and then left Lt. Nelson Orcelus Reynolds and a small detachment behind to keep things quiet. Returning in late July after Reynolds and his men had rounded up the Horrells, Jones got each faction to sign letters amounting to a peace treaty, one of the more unorthodox (if successful) feud mitigations in the history of the Old West.

The wooden frame around the door of a Lampasas barber shop (413 East 4th St.) still has some shotgun pellet holes in it. A historical marker summarizing the feud stands on the west side of the courthouse, along with another marker detailing the gunfight.

Another historical marker was placed at the site of the March 26, 1877, battle (three and eight-tenths miles east of Lampasas on US 190; GPS coordinates: N31° 03.08', W98° 05.82'), near a stream that came to be called Battle Branch.

The **Lampasas County Museum** (303 South Western Ave.; 512-556-2224) and the adjacent **Keystone Square Museum** (304 South Western Ave.) have exhibits and artifacts related to the bloody feud and other aspects of the county's history.

Langtry (Val Verde County)

Judge Roy Bean—the Law West of the Pecos—got his title because he was justice of the peace for the Val Verde County precinct that included Eagle Nest, a raucous town just across from Mexico on the newly completed southern transcontinental rail line. With a makeshift office, law library (one book of Texas statutes), and courtroom in his saloon, Bean had nowhere near the judicial authority conferred on him by legend. As a JP, he could adjudicate misdemeanor violations, accept fines, conduct inquests, and a few other things, but his authority fell far below that of a district judge. Still, the judge was a character. He once famously fined a dead man for carrying a pistol, the amount due the court being identical to the coin and cash found on the deceased. Seldom sober as a judge, Bean had three abiding interests—whiskey, making money, and the beautiful British actress Lilly Langtry. He changed the town's name to Langtry and named his saloon the Jersey Lilly in her honor. Despite his age, the crusty judge pined for her like a teenager. A few years after Bean died in 1906, the famous performer, on the way from one coast to another, got off the train at Langtry to take a quick look at the Jersey Lilly. Before she left, townspeople presented her with a pistol that had belonged to Bean, a firearm her estate left to a museum in her native Jersey Isle.

Judge Roy Bean Visitor Center (526 State Loop 25; 432-291-3340) has exhibits and artifacts on the West's most famous JP. The restored Jersey Lilly stands adjacent to the visitor center operated by the Texas Department of Transportation. Bean's grave is sixty miles to the southeast on the grounds of **Whitehead Memorial Museum** (1308 South Main St., Del Rio).

Fitzsimmons-Maher Match

In 1896, a promoter began touting a boxing match in El Paso pitting Robert James Fitzsimmons against heavyweight champion James J. Corbett. But prizefighting was illegal in Texas, and the governor sent a trainload of rangers to the City of the Pass to make sure no fists swung there for money. Then Corbett decided to designate pugilist Peter Maher as his successor. But where to have the fight remained a problem.

Judge Roy Bean, figuring to greatly boost the sale of alcoholic beverages at his Jersey Lilly saloon, announced he would host the contest on a sandbar in the Rio Grande. That, technically, would allow the fight to take place in the absence of any state or nation's laws. Just to make sure the match did not occur in the Lone Star State, numerous rangers rode the train carrying the fighters and their fans to Val Verde County. On February 22, with the rangers enjoying the fisticuffs as well as anyone, the much-ballyhooed main event lasted all of ninety-five seconds before Fitzsimmons KO-ed Maher.

Flooding washed away the sandbar where the international prizefight took place long ago, but a historical marker (Torres Avenue and Texas 25 Loop) tells the story.

Laredo (Webb County)

Laredo was founded on the Rio Grande in 1755 when what is now Texas was part of Spain's colonial empire. After Mexico became an independent nation in 1821, Laredo continued as a ranching and trade center. During the Texas Revolution in 1835–1836, Mexican troops passed through Laredo on their way to put down the rebellion. Even after Texas won its independence, Mexico continued to claim Laredo. In 1838 some of the area ranchers attempted to form a separate country, the Republic of the Rio Grande, with Laredo as capital. Mexican federal forces violently suppressed the revolution, and despite Texas's claim that the Rio Grande was the border between Mexico and the new republic, Laredo continued to consider itself a Mexican city until after the Mexican War of 1846 to 1848. The US Army established Fort McIntosh at Laredo in 1849. The arrival of the railroad in 1881 spurred further growth.

Villa Antigua Border Heritage Museum (810 Zaragosa St.; 956-718-2727) focuses on the region's people, culture, and history.

Housed in one of Laredo's oldest buildings, the **Republic of the Rio Grande Museum** (1005 Zaragosa St.; 956-727-3480) tells the story of Laredo's brief tenure as capital of an independent republic.

Abandoned after World War II, **Fort McIntosh** (end of Washington St.) is a National Register of Historic Places Historic District and State Archeological Landmark. An important border post for nearly a century, it is now the home of Laredo Community College. Several historical markers on the campus interpret the fort's history.

The Streets of Laredo

One of the best-known Western ballads chronicles a Laredo gunfight that never took place. Not that Laredo did not see its share of fatal shootings during the nineteenth century, but the song *The Streets of Laredo* actually traces to an old Irish ballad called *The Unfortunate Rake* and is not based on anything that happened in this border city.

In 1924, old-time trail driver Frank H. Maynard (1853–1926) claimed to be the one who converted the Irish piece into a ballad told by a young cowboy "wrapped in white linen and cold as the clay" who was about to die from a bullet wound suffered on the streets of Laredo. Covered over the years by numerous artists, the song remains a classic.

Quarantines Don't Stop Bullets

With an outbreak of smallpox rapidly spreading in Laredo, Texas Ranger Capt. J.H. Rogers and one of his men came to the border city in 1898 to assist state health authorities with preventative measures, including a quarantine. Some residents decided to forcibly resist.

As rumors to that effect began circulating, Rogers wired for more rangers. When a local hardware store notified the sheriff's office that a former city policeman had placed an order for two thousand rounds of buckshot shells, officers raided his residence. Captain Rogers and his rangers accompanied the local lawmen, and the situation soon deteriorated into a shooting that mutated into a riot.

The captain caught a rifle bullet that nearly took his arm off, but he and another ranger killed the gunman. Numerous residents suffered wounds of varying severity in the riot, which continued through the night, but no one else died. Cavalrymen from Fort McIntosh finally restored order.

The riot spread from a southeast Laredo residential neighborhood to the combination city hall and public market now known as **El Mercado** (500 Flores Ave.) an 1884-vintage brick structure that still stands.

Rangers carried their badly wounded captain to the newly opened **Hamilton Hotel** (815 Salinas St.). Listed on the National Register of Historic Places, the old hotel is now an apartment building.

Longview (Gregg County)

In the spring of 1894, Oklahoma outlaw Bill Dalton and two of his gang members decided to take care of a little banking business in Texas. They hit the First National Bank (200 North Fredonia St.) in the piney woods town of Longview on May 23 and collected $2,000. However, before they could make their getaway, bullets started flying. In a twenty-minute exchange of gunfire with numerous townspeople, gang member James Wilson (Jim) Wallace (1865–1894) died along with two citizens. The rest of the outlaws made it out of town. The killing of two innocent men and the wounding of two other residents, not to mention the uninsured loss from the bank, so outraged the populace that just for good measure they lynched the dead outlaw from a telephone pole. Two weeks later, in Ardmore, Oklahoma, someone recognized a bank note Dalton tried to pass. A posse went after him, and he died in a gunfight.

Three years passed before anyone faced prosecution for the robbery. Arrested in Kimble County for cattle theft after a shoot-out with county lawmen, Jim Nite stood trial in Longview in 1897 for his part in the caper. Nite got twenty years, but Governor Oscar B. Colquitt later pardoned him. Still not rehabilitated, he later died in a gunfight in Tulsa, Oklahoma.

A historical marker on the Fredonia Street side of Citizens National Bank marks the site of the Longview shoot-out. The **Gregg County Museum** (214 North Fredonia St.; 903-753-5840) has a comprehensive exhibit on the robbery, including some of the weapons used that day and other artifacts.

One of the citizens killed during the robbery, George W. Buckingham (1859–1894), is buried in Greenwood Cemetery (705 East Magrill St.). Jim Wallace, the slain robber, was buried in the same cemetery, but his grave was not marked.

Lubbock (Lubbock County)

Ranching in the area that would become Lubbock began in the 1880s, but no one thought of building a town until 1890. That year, two competing developers laid out separate townsites. One real estate investor called his town Monterrey, the other called his Old Lubbock, for former Texas ranger and Confederate officer Tom Lubbock. The "Old" did not refer to the new town, but its namesake, as in "Old Jones" or "Old Smith." Neither Monterrey nor Old Lubbock did well financially, so in 1891 the two land sellers decided to promote one town at a new location. For that community, they dropped "Old" but kept "Lubbock." The new town grew slowly as a ranching center and was not incorporated until 1909.

When a tornado ripped through Lubbock on May 11, 1970, leaving twenty-six people dead, no one would have thought anything positive could come out of the disaster, but something did—the **National Ranching Heritage Center** (3131 4th St.; 806-742-0498). On the north edge of Texas Tech University, the twenty-seven-acre complex has nearly fifty restored historic ranch-related structures brought to Lubbock from their original locations for preservation. Conceived in 1966 and dedicated a decade later, the center is mostly surrounded by several high, grass-covered berms that separate it from modern Lubbock. Built with tons of debris left by the tornado, the berms allow visitors to imagine they were back on the High Plains when it first opened to settlement, or even before. In addition to the restored structures on the property, which range from dugouts to a two-story ranch house, the center's main building houses a museum that explores Western ranching.

The wind blows frequently in Lubbock and elsewhere on the South Plains. That makes the city a perfect place for the **American Windmill Museum** (1701 Canyon Lake Dr.; 806-747-8734), which has the world's largest collection of wind-powered water-pumping towers. First developed in the 1850s, the so-called "wind engines" helped win the West.

Marfa (Presidio County)

One night, not long after Marfa's founding as a water stop on the Texas and Pacific Railway in 1881, a cowboy noticed strange bright lights that appeared to be moving around in the mountains east of town. That was in 1883 and no one has ever figured out what causes the **Marfa Lights**, which are still seen most nights. The Texas Department of Transportation maintains a **Marfa Lights viewing area** on US 67/90, eight miles east of Marfa.

Marfa is the Presidio County seat and was home to the cavalry post of **Fort D.A. Russell** from the time of the Mexican Revolution through the end of World War II. In 1955 the classic movie *Giant* was filmed in the area, the crew and cast—including actress Elizabeth Taylor—staying in the 1929-vintage **Hotel Paisano** (207 North Highland Ave.; 432-729-3669).

The **Marfa and Presidio County Museum** (110 US 90 West; 432-729-4772) focuses on the history of one of Texas's largest counties and also includes an extensive collection of vintage photographs.

Built in 1886, the **Old Presidio County Jail** (310 Highland St.) housed many a miscreant and felon in its time, but now stands vacant. The lockup continued in use for more than a century before being replaced by a new jail in 1993.

Writing Ranger

James (Jim) Buchanan Gillett (1856–1937) joined the Frontier Battalion in 1875, and distinguished himself as an American Indian fighter and state lawman. He left the Rangers in December 1881 to become assistant city marshal in El Paso, and less than a year later was named marshal. In 1885 he went to work for the Estado Land and Cattle Company before buying his own ranch. Elected Brewster County sheriff in 1890 he served a two-year term while continuing to run his ranch. He moved to nearby Jeff Davis County in 1907 and stayed there the rest of his life.

In 1921 he published his memoir, *Six Years with the Texas Rangers*, a book generally regarded as one of the most detailed and readable accounts of nineteenth-century ranger life.

Gillett is buried in Marfa Cemetery (210 West San Antonio St.).

Mason (Mason County)

Mason developed downhill from Fort Mason, a frontier post established beyond the frontier in 1851. The army left in 1871 but the town remained a ranching center and county seat.

Mason County Museum (210 Bryan; 325-347-6583) focuses on the county's history.

One of old Fort Mason's officer's quarters was reconstructed at the site of the fort (204 Spruce St., five blocks south of the courthouse) in the mid-1970s on what is now called Post Mountain. There are also foundation remnants of the fort's more than twenty buildings.

The Hoo-Doo War

The near anarchy that gripped Mason County from 1874 to 1877 resulted from a volatile mix of lingering post–Civil War grudges, cultural differences ("Americans" versus settlers of German heritage), and ranchers bent on exterminating cattle thieves. Overzealous law enforcement at the county level and indifference on the part of some rangers added to the problem.

What came to be called the **Hoo-Doo War** started when a posse under newly elected Sheriff John Clark jailed a number of Llano County residents for rustling. After their release they were escorted by a delegation of partisans back to Llano County. A Methodist church mysteriously burned down about the time they rode by.

Clark jailed another ten men for rustling in early February. Out on bail, they fled the county, which they weren't supposed to do. Soon the sheriff had five of them back in the Mason County lockup.

Meanwhile, on February 15, someone found a seventeen-year-old "American" shot to death. A note pinned on his coat observed, "He would not stop rustling." Three days later, a group of concerned citizens forcibly removed the five alleged cow thieves from jail and took them to a large oak tree on the south side of town. Substantially outgunned, Sheriff Clark and Ranger Lt. Dan Roberts could only watch as the vigilantes strung up four of the men and shot the fifth. At least the officers cut down one of the men in time to save him.

In March, the anti-rustling crowd even threatened to lynch rancher Tom Gamel for declining to participate in the mass hanging the month before. Clearly the flame of law and order had flickered out in Mason County. Equally as plain, Roberts, the ranking ranger in charge, did not see the extra-legal adjudication of cattle thieves as a threat to social order.

On May 13, suspected rustler Tim Williamson died of sudden onset lead poisoning as Deputy Sheriff John Worley escorted him to the county seat for a bond hearing. That summer, a man hunting stray cattle on Gamel's ranch found death instead. Not three weeks later, the sheriff and his volunteer force killed a suspected rustler and wounded another man in a shoot-out at a rural general store.

Four days after that in-the-name-of-the-law killing, on August 10, former Texas Ranger Scott Cooley killed and scalped Deputy

Worley. The man killed while in Worley's custody had been a friend of Cooley's.

On September 28, four additional murders later, Major John B. Jones—determined to end the violence—led a large contingent of rangers into Mason County. But the following day, while the rangers vigorously scouted elsewhere, Cooley and pal John Ringo (later famously known as Johnny Ringo) shot and killed Mason County hide inspector Dan Hoerster in front of the Mason House Hotel.

With two county officials already dead, Sheriff Clark concluded the time had come to pursue other career opportunities and vacated both his office and Texas. One more payback murder happened in Llano County, and that summer, Cooley died in Blanco County, possibly of poisoning.

Thirteen men had died violently, and a fourteenth had died young under highly suspicious circumstances. Only one person was convicted in any of the deaths, and he spent only a short time in prison before paroled.

Any hope of widespread prosecution in connection with the feud went up in smoke when the Mason County Courthouse burned in 1877. Metaphorically, the intentionally set fire ended the feud, though hard feelings between certain Hill Country families smoldered for years.

Mason Square Museum (130 Fort McKavett St.; 325-347-0507), has a permanent Hoo-Doo War exhibit.

A historical plaque (near Westmoreland Street and Avenue F) marks the site of the rock-lined well Worley was digging when he was killed.

Dating to 1870, the two-story **Mason House** (100 Live Oak St.) was Mason's earliest hotel, serving as a stage stop on the San Antonio to El Paso route. Ranger Lieutenant Roberts was staying there when mob action broke out on the nearby courthouse square. Scott Cooley and John Ringo breakfasted there before killing hide inspector Hoerster. After the hotel closed, the owner converted the building into rental units.

Built in 1894, the two-story stone **Mason County Jail** (122 Westmoreland St.), just south of the courthouse, remains in use.

Midland (Midland County)

Since the 1920s, Midland basically has been about only one thing: pumping oil from the ground. Before then, getting its start in 1881 as a depot out in the middle of nowhere on the newly laid Texas and Pacific tracks, it was a cattle town surrounded by sprawling ranches.

The Last Ranger-Comanche Fight

The Comanches had been relegated to a reservation in Oklahoma, but trouble broke out again in the summer of 1879 when the federal government granted Chief Black Hawk permission to hunt buffalo in Texas. Armed with rifles and ammunition graciously furnished by the US, the chief and twenty-five warriors began hunting something more precious to them than buffalo—Texas horseflesh.

A troop of cavalry from Fort Concho began searching for the renegades, but it was a squad from Texas Ranger Capt. June Peak's Company A that found the warriors in present Martin County.

Clashing near a reed-lined playa lake that gave the Indians excellent cover, Ranger William Anglin (circa 1850–1879) had his horse shot from under him. Disentangling himself, he managed one pistol shot before another rifle volley killed him. Outnumbered, the rangers rode for reinforcements. When cavalry troopers and two rangers returned several days later, they found Anglin's body, wrapped it in a saddle blanket, and buried him where he had fallen. Pony tracks led away from the lake in the direction of Oklahoma.

A 1967 historical marker just inside the entrance of **Midland's Fairview Cemetery** (Noble and North Pecos Streets) commemorates the incident, the last fight between Texas rangers and the Comanches. But Anglin's unmarked grave has never been located.

The battle is believed to have occurred on the Mabee Ranch in present Martin County, just north of Midland. **Midland County Historical Museum** (301 West Missouri; 432-688-8947) documents the history of the city and county.

Old Maude

Writer-historian **J. Evetts Haley** (1901–1995) learned about **Old Maude** while researching his biography of cattleman Charles Goodnight. She was a longhorn in the herd Goodnight drove from Texas to Colorado via the Goodnight-Loving Trail. Goodnight later took the already well-traveled cow with him when he left Colorado for the Texas Panhandle, where he established a ranch in Palo Duro Canyon in 1876. Old Maude, as Goodnight first called her, had twenty-seven calves, and lived so long she lost all her teeth.

Using a later-generation longhorn as her model, artist Veryl Goodnight—a distant relative of the famous stockman—sculpted Old Maude for a life-size bronze statue commissioned by Haley for his **Haley Memorial Library and Research Center** (1805 West Indiana Ave.; 432-682-5785). With more than twenty-five thousand books, documents, and photographs related to the Old West and over seven hundred pioneer interviews done by Haley, the library opened in 1976. *Old Maude* was dedicated seven years later and stands in front of the building along with a statue of a horseback cowboy.

Mobeetie (Wheeler County)

Late-nineteenth-century maps showed that the new army post of **Fort Elliott**, established on Sweetwater Creek in 1875, lay in Texas. While that was technically correct, the fort may as well have been in far southwestern Kansas. Supplies came from Dodge City as did most of the nonmilitary types who always roosted near army installations—saloonkeepers, gamblers, prostitutes, and men who for legal reasons found it best to hang out in less civilized areas. Adding to the mix were the buffalo hunters, whose camp near the fort was known as Hide Town, and cowboys. When enough people lived in the vicinity of the fort to merit a post office, Washington rejected the proposed town name of Sweetwater. But the government did approve someone's suggestion of "Mobeetie," an American Indian word that translated to "Sweetwater." Mobeetie became the Panhandle's first town.

Lust and Lead

Among those who came to the new Texas town was a young Kansan named **Bartholomew "Bat" Masterson**. He did some survey work but made most of his money as a faro dealer. On January 24, 1876, in one of Mobeetie's many saloons, Masterson and Cpl. Melvin King got into a disagreement the soldier decided to settle with his revolver. Whether the difficulty was over the way Masterson played his cards or involved the affections of blue-eyed, black-haired prostitute Mollie Brennan is not known, but the young woman rushed to shield Masterson just as King pulled the trigger. The bullet killed Brennan and kept going, tearing into Masterson's hip. While seriously wounded, Masterson shot and killed King. Brennan became the first, or one of the first, occupants of **Mobeetie Cemetery** (west of County Road H, just south of State Highway 152; GPS coordinates: N35° 30.06', W100° 26.28'). Masterson survived but walked with a limp for the rest of his life.

The **Mobeetie Old Jail Museum** (300 Olaughlin St.; 806-845-2028) tells the story of Fort Elliott and Mobeetie's wild and wooly days. A 1936 state historical marker stands at the site of the old fort (eight-tenths of a mile west of the intersection of State Highway 52 and Farm to Market Road 48). Abandoned in 1890, no trace of the fort remains, but someone did think to save the post's fifty-foot cedar flagpole, which now stands in front of the old jail. Another historical marker outside the two-story stone former lockup summarizes the life of George Washington (Cap) Arrington (1844–1923), a former Texas ranger captain and later Wheeler County sheriff from 1882 to 1890.

Pecos (Reeves County)

Named for the nearby Pecos River, the only river in far West Texas other than the Rio Grande, Pecos was founded in 1881 along the newly laid tracks of the Texas and Pacific Railway. Two years later, during a July Fourth celebration, a gathering of cowboys from nearby ranches demonstrated their roping and riding skills to the entertainment of onlookers. Pecos later claimed this was America's first rodeo. At least five other western cities make the same claim.

Orient Hotel

Pecos may or may not have staged the nation's first rodeo, but the town's saloons saw plenty of Wild West action. Not long after former Texas Ranger R.S. Johnson built a red sandstone saloon in 1896 just an easy amble from the railroad depot, Barney Riggs dispatched cowboys John Denson and Bill Earnhart in the popular drinking establishment.

In 1904, Johnson built the three-story **Orient Hotel** next to his Number 11 Saloon. The two historic properties have, since 1963, been the home of the **West of the Pecos Museum** (120 East Dot Stafford St.; 432-445-5076). The museum has fifty rooms of exhibits and artifacts on the history of Pecos and far West Texas. Bullet holes from the gunfight in the old saloon are still visible and tags on the wooden floors mark where the victims fell.

Clay Allison

A Tennessean who came to Texas after the Civil War, **Robert Clay Allison** (1841–1887) is remembered in two ways: as a psychopathic killer and as a nice guy. So maybe he was only an ill-tempered, hard-drinking sociopath. The so-called "Gentleman Gunfighter" (he was also known as the "Wolf of the Washita") didn't kill nearly as many men as some writers have given him credit for, but he did put at least three fellows in an early grave—two in shootings and one by lynching.

Allison's life was cut short as well, but in an accident, not a gun fight. On July 3, 1887, he left Pecos with a wagonload of supplies headed to his ranch on the Texas–New Mexico border. Likely drunk, he fell from the wagon and was fatally injured when it ran over him.

As an area rancher, about all Allison contributed to the Pecos economy was the money he spent on supplies and liquor, but in the 1970s it occurred to civic leaders that the long dead gunfighter might help attract tourists to town. In 1975, Allison's remains were exhumed from the original burial site and reburied adjacent to the West of the Pecos Museum. Next to his grave in Pecos Park is a replica of Judge Roy Bean's Jersey Lilly saloon.

PLEASANTON (ATASCOSA COUNTY)

Settled in 1858, Pleasanton refers to itself as the "Birthplace of the Cowboy." While some historians would argue that when Texas was part of Spain's colonial empire, men on horseback worked cattle on ranches along the San Antonio and Guadalupe Rivers, Pleasanton says the wrangling techniques that became standard across the West were developed in this area. They even put it on a bronze, eight-foot cowboy statue dedicated in 1970 in front of Pleasanton City Hall (153 2nd St.).

The **Longhorn Museum** (1959 State Highway 97 East; 830-569-6313), tells the story of the storied cattle breed and the development of the cowboy in South Texas.

Cowboy Tree House

Many a Wild West town had its hanging tree, but Pleasanton may be the only place that had a **cowboy tree house**.

When profit-minded Texans began pushing longhorns up from the South Texas brush country to the railhead in Kansas in the early 1870s, Pleasanton made a convenient stopping place on the Chisholm Trail. The town boomed as a place where drovers could replenish supplies, drink, consort with women of easy virtue, and gamble.

Local lore has it that one saloonkeeper became so tired of all the ruckus connected to poker playing that he took an unusual step to separate the rowdy gamblers from his place of business: He built them a tree house to play in.

The elevated saloon annex quickly became a popular cowboy roost. All continued well with the high-rise casino until something bigger than an acorn dropped from the tree—a drunken cowboy. The fall broke the drover's neck (maybe fatally, though that detail does not seem to have survived), and the city government ordered the removal of the cowboy tree house.

Pleasanton has plenty of large, sturdy oak trees, but where the cowboy treehouse stood is not known.

Presidio (Presidio County)

Dating back to the Jumanos, people have been living where the Rio Conchos flows into the Rio Grande from Mexico for nearly a thousand years. Spanish explorers visited this area in the 1500s and by the late 1600s had established a mission and presidio here. Anglo-American settlement began here in the 1840s.

Fort Leaton

When **Juana Padrasa** married **Benjamin Leaton** in 1851, the bride wore black. That's because her new husband lay dead in his grave. A priest posthumously married the couple so Juana would legally be a widow and thus entitled to inherit her late husband's estate.

Not that Juana rushed into matrimony—the couple had been together long enough to have three children. In 1848 they had moved from Chihuahua City, Mexico, to land on high ground above the Rio Grande near Presidio. Benjamin had purchased the acreage in 1832 when it was still part of Mexico. The couple expanded an existing adobe structure, turning it into a forty-room complex that came to be known as **Fort Leaton**. Benjamin ran a trading post at the fort and hauled freight along the Chihuahua Trail, supplementing his income by being a bounty hunter, collecting money from Mexico for every Comanche or Apache scalp he could produce.

Soon after Benjamin's death, Juana married Edward Hall. Together they ran a trading post at the fort until the 1860s. At some point, Hall became indebted to John Burgess, Benjamin's former business partner. Burgess foreclosed on Hall and took control of the fort and surrounding property. Benjamin and Juana's son William felt the foreclosure had ended any chance he had of realizing his share of his father's property and murdered Burgess in 1875.

Even with Burgess out of the picture, the property remained with the Burgess family until the mid-1920s. After that, it fell into disrepair. A decade later, new owners attempted to restore the old fort, but the Great Depression stymied that effort. Not until the state acquired the property in 1967 was its preservation assured. Listed on the National Register of Historic Places in 1973, the fortified residence opened to the public in 1978 as **Fort Leaton State Historic Site** (16951 Farm to Market Road 170; 432-229-3613).

Quanah (Hardeman County)

The Fort Worth and Denver Railway, which was building across northwest Texas in 1887 on its way to Colorado, sold lots along its right of way to develop a new town named for Comanche chief Quanah Parker. In 1890 it became the county seat and grew as a ranching and agricultural center.

The **Hardeman County Historical Museum** (105 Green St.; 940-663-5272) is in the former Quanah, Acme, and Pacific Railway depot, built in 1908. The museum documents the history of the county and the life of the town's famous namesake. Among its holdings is an ornately decorated rifle once owned by the chief.

The 1890-vintage former **Hardeman County Jail** (101 Green St.) had additional exhibits related to area history.

"Americano!"

Nearly a quarter of a century had passed since that spring morning in 1836 when Comanches overwhelmed Fort Parker, killing five settlers and taking one woman and three children captive. All but one of those taken had been fairly quickly accounted for. Blonde-haired, blue-eyed **Cynthia Ann Parker** (1827–1871) remained lost. Tragic as it had been, the East Texas massacre had virtually been forgotten and plenty of blood spilled since. Even the Parker family, though they had tried hard to find her, had given up hope.

On December 19, 1860, a company of Texas rangers under Capt. Sul Ross and a detachment of US cavalry rode into the face of a norther, following a trail their guides said would lead to a Comanche village.

When the armed men topped a rise along the Pease River in present Hardeman County near future Quanah, they saw a small collection of teepees and charged. Taken by surprise, the Indians tried to flee, but the rangers and soldiers rode them down and killed several. Someone—accounts vary—aimed at a warrior wrapped in a buffalo robe. He did not realize it, but the rider was a woman. Before the ranger could pull the trigger, she turned, bared her breasts, and held up a baby. "Americano!" she screamed. The rangers held their fire and rode closer. It was an Anglo-woman, and she had blue eyes.

Returning to Camp Cooper, a military post in what is now Throckmorton County, the rangers turned the woman and her young daughter over to the army. No one knew who she was, only that she belonged with her family. But it was too late. Cynthia Ann Parker had just lost the only family and culture she knew.

In early January 1861, when word reached her Uncle Isaac Parker that a white woman had been captured in the Pease River fight, he believed she might be his long-lost kin. He traveled from Birdville to Camp Cooper, and through an interpreter confirmed her identity. Parker took the woman and her baby daughter Prairie Flower (1859–1863) to his cabin in Birdville, and he and his family cared for her until she moved to Anderson County.

Two historical markers discuss the battle. A 1936 granite marker stands five miles east of Crowell on US 70. The marker notes that the fight occurred four miles to the north on land that is now privately owned. A second marker stands in **Crowell City Park** (South Main Street at West Austin Street).

The Quanah Parker Trail

Starting in 2011, a nonprofit consortium of history-minded citizens, historians, museum directors, and others, working with the Texas Historical Commission, began placing twenty-two-foot metal arrows to mark places in northwest Texas with a historical connection to Quanah Parker and the Comanche people. By 2021 eighty-eight such markers, each painted in red, yellow, and blue (the colors of the Comanche Nation) dotted the Plains region along what the organizers labeled the **Quanah Parker Trail**. Sites marked by a giant arrow rising from the ground range from museums with collections of Plains Indian artifacts to battle sites to physical features. A map showing all the locations can be found at quanahparkertrail.com.

Medicine Mounds

Four cone-shaped hills rise 350 feet above the surrounding plains a dozen miles southeast of Quanah. The Comanche people considered two of these geologic features sacred: the tallest, which became known as **Medicine Mound**, and the next highest, **Cedar Mound**. Young Comanche men would come to Medicine Mound on their vision quest, a ritual in which the seeker would isolate himself and use the hallucinogenic plant peyote to connect himself with nature and the spirit world.

In the early 1900s a small community named Medicine Mound developed near the mounds. Devastated by fire in the 1930s, today it is a ghost town.

The **Downtown Medicine Mound Museum** (292 Spur 91 South; 940-839-4451) has exhibits and artifacts related to the history of the mounds.

Ranger Captain vs. Sheriff

Texas Ranger Capt. **Bill McDonald** got into a gunfight in downtown Quanah on December 9, 1893. His opponent was Childress County Sheriff John P. Matthews.

At first, just McDonald and Matthews were shooting at each other, but two of Matthews's friends soon joined in. When one round tore into the ranger and temporarily paralyzed his right hand, McDonald cocked his six-shooter with his teeth. After the shooting stopped, both lawmen had life-threatening wounds. Friends took Matthews back to his county, where he lingered until December 30 before dying. The sheriff would have died the day McDonald shot him, but a notebook and two plugs of tobacco stopped two bullets from tearing into his heart. McDonald had a long convalescence but finally recovered. He was tried for murder and acquitted.

McDonald left the Rangers in 1907. After that, he served as a state treasury agent, a bodyguard for President Woodrow Wilson, and finally as a US marshal. He died of pneumonia on January 15, 1918. After a well-attended funeral in Fort Worth, he was returned to Quanah for burial in **Quanah Memorial Park Cemetery** (Prairie Street off Farm Rd. 2640, just north of town).

The shoot-out began in front of the old First National Bank in the 100 block of Mercer Street at 3rd and continued a block to the Fort Worth and Denver Railway depot, since razed.

Richmond (Fort Bend County)

One of the Wild West's more unusual memorials is a marble obelisk with a stone jaybird sitting on top of it. Dedicated March 18, 1896, the monument commemorates the victims of a war most people have never heard of. This monument is sacred to the memory of those who died in what became known as the **Jaybird-Woodpecker feud**.

Most of Texas had settled down by the late 1880s, but in Fort Bend County the Civil War continued to be fought in a political sense. The Jaybirds were the democrats, die-hard Confederates who had no use for northerners and the freedom the north had won for blacks. The Woodpeckers were the republicans, members of Lincoln's party. Some of them, including some county office holders, were black.

On June 21, 1889, a prominent Fort Bend County Woodpecker killed an equally prominent Jaybird in nearby Wharton County. Texas rangers had to be rushed in to make sure the Jaybird survived his arrest and arraignment. The rangers succeeded in doing that, but tensions continued to build between both factions. The cork blew out of the bottle on August 16, 1889, in downtown Richmond when the county judge, a Woodpecker, was shot and wounded by a Jaybird. Armed supporters of both sides poured out into the streets and soon two mobs faced each other in front of the courthouse.

Three mounted Texas rangers tried to defuse the crowd, but passions ran too high. When the smoke cleared, two men, including the Woodpecker party county sheriff, lay dead. A young black girl, an innocent bystander, had been felled by a stray bullet. Six men, including one of the rangers, were wounded. Of those, two would die, including the ranger. Two companies of militia, more rangers, and Governor Sul Ross rushed to Richmond to restore order. The gun battle marked its worst outbreak of violence, but the feud simmered on well into the twentieth century.

The 1896 monument to the three Jaybirds who died in the feud stood initially on the courthouse square. When a new courthouse was built in 1909, the statue was moved to a plot adjacent to the Richmond city hall. On October 6, 2021, the monument was moved again, this time to the **Hodge's Bend Cemetery** (17245 Old Richmond Rd., Sugar Land; 281-704-8925).

Fort Bend County Museum (500 Houston St.; 281-342-6478) has an exhibit on the gun battle and the feud that sparked it.

Round Rock (Williamson County)

Round Rock is named for a distinctive round rock in Brushy Creek, once a landmark on the Chisholm Trail. A post office opened in 1851, but Round Rock remained a small farming community until the International–Great Northern Railroad came through Williamson County in 1876. To be adjacent to the tracks, most residents and businesses left what became known as Old Town and started over. Initially the town was known as New Round Rock, but the "New" eventually wore off.

Williamson Museum on the Chisholm Trail (8 Chisholm Trail; 512-943-1670) opened in 2017 in a historic two-story rock house in Old Town. The museum is a branch of the **Williamson Museum** (716 South Austin Ave.) in the county seat of Georgetown.

". . . Took to Robbing Stagecoaches"

Born and raised in Indiana, **Sam Bass** spent some time in Mississippi before coming to Denton, Texas, in 1870. He aspired to be a cowboy, but at first had to settle for being a farmhand and teamster. Later he bought a sorrel mare that earned him some nice horseracing purses. In 1875 he finally got a taste of the cowboy life, pushing a herd from San Antonio to Nebraska with friend (and future fellow outlaw) Joel Collins. With the money they made from that, the two went to the Black Hills of North Dakota to prospect for gold. That left them broke, but as Bass later said, they "took to robbing stagecoaches."

Back in Nebraska, his biggest heist came on September 17, 1877, when he and five others held up a train and escaped with

$60,000 in gold. With a new group of associates (Collins had been shot dead shortly after the robbery), Bass started robbing trains in the Dallas area—four brazen holdups inside two months.

By this time, he had gained the attention of Texas rangers, who were eager to get him in jail. But Bass proved embarrassingly difficult to capture, outriding citizen posses in North Texas and surviving running gunfights with rangers. What finally did him in was an informant, a criminal defendant who agreed to trade information on Bass's plans in exchange for immunity. With the informant riding along, in July 1878, Bass and his gang headed toward Round Rock. There they intended to rob the community's bank.

Learning Bass's intention, Maj. John B. Jones dispatched Rangers Chris Connor, George Herold, and Dick Ware from Austin to Round Rock. Before leaving to join them, he sent orders for additional rangers to get to Round Rock as soon they could.

About four o'clock in the afternoon on July 19, Bass, Seaborn Barnes, and Frank Jackson walked along Round Rock's Main Street, headed toward Henry Kopperal's store to buy tobacco. As they did, Williamson County Deputy Sheriff Ahijah W. Grimes and Maurice Moore, a Travis County sheriff's deputy who had joined Jones on the train to Round Rock, followed them discretely. Moore told Grimes he thought one of the strangers had a concealed gun.

When the trio walked into the store, Grimes followed and asked if they were armed. They were. All of them drew their pistols and started shooting at Grimes, who fell dead just outside the store. Moore began firing on the outlaws while they were still inside the gun smoke–filled store, shooting off one of Bass's fingers but causing no other harm. Seconds later, as they burst from the building one of the outlaws put a bullet into Moore's chest.

Hearing the shooting, Jones and his three rangers came running as the outlaws hurried toward the alley where they had hitched their horses. Ranger Ware put a .44-40 Winchester round through Barnes's head, ending his story. Bass caught a rifle bullet from Herold, but Jackson escaped unscathed. He helped the gravely wounded Bass mount up, and together they galloped out of town.

The next day some of the additional rangers Jones had requested found Bass sitting against a tree a short distance from town. Jackson, realizing his friend would die, had ridden on and was never seen again in Texas. Bass died on Sunday, July 21, his twenty-seventh birthday.

The one-story limestone building where Grimes died and Moore took a bullet (the former ranger survived only to be killed in the line of duty in Travis County on November 10, 1887) still stands at the southeast corner of Main and Mays Streets in Round Rock. A bar (105 South Mays St.) now occupies the building. A historical marker (West Main and Round Rock Avenue) is located at the approximate site of Bass's death.

Old Round Rock Cemetery

Dating to 1851, **Old Round Rock Cemetery** (off Sam Bass Road just east of Clark Street) has the graves of Sam Bass (1851–1878), Seaborn Barnes (1854–1878), and Ahijah W. Grimes (1855–1878). The young deputy's widow and other members of his family strongly objected to the two outlaws being buried in the same cemetery with her husband, but the pair stayed put.

Grimes has three gravestones—a Masonic monument placed soon after his death, one set in 1978 on the centennial of the shoot-out, and one erected by the Williamson County Sheriff's Office in 2015.

Round Rock's police headquarters (615 East Palm Valley) has a plaque dedicating the building to Grimes's memory. In 2018, the Williamson County Sheriff's Department training facility in Hutto was named for Grimes.

Bass had no tombstone until his sister had one put over his grave a few years after his death. Its epitaph read, "A brave man reposes in death here. Why was he not true?" Souvenir hunters chipped pieces from the stone until it practically disappeared, so in 1953 another marker was placed on his grave. A third marker with details of his death was added in 1978.

Barnes, buried next to Bass, has a modern gravestone.

SAN ANGELO (TOM GREEN COUNTY)

San Angelo, first called Saint Angela, developed on the other side of the Concho River from Fort Concho, a frontier cavalry post established in 1867.

From 1875 to 1882 the fort was the regimental headquarters of the Tenth Cavalry, whose African-American troopers the Comanches and Kiowa called Buffalo Soldiers. Vacated by the military in 1889, the fort eventually became a National Historic Landmark.

Fort Concho National Historic Landmark (630 South Oaks St.; 325-481-2646) is one of the best-preserved former cavalry posts in the West, with twenty-three original and restored buildings.

The community of San Angelo survived the later abandonment of the fort and grew as a ranching and trade center.

Miss Hattie's

Many a marriage has ended over an unfaithful husband's patronization of a house of ill repute, but San Angelo may be the only western town in which the dissolution of a couple's matrimonial bond resulted in the establishment of a bordello.

In 1902 someone known only by the last name of Hatton purchased a six-year-old, two-story, stone building on Concho Avenue, then a rowdy thoroughfare of bars and other good time places. Mr. Hatton operated a saloon downstairs and he and his wife lived upstairs. When trouble came to paradise and the Hattons divorced, the couple reached an agreement whereby Mr. Hatton would retain ownership of the first floor while Mrs. Hatton would own the second floor. A grass widow had to get by, so the former Mrs. Hatton converted her half of the building into a pleasure palace that under various owners continued in operation until Texas rangers shut it down in 1952.

At least that's the story. Whatever the truth, the building still stands. And since the 1970s its upstairs has been operated as a bordello museum known as **Miss Hattie's** (18½ East Concho Ave.; 325-653-0112).

Counting Sheep

San Angelo has always been a ranching town, cattle or sheep and goats. In recognition of the city's stature in the wool and mohair industry, a flock of more than a hundred fiberglass sheep statues "graze" across the city. Vividly painted by local artists, the sheep look like sheep in shape only. For statue locations, see sanangelosheep.info.

Sponsored by a nonprofit group called Historic Murals of San Angelo, the downtown area has fourteen murals at various locations illustrating some aspect of the city's history.

San Antonio (Bexar County)

On June 13, 1691, an expedition led by Domingo Terán de los Ríos, first governor of New Spain, encountered a small, winding river roughly 150 miles above the Rio Grande. Terán noted in his journal, "We camped on the banks of a stream adorned by a great stand of trees . . . I named it San Antonio de Padua because we reached it on his day." Terán's *entrada* moved on, but something else he wrote foreshadowed the settlement that became San Antonio. Observing that American Indians in the area were "docile and affectionate, naturally friendly, and very well disposed toward us," he "saw the opportunity of using them to form missions."

In 1718, Spain finally began constructing a series of missions along the river Terán named. With an infusion of colonists from the Canary Islands in 1731, San Antonio grew into one of New Spain's more important towns. By this time, however, raiding Lipan Apaches and Comanches made it clear that not all Indians in the area were "docile and affectionate."

San Antonio Missions National Historic Park preserves the four missions Spain established: Mission Concepción (807 Mission Rd.); Mission San Jose (6701 San Jose Dr.); Mission San Juan (9101

Graf Rd.); and Mission Espada (10040 Espada Rd.). They are connected by a hiking and bike trail.

After Spain lost the last of its North American territory in the revolution that gave birth to the Republic of Mexico, San Antonio continued as a settlement.

Once Texas joined the Union, San Antonio—finally safe from invading military forces and unwelcoming American Indians—grew rapidly. San Antonio was the western-most town in Texas, a supply point for anyone venturing into the vast unsettled West. When the Civil War began in 1861, San Antonio, with more than eight thousand residents, was Texas's largest city.

Following the war, San Antonio prospered as a stopping place for northbound cattle drives and as a business and military center. The arrival in 1877 of its first railroad brought more growth.

The Alamo

One of the world's best-known nineteenth-century historical events, the thirteen-day siege of the **Alamo** during the Texas Revolution was of no real strategic value to either side as Texas fought to separate from Mexico. But the garrison's fall strengthened the Texans' resolve and gave Gen. Sam Houston more time to organize and drill the volunteer army that ultimately would prevail. Later, what happened at the old Spanish mission that winter of 1836 would become a metaphor for courage and the desire for freedom.

The end of the siege came about 5:30 a.m. on March 6, 1836, a chilly Sunday morning, when Mexican troops made a final assault. At least 189 defenders died in the brutal hand-to-hand fighting that followed, though historians believe there were probably 200 to 250 men trying to hold the makeshift fortification. The known defenders came from twenty-two different states and six foreign countries. Taking the mission proved costly for Gen. Antonio Lopez de Santa Anna, who lost somewhere between three hundred and five hundred soldiers, either killed or wounded. That amounted to as much as a third of the force he had on hand.

While that distant day marked the last military conflict at the Alamo, the scene of the battle has continued to be an area of conflict. The first fight, beginning in the late-nineteenth century, involved saving the historic site from demolition. That accomplished, the Daughters of the Republic of Texas (DRT) took over management of the site. The second fight came early in the second decade of the twenty-first century, when, after heated debate, the Texas legislature transferred control of the Alamo (300 Alamo Plaza; 210-225-1391) to the state's General Land Office. The third fight was how the Alamo should be remembered going forward.

A master plan developed in 2018 called for expanding the Alamo property to include much more of the original site, stabilizing the existing ruins, building a larger museum, and altering traffic flow with the goal of making the scene of the battle a more reverent setting that accurately tells the Alamo story from all cultural perspectives.

The centerpiece of the plaza in front of the iconic mission chapel is the **Alamo Cenotaph**, a massive marble monument completed by sculptor Pompeo Coppini in 1939. It lists the known names of those who died at the Alamo.

The Council House Fight

The Alamo was not the only bloody battle in San Antonio's three-hundred-plus-year history. More than forty Comanches and seven Texas soldiers or officials (including Bexar County's first sheriff) died on March 19, 1840, in what came to be known as the **Council House Fight**. The incident took place inside the local government building called the Casa Reales during a meeting between Texas authorities and twelve Comanche leaders over the return of women and children captured by the Indians. When the Indians handed over only one of a dozen or more known captives, the officials said the chiefs would be held until the other captives were delivered. At that, fighting erupted as the chiefs tried to escape. Not only did the incident claim more than two score lives, it only heightened the Comanche people's animosity toward Texans.

Casa Reales continued to serve as a government building until 1850. After that it saw a variety of usages until razed in the early 1920s. A 1924 engraved stone plaque and a 1971 state historical marker on the side of the building (the intersection of Market Street and West Main Plaza) that occupies the site today summarize the story.

Menger Hotel

Adjacent to his brewery on Alamo Plaza, German immigrant William Menger opened a two-story, fifty-room hotel on February 1, 1859. Considered the Alamo City's finest hostelry throughout the nineteenth century, the **Menger Hotel** (204 Alamo Plaza; 210-223-4361) hosted presidents, generals, cattle kings, actors, famous writers, and other notables. Legendary ranch founder Richard King died in the hotel in 1885. Future president Theodore Roosevelt recruited some of his Rough Riders in the Menger bar in 1898. Much expanded and remodeled, the Menger remains in business.

The US Army has had a continuous presence in San Antonio since Texas joined the Union in 1845, but more than thirty years went by before the military started construction of the permanent post called **Fort Sam Houston**. The first building at the post was a large stone quartermaster depot and headquarters forming a large square with a tall stone watchtower rising from the center. Early on, it was referred to as the Quadrangle, later often shortened to simply "the

Quad." In 1882, with American Indian raids no longer a consideration, the watchtower was converted into a clocktower.

Four years later, American Indians did appear at the Quadrangle, but they came as prisoners of war. Having finally surrendered in Arizona, Geronimo and thirty-one of his followers were moved by train to San Antonio. They camped inside the Quadrangle under guard until continuing their journey to an island prison in Florida.

Later in the nineteenth century, as the fort grew both in size and importance, the army landscaped the interior of the Quadrangle. Soon, the open space took on a park-like atmosphere, with peacocks strutting around and whitetail deer munching on the grass. The Quadrangle houses a museum focusing on the history of the fort but is still the post headquarters.

Fort Sam Houston Museum (1405 East Grayson St., Building 16; 210-221-1886) tells the story of the longtime post. Also on post is the **US Army Medical Department Museum** (2310 Stanley Rd., Building 1046; 210-221-6358).

Old Bexar County Jail

In 1879 Bexar County built a two-story limestone jail designed by noted architect Alfred Giles. The new lockup could accommodate seventy prisoners. "This jail has stood the test of three years' use, during which time the worst characters from San Antonio to the Rio Grande have been sent here for safe keeping . . ." a governmental evaluation in 1873 noted. "The modern method of jail building, as shown in the Bexar County jail, is perfection for light, air, space, and ventilation, combined with security."

But by 1912 the city and county had grown to such an extent that more prisoner space was needed, so another architect was hired to design a third-floor addition. The expansion project also included indoor gallows for more discrete executions. In 1926 two more floors were added.

The jail continued in use until 1962 when a much larger facility was opened. Bexar County used the old hoosegow for record storage until selling it in 2002 to investors who intended to convert the old "cross bar hotel" into a real hotel. The interior was extensively remodeled, but city historical preservation ordinance prohibited any significant change to the exterior of the building. Accordingly, the **Holiday Inn Express (Old Bexar County Jail)** (120 Camaron St.; 210-281-1400) may be the only overnight public accommodation anywhere with bars over the windows.

The hotel's website suggests anyone interested in a paranormal experience should ask for Room 218, which is where the trapdoor of the gallows used to be, or Room 108, where the condemned would end up dangling.

Buckhorn Saloon

Working as a bartender and bellhop at the old Southern Hotel, at some point it occurred to seventeen-year-old Albert Friedrich that there might be more money in saloon ownership and management than pouring drinks or carrying luggage. In 1881 he opened the **Buckhorn Saloon** (318 East Houston St.; 210-247-4000). Soon discovering that not every cowpoke who hit town had enough money for a cold brew, Friedrich decided to accept cattle horns and deer antlers in lieu of cash. Before long, he had the saloon's walls covered with wide longhorn mounts and trophy whitetail deer antlers. The Buckhorn became one of the Alamo City's first tourist attractions. The horns and the saloon are still there. Additionally, since 2006, the Former Texas Rangers Association has had an agreement with the Buckhorn to maintain an eight-thousand-square-foot Ranger museum at the popular downtown destination.

Samuel Walker

For three good reasons, his fellow rangers called **Samuel Hamilton Walker** (1817–1847) lucky. But any gambler knows that whatever the game, sooner or later, the odds turn against you.

Born in Maryland, Walker came to Texas in 1842 by way of Florida, where he fought in the Seminole Indian War. In Texas, he soon took part in the unsuccessful Texas military incursion into Mexico known as the Somervell and Mier Expeditions and, along with other captured soldiers, endured confinement in the infamous, castle-like Perote Prison near Mexico City. His first piece of good luck came in selecting a lifesaving white bean when the prison's military commander complied with orders to execute every tenth Texan. Later escaping, in late 1843 or early 1844, Walker joined Capt. Jack Hays's ranger company and rode with the rangers for most of the next three years.

In addition to other scraps, on June 8, 1844, in what is known as the Walker's Creek Battle, Walker and other rangers under Jack Hays participated in the West's first American Indian fight in which Colt revolving pistols were used. The state-of-the-art weapons carried the day, but during the fierce fight, a Comanche warrior pinned Walker to the ground with a lance. Still, he survived the serious wound, his second big piece of luck.

As a ranger captain, Walker and his men guided Gen. Zachary Taylor's army through South Texas as he marched to war with Mexico in the spring of 1846. In the first major battle, Walker had his horse shot out from under him, and as a Mexican lancer rode hard in his direction with his long-bladed pike lowered, Walker shot and killed him. That proved the third and last time his luck would hold.

During a break in the hostilities, he returned to Maryland and accepted an invitation to meet with gun designer Samuel Colt to discuss possible improvements to his five-shooter. The battle-hardened ranger had two major suggestions: allow for larger caliber bullets with more powder behind them and increase the size of the cylinder to accommodate six rounds instead of five. Colt made those changes and named the new weapon the Walker Colt.

Back in Mexico and armed with a set of the new Colts, Walker was shot and killed on October 9, 1847, at Huamantla, Mexico, in the last major battle of the war. His dying request was to be buried next to his old friend and fellow ranger Robert Addison (Ad) Gillespie (1815–1846), who had been killed the year before in the Battle of Monterrey.

Walker's request to be buried next to his ranger comrade Gillespie was honored, but it took a decade before the remains of the two soldiers could be exhumed in Mexico and returned to San Antonio for re-interment. Walker is buried in the Odd Fellows Cemetery (northeast corner North Pine and Paso Hondo Streets).

The **South Texas Heritage Center at the Witte Museum** (3801 Broadway St.; 210-357-1900) is a large addition to the venerable Witte that focuses on the diverse cultures that shaped South Texas, from the Comanche people, the nemesis of the Texas Rangers, to the Spanish, Mexicans, Germans, and others, as well as cowboys and outlaws. There is also an exhibit on the *carretas*, the ox-drawn carts that figured in the Cart War of 1857.

Named for former Gov. Dolph Briscoe, who provided the donation that made the museum possible, the **Briscoe Western Art Museum** (210 West Market St.; 210-299-4499) holds an extensive collection of Western art and artifacts. Pieces on display range from sculptures to a restored stagecoach to a saddle that belonged to Mexican bandit Pancho Villa. Opened in 2013, the museum is housed in the renovated 1929 former San Antonio Public Library.

Fatal Corner

Where Commerce and Soledad Streets meet is an unremarkable-looking urban scene today, but in the nineteenth century the northwest corner of this intersection saw more one-on-one bloodshed than any other place in the city. Because of that, it became known as the **Fatal Corner**.

The most famous of those killed at the corner were Jack Harris (1834–1882), Ben Thompson, and John King Fisher. All three died in or in front of Harris's Vaudeville Variety Theater. Harris, a former San Antonio policeman and king of the Alamo City's gambling and saloon scene, had been called the "wickedest man in San Antonio." He and Thompson, no acolyte himself, had an ongoing grudge of several years standing. That culminated on July 11, 1882, when Thompson and Harris got into a shoot-out and Thompson won.

Though tried and acquitted, Thompson made the mistake of returning to the vaudeville theater on March 11, 1884. He arrived with his friend John King Fisher at about 11 p.m. after a boozy train ride from Austin and a night on the town. For a time, Thompson and Fisher sat, drank, and smoked with theater co-owners Joe Foster (1837–1884) and William H. (Billy) Simms (1856–1909). Also present was Jacob Coy, a San Antonio policeman who worked as bouncer there.

Several versions exist of what happened next, but when Thompson and Foster got into a heated discussion of Harris's killing, Fisher stood and tried to get Thompson to leave. Then Coy told Thompson to settle down. Instead, Thompson slapped Foster and stuck his pistol into Foster's mouth. Coy grabbed the gun as he, Thompson, and Foster began scuffling. Thompson's revolver went off and a fusillade of eighteen or nineteen gunshots followed. Foster took a bullet in the leg, Coy sustained a non-life-threatening wound, and Thompson and Fisher fell dead. The former Austin marshal had fired only one round and Fisher none. Authorities never determined who killed the two men.

Harris and Foster are buried in **City Cemetery No. 1** (1301 East Commerce St.). Foster, who died of his wound ten days after the shooting, is buried under a tall marble monument not far from Harris. Harris had no tombstone until one was placed at his grave on the centennial of his death. A nearby historical marker summarizes what happened to the two men.

William H. (Billy) Simms is buried in **City Cemetery No. 4** (intersection of Commerce Street and New Braunfels Avenue).

Phillip (Phil) Shardein (1839–1905), the city marshal who led the investigation into Thompson and Fisher's deaths, is buried in the **Masonic Cemetery** (1801 East Commerce St.).

Vaudeville Theater, a two-story limestone building constructed in the 1850s, burned down in 1886.

Opened as the Texas Pavilion during the 1968 HemisFair in San Antonio, the **Institute of Texan Cultures** (801 East Cesar E. Chavez Blvd.; 210-458-2300) focuses on all the ethnic groups that made Texas what it is. The multimedia museum, operated by the University of Texas at San Antonio, is a Smithsonian affiliate. Its three-story building has sixty-five thousand square feet of exhibit space and an extensive research library and photography collection.

San Marcos (Hays County)

When the Texas legislature took land from southwestern Travis County to create a new political subdivision in 1848, they named it for **John Coffee (Jack) Hays** (1817–1883). A larger-than-life bronze statue for this larger-than-life ranger was dedicated on the courthouse square (111 East San Antonio St.) in San Marcos 153 years later. Authorized by the San Marcos Arts Commission and designed by artist Jason Skull, the 2001 statue stands fourteen feet high on a limestone base. A plaque on the base gives a summary of Hays's life.

The Wittliff Collections

Part of the **Wittliff Collections** at Texas State University's Alkek Library, the Southwestern Writer's Collection has a room dedicated to the now classic made-for-TV miniseries *Lonesome Dove*.

Based on Larry McMurtry's 1985 Pulitzer Prize–winning novel, the 1988 series is an action-filled saga built around a cattle drive from Texas to Montana led by two ex–Texas rangers, Capt. Woodrow Call (Tommy Lee Jones) and Gus McCrae (Robert Duvall).

Bill Wittliff, who founded the writer's collection, wrote the screenplay, and later donated material related to the series. Visit thewittliffcollections.txstate.edu for specific on-campus directions and parking information.

San Saba (San Saba County)

Forty-three homicides have been linked to an outbreak of vigilantism in the 1890s attributed to what came to be called the **San Saba Mob**. One early-day writer called it "nothing less than a murder society."

Four Texas rangers under Sergeant W. John L. Sullivan arrived in San Saba in June 1896 to deal with the trouble. Despite two hung juries, with the help of a fearless prosecutor and a gutsy local newspaper editor, the rangers succeeded in getting the worst member of the lawless crowd prosecuted and sent to prison for life. It took the rangers (others would take part in addition to the original five) and local authorities fourteen months to break up the mob, mostly just by their intimidating presence.

The final assertion of ranger control came when a drunk mob member with a rifle confronted Ranger Dudley Barker outside the courthouse. Barker pulled his revolver and put five bullets in him.

The courthouse that stood during the mob's reign was razed in 1910. A historical marker summarizing the violent period stands outside the 1911 courthouse (East Commerce and South Water Streets). The only surviving building directly connected to the violent period is the 1884 **San Saba County Sheriff's Office and Jail** (104 South Water St.; 325-372-3277). The two-story stone lockup continues in use, the oldest operating jail in the nation. A 1969 historical marker relates its history.

San Saba Historical Museum (Mill Pond Park, US 190, half a mile east of courthouse) focuses on the history of the town, the area, and the reign of the mob.

Santa Anna (Coleman County)

When the Former Texas Rangers Association began holding annual reunions in the 1920s, former Ranger Caleb Grady seldom missed one. In 1935, the association met at Santa Anna. Given that many of the former rangers once served in the vicinity, the organization's leadership decided to adopt Santa Anna as their regular meeting place.

With help from local donors, the association bought twenty-five acres on the slope of Santa Anna Peak—a high point the Rangers once used as an observation post—to serve as a reunion ground. Grady helped secure federal Works Progress Administration money for construction of a rustic, native stone meeting hall with a fireplace on each end. The work began in 1936, and the association held its first reunion there in 1937. From then, the rangers came back to their old stomping grounds every summer until 1951, when only one aged ex-ranger attended.

The local Veterans of Foreign Wars post took over the property after the reunions ended. Later, the property went to the Texas Highway Department and continued in use as a park. The state later deeded the acreage to the City of Santa Anna. In 1979, then Sheriff H.F. Fenton purchased the old meeting hall and built a ten-unit motel adjacent to it. He didn't have any trouble coming up with a name—the **Texas Ranger Motel** (401 US 67; 325-349-3150). Visitors are welcome to check out the historic reunion hall. Rangers standing sentinel on Santa Anna Peak in the 1870s carved their names on two large rocks now sitting in front of the structure.

The **Santa Anna Visitor Center** (704 Wallis Ave.; 325-349-3151) has exhibits on the town's history.

Shafter (Presidio County)

The Presidio and Cibola Mining Company had three hundred men working its silver mine at Shafter during the last decade of the nineteenth century. Twenty-two-year-old Ranger John R. Gravis and three other local and federal officers constituted the town's ad hoc police force, and they kept busy. Gravis and a Presidio County deputy sheriff had the watch the night of August 4, 1890, when a group of drunk miners started shooting up the town. As the two officers approached, the pistol-packing drunks began firing on the ranger and his colleague. Gravis fell dead; the deputy went down with an arm wound.

When word reached the ranger camp at Marfa the next morning, Capt. Frank Jones ordered his men to saddle up and made the forty-three-mile ride south to Shafter in less than six hours. The state lawmen rounded up numerous suspects and packed the young ranger's body back to Marfa for shipment by train to his home community of Laredo for burial.

Production at the mine slowed in the early twentieth century. It closed for good in 1942, and Shafter quickly became a ghost town.

There's a small museum at the **Brooks-Fuentes Cemetery** (GPS coordinates: N29° 48.68', W104° 18.34') that gives an overview of the ghost town's history.

Snyder (Scurry County)

The rifle roared, a .50-caliber hunk of lead smacked into the side of the buffalo, and the huge beast went to its knees and then tumbled over. Hide hunters killed bison by the tens of thousands in the 1870s, but this was no ordinary bison. It was all white, one of only seven albino buffalos known to have been killed in North America. **J. Wright Mooar** (1851–1940) brought the shaggy beast down on October 7, 1876, near future Snyder. American Indians considered the white buffalo sacred and would not kill one, but Mooar was not superstitious. He kept the unusual hide and had it tanned. After the buffalo were gone from the Plains, Mooar took up ranching and remained in

Scurry County for the rest of his long life. He later wrote a book on his frontier experiences and enjoyed regaling youngsters with tales of the Old West as he saw it. He lived to eighty-eight, but to his dying day never expressed regret over his role in nearly exterminating a species—or for killing the white buffalo.

A bronze statue of a white buffalo stands on the **Scurry County Courthouse** square (25th Street and College Avenue). It is eight feet long and five and a half feet high at the shoulder, but said to be smaller than the buffalo Mooar killed. Nearby is a state historical marker summarizing the white buffalo story.

Mooar is buried in **Snyder Cemetery** (Avenue E and Camp Springs Road).

The **Scurry County Museum** (6200 College Ave.; 325-573-6107) tells the local history story.

Sonora (Sutton County)

Charles Adams, a merchant and rancher from Fort McKavett, acquired four sections of land in the mid-1880s in present Sutton County. He drilled a well on his ranch in 1889 and soon offered free town lots, naming the new community Sonora for Sonora, Mexico. Sonora opened a post office the same year and in 1890 was named county seat of Sutton County. A ranching and trade center, Sonora attracted good folks and bad.

One Less Wild Bunch Member

Wild Bunch member **William Richard (News) Carver** (1868–1901)—forever immortalized in the 1900 group photograph of Carver, Butch Cassidy, Ben Kilpatrick, Harvey Logan, and Harry Longabaugh taken in Fort Worth—made news in Sonora on April 2, 1901. But he didn't get to read about it in the papers. When Sheriff E.S. Briant and some of his deputies tried to arrest him for a killing in Concho County, Carver went for his six-shooter. Before he could get off a shot, the lawmen put six bullets into the outlaw and ended Carver's run.

Carver is buried on the east edge of town in **Sonora Cemetery** (516 North I-10 Service Road; GPS coordinates: N30° 34.75', W100° 38.34'; front area of section B).

Had Carver been arrested, he would have been held in the stone two-story **Sutton County Jail** (309 East Oak St.) that still stands on the courthouse grounds. Built in 1891, the jail continued in use until 1980. Tours of the old jail can be arranged at the **Old Icehouse Ranch Museum** (206 South Water St.; 325-387-3754), which has an exhibit on Carver's demise and covers all other aspects of Sutton County history.

Tascosa (Oldham County)

Once the army forced the Comanche, Kiowa, and Cheyenne people from their hunting grounds on the far high plains of Texas, several New Mexican sheepherders began grazing their flocks in what is now Oldham County at a boggy crossing of the Canadian River where Atascosa Creek enters the river. Soon Casimero Ramero and roughly a dozen families had settled there, living in small adobe houses. The first Anglo in the area was Henry Kimball, a recently discharged soldier who first saw the crossing while in the army. Kimball began ranching near the *placita*, which in a minor corruption of "Atascosa" began to be called Tascosa. As more ranchers came to the Panhandle, Tascosa attracted freighters, merchants, cowboys (honest and not-so-honest), and purveyors of whiskey, women, and games of chance. Billy the Kid, Pat Garrett, Bat Masterson, and other noted Wild West characters spent time here during the town's heyday.

Two Dead Ducks

Sitting in Tascosa's Equity Bar, Oldham County Sheriff Caleb Berg (Cape) Willingham heard a commotion outside. Suddenly one of the town's few ladies did something most ladies of the era would not—she ran into the drinking establishment. "He killed my duck!" she yelled, pointing to a man outside. "Shot it just now."

Willingham recognized the shooter as LS Ranch foreman Fred Leigh. Known for his excessive drinking, Leigh had been warned before about carrying a pistol in town. Armed with a double-barreled shotgun, the big sheriff approached the mounted cowboy. "You're in debt to this woman for that duck you shot just now," the sheriff said. "You going to pay for it?"

"Hell, no, I ain't going to pay for no duck," the cowboy replied. As Leigh said that, Willingham saw the drover reach for his six-shooter. That ended the talking. The sheriff let loose with both barrels of his scatter gun and the cowboy tumbled from his horse, as dead as the duck he'd blasted.

Not only had he been killed on account of a duck, Leigh had the honor of being the first person buried in Tascosa's **Boot Hill** (GPS coordinates: N35° 19.11', W102° 09.47'). The hilltop graveyard went on to accommodate thirty-two graves. Twenty-three of the occupants, like Leigh, died with their boots on.

Bypassed by the railroad in 1887, Tascosa went into decline. It lost its county seat status to Vega in 1915, and the last resident moved away in 1939. The same year, Amarillo boxer Cal Farley acquired the old townsite and converted it into **Cal Farley's Boys Ranch** (8 Julian Bivins Blvd.; 806-372-2341), a home for troubled or underprivileged children.

The two-story, 1880 stone courthouse still stands on the Boy's Ranch property and houses the **Old Tascosa Courthouse and Julian Bivins Museum** (806-533-1202). The museum's collection ranges from American Indian artifacts to items related to the history of the old cow town to pieces relative to the history of Boys Ranch. There also is material related to Panhandle rancher Julian Bivins, who donated to Farley the 120 acres that included the old townsite.

Uvalde (Uvalde County)

In 1849, as part of a north-south line of posts the army built along the state's western frontier, Fort Inge was established three miles south of future Uvalde. Named for Spanish colonial governor Juan de Ugalde but corrupted to "Uvalde," the town was founded in 1856. The nearby fort was vacated by federal troops in 1861 but it was regarrisoned after the Civil War and continued in use until it was abandoned in 1869. Uvalde grew as the county seat and as a ranching and agricultural center.

King Fisher

If an outlaw didn't get killed or hanged, it wasn't unusual for them to eventually give up their criminal ways. Some sought anonymity, some hungered for notoriety, some turned to preaching, and a few went from one side of the law to the other and became peace officers. One bad man who went into law enforcement was **John King Fisher** (1854–1884), who started off as a horse thief, expanded his field of interest to cattle, and killed several men along the way. The Texas Rangers made numerous cases against him, but Fisher never was convicted. (He did do time for his first horse theft, but that was all.) In 1881 he was appointed as an Uvalde County deputy sheriff and two years later became acting sheriff. He had become roundly popular in South Texas, but on the night of March 11, 1884, at Jack Harris's Vaudeville Variety Theater in San Antonio, someone shot Fisher to death along with another nefarious character, Ben Thompson. No arrests were ever made.

Fisher is buried in Uvalde's **Pioneer Park Cemetery** (500 block of North Park Street). In 1959, to make room for a new road, Fisher's grave and nineteen others were moved from their original location to the newly established Pioneer Park. When the old grave was opened, workers might have found a layer of ash on top of it, remnants of the annual visit of the mother of a man Fisher had killed. On her son's birthday, legend has it, the woman would build a fire over the grave and gleefully dance around the flames.

Pat Garrett and his Ghostwriter

The man credited with transforming Billy the Kid from dead outlaw to Old West icon was **Marshall Ashmun (Ash) Upson** (1828–1894), a New Mexico newspaper journalist Pat Garrett hired to ghostwrite his book *The Authentic Life of Billy the Kid*. The book saw only modest sales following its publication in 1882, but it created an enduring legend. And Garrett and Upson remained lifelong friends.

In April 1891, ten years after killing The Kid, Garrett moved his family to Uvalde County. A month later Garrett sold his ranch near Lincoln, New Mexico, and used the money to buy a ranch in Uvalde County on which he raised horses. When Upson died in 1894, he was buried in Uvalde in a cemetery lot Garrett owned. Two years later, the former Lincoln County sheriff left Uvalde and returned to New Mexico.

While in Uvalde, Garrett and his family lived in a house in the 900 block of West Main St. (US 90) that was later destroyed by fire. A state historical marker placed in 1970 at what is now the Texas Department of Transportation's area maintenance yard (994 Main St.) marks the location.

Garrett's barn still stands on private property at 909 Fort Clark Road.

Upson is buried in **Uvalde Cemetery** (228 West Canales St., lot 54). His grave had been unmarked until the Wild West History Association placed a new tombstone over it in 2021.

Van Horn (Culberson County)

Founded in 1881 when the Texas and Pacific Railway built across West Texas, and named for a nearby robust water source known as Van Horn Wells, the town is the county seat, ranching center, and has been a waypoint for east-west travelers since stagecoach days.

Where the Dove Flew

When the stagecoach did not show up, Capt. George Baylor and his Texas ranger company followed the route until they rode up on the wreckage of the stage in Quitman Canyon in present Hudspeth County. The rangers expected to find the bodies of its driver and passengers, but they were missing. Also missing were all but one of the mules that had been pulling the coach. The remaining animal lay dead. Determined to catch up with the Apache perpetrators and their presumed captives, the rangers followed the warriors' tracks into Mexico and back into Texas.

From the Rio Grande, the trail headed north into the Eagle Mountains, thirty-plus miles above present Van Horn. The sign had grown increasingly fresh. On the evening of January 28, 1881, Baylor noticed mourning doves flying toward what he knew must be a water source in the mountains. That, he also knew, would be a logical place for the Apaches to camp.

The next morning, the rangers' Pueblo scouts found the Indians, and the lawmen attacked as they cooked breakfast. Killing four warriors, two women, and two children, the rangers captured several others. Some of the men did not like having killed women and children, but it was done. As it turned out, the attack marked the last fight rangers ever had with American Indians.

After the shooting ended, Baylor and his men sat down to eat the breakfast the Indians had been preparing. Once full, the rangers took the prisoners to Fort Davis. The stagecoach occupants were never found.

The battle occurred in the Sierra Diablo Mountains on what is now the Figure 2 Ranch. A historical marker telling the story of the fight and giving a history of the ranch is located thirty-two miles north of Van Horn on State Highway 54.

The **Culberson County Historical Museum** (112 West Broadway St.; 432-283-8028) has an exhibit on the battle.

VERNON (WILBARGER COUNTY)

Surrounded by the giant Waggoner Ranch, a place called Eagle Flat was the next to last place for drovers pushing herds up the Western Cattle Trail to get supplies before undertaking 250 miles of federal no-man's-land in what is now Oklahoma. **Doan's Crossing** was the last supply point. Eagle Flat was renamed Vernon in 1880 for Mount Vernon, George Washington's home. It prospered when the Fort Worth and Denver Railway reached there in 1887 and continued to develop as a ranching center.

Red River Valley Museum (4600 College Ave.; 940-553-1848) focuses on area history and the trail-driving era.

Wilbarger County Museum (1826 Cumberland St.; 940-886-7993) interprets the history of the city and county.

Doan's Crossing

The term "convenience store" was unknown in the 1870s and '80s when Jonathan Doan and his nephew **Corwin F. Doan** (1848–1929) ran a general store on the Western Cattle Trail just south of the Red River. But trail bosses and cowboys found Doan's in-the-middle-of-nowhere store mighty convenient. Customers, as one of the historical markers at the site notes, ranged from English noblemen to reservation Indians from Oklahoma. An estimated six million longhorns passed by the store during the trail-driving days, splashing across the river separating Texas from Oklahoma at a point called **Doan's Crossing**.

Doan's 1881 adobe house (thirteen miles north of Vernon off US 283 on Farm to Market Road 2916) still stands and is open to visitors. The site has four historical markers or memorials. One, placed by the state in 1936 during the Texas Centennial celebration, features a still appropriate quote from cowboy humorist Will Rogers: "You don't need much monument if the cause is good. It's only these monuments that are for no reason at all that has to be big." Also among the markers at the crossing is a gray granite monument engraved with numerous Texas cattle brands.

Corwin F. Doan is buried in **Eastview Memorial Park** (8271 County Road 105 South; plot 9-6-2).

Waggoner Ranch

Covering a little over a half million acres, the famed **Waggoner Ranch** is not the nation's largest ranch, but it is the largest ranch behind one fence. Dan Waggoner founded the ranch in Wise County in 1849. In 1873, he and his son, W.T. (Tom) Waggoner, pushed a herd of cattle from their land to Kansas and came back to Texas with $55,000—a fortune for the time. Waggoner used the money to buy more land, the Waggoner holdings eventually extending across six counties and covering a million acres. The Waggoners raised cattle and horses on their land, which they also farmed. Later, the discovery of oil on their property added another profit point. The huge enterprise, now 525,000 acres, remained in the Waggoner family until 2016 when it was sold.

The sprawling ranch's headquarters, known as Zacaweista, is thirteen miles south of Vernon. Tom Waggoner lived for a time in an 1890 two-story Queen Anne–style house (2720 Paradise St.), a property he later deeded to his son, banker Guy Waggoner. Now known as the Waggoner-Hicks House, the private residence is a recorded Texas Historic Landmark.

Waco (McLennan County)

Drovers pushing cattle up the Chisholm Trail from South Texas to Kansas had to cross a succession of rivers that could be as cantankerous as any longhorn steer. Fed by springs in the area, the Brazos usually ran fast and wide at Waco and cattle and men sometimes drowned trying to get to across. That changed in 1870 when a private company built a toll bridge over the river, an engineering marvel that for a time was the longest span anywhere west of the Mississippi. Pedestrians, horseback riders, buggies, wagons, and cattle could use the bridge for a fee.

Waco was laid out in 1847 where a Hueco (Waco) Indian village once stood, but it did not grow significantly until after the Civil War and the opening of the bridge. For all the 1870s and part of the 1880s, Waco saw multiple thousands of cattle come through town. The rich bottom land along the Brazos produced a lot of cotton and for decades Waco was the nation's largest inland cotton market. The development of railroads in Texas ended the trail-driving days but the iron rails only accelerated Waco's growth, which by the 1890s had become one of the state's largest cities.

Still used as a pedestrian bridge, the **Waco Suspension Bridge** is off University Parks Drive between Washington and Franklin Avenues.

The **Mayborn Museum Complex** (1300 South University Parks Dr.; 254-710-1110) explores the area's natural and cultural history.

Sul Ross

As a young Texas ranger, future governor **Sul Ross** (1838–1898) led the ranger company that found Cynthia Ann Parker in 1860. By then, twenty-four years after her capture by Comanches in the attack on Fort Parker, it was too late for the young mother of three Indian children to readjust to white ways. Ross later distinguished himself as a Confederate general during the Civil War. He served as McLennan County sheriff from 1873 to 1875, followed by four terms in the state senate. Elected governor, he held office from 1887 to 1891. After leaving Austin, he became president of what is now Texas A&M University and held the post until his death. Ross is buried in **Oakwood Cemetery** (2124 South 5th St.; GPS coordinates: N31° 32.28', W97° 06.78').

Tough Town for Newspapermen

On November 19, 1897, **G. B. Gerald** and newspaper editor **J.W. Harris** began blazing away at each other at 4th and Austin Streets in downtown Waco. The shoot-out, as newspapers put it, "created quite a sensation," but the incident did not overly burden the local judicial system, since each participant in the gunfight died of his wounds. Everyone knew that both victims had essentially been stand-ins for the principals in the big fight to come, a clash between nationally known editor **William Cowper Brann** (1855–1898), who published an acerbic if well-written monthly called *Brann's Iconoclast*, and whoever would finally decide to kill him. That turned out to be **Tom Davis**. Brann had been particularly critical of Waco's Baylor University in his publication, and Davis was a loyal Baylor defender.

The situation finally came to a head on April Fool's Day 1898. Again, neither combatant lived to face trial. Brann killed Davis outright but soon died of his wounds.

Thanks to those well-publicized shootings and others, the home of Baylor University and numerous churches became known as Six-Shooter Junction. In fact, the standing joke was that when passenger trains approached Waco, the onboard ticket punchers would call out, "Waco, twenty minutes for dinner; walk a block and see a killing."

Brann was buried in Oakwood Cemetery (2124 South 5th St.; GPS coordinates: N31° 32.28', W97° 06.78'). The editor's supporters chipped in to have a large memorial in the shape of the lamp of truth placed at his grave, its only marking his initials, "WCB" and the word "Truth." A few days after his funeral, someone fired a couple of shots at the stone, leaving pockmarks at the bottom of the lamp that were still visible until the sculpture was stolen in 2009. Now all that remains is the base with the lettering. A state historical plaque summarizing the shoot-out is on the side of a building on South 4th Street between Franklin and Austin Avenues.

Texas Ranger Hall of Fame and Museum

Texas rangers under **Capt. Thomas Hudson Barron** (1796–1874) worked their way up the Brazos River in 1837 clearing a wagon road from a small downstream settlement called Falls of the Brazos to what would become Waco. The men built a few log cabins near a spring on the river, but less than a month later, a courier arrived with orders relocating the company. Though not much of a fortification, the outpost was named **Fort Fisher** for the Republic of Texas's secretary of war, William S. Fisher. The fort fell to ruin and eventually no trace of it remained, but the Texas Rangers endured, evolving over the decades from American Indian fighters to state lawmen.

In 1964, 127 years after the establishment of Fort Fisher, the Waco Chamber of Commerce approached the Texas Department of Public Safety (which includes the Rangers) proposing to construct a building that would serve both as a Ranger field headquarters and museum. Then DPS director Col. Homer Garrison accepted the offer, and four years later, on October 25, 1968, dignitaries gathered for the dedication of the new facility—Fort Fisher returned. The name of the complex, which sits on thirty-two acres along the Brazos adjacent to downtown, was later changed from Fort Fisher to the **Texas Ranger Hall of Fame and Museum** (100 Texas Ranger Trail; 254-750-8631).

Barron must have liked what he saw when he first beheld the mid-Brazos River. In 1847, a decade later, he homesteaded 340 acres there and built Waco's first residence. Later, he served as McLennan County tax assessor-collector. Barron died February 2, 1874. One hundred and two years later, the former ranger's remains were moved from his original burial site to **First Street Cemetery** (University Parks Drive and I-35). A historical marker stands near his grave. Listed on the National Register of Historic Places, the cemetery is part of Fort Fisher Park, adjacent to the museum.

Two works of Ranger-related public art stand outside the museum. The first, *Major George B. Erath—Frontiersman,* is a bronze by artist Robert Summers of noted ranger and surveyor George B. Erath, placed in 1976. The second, *Texas Ranger,* a larger-than-life bronze by sculptor Don Hunt of an early-day horseback ranger bearing the Texas flag, was placed in 2008 to mark the museum's fortieth anniversary. Inside the museum is a third piece, a life-size ranger statue, *Old Ranger,* also by Summers.

WEATHERFORD (PARKER COUNTY)

Isaac Parker (1793–1883) never quit trying to find his niece Cynthia Ann.

One of elder John Parker's sons, Isaac fought in the Texas Revolution and rode as a Texas ranger. He served as a senator in the republic's congress and, following statehood, won election to the state senate. After rangers recaptured his niece from the Comanches in 1860, Parker took her and her young daughter to his home and did all he could to help her readjust, even sponsoring legislation granting her a pension and land. He moved from Tarrant County to Parker County in 1872 and remained there the rest of his long life.

Parker is buried in **Turner Cemetery** (Ragle Road). A granite historical marker was placed near his grave in 1936, with a more detailed marker erected in 1986.

Doss Heritage and Culture Center (1400 Texas Dr.; 817-599-6168) focuses on the history of the area.

WICHITA FALLS (WICHITA COUNTY)

In a part of Texas that gets so hot and dry it's hard to imagine that the Wichita River once had a waterfall (albeit a modest one), but it did. And that's how Wichita Falls got its name. The city started as a buffalo hunter camp in 1876 and didn't amount to much until the Fort Worth and Denver Railway came through in 1887. The town grew as a trade center and cattle shipping point for the large ranches in the area, but that was nothing compared with the boom it experienced in 1911 with the discovery of oil in the area.

The **Museum of North Texas History** (720 Indiana Ave.; 940-322-7628) focuses on Wichita Falls and the area around it.

Rangers Couldn't Be Everywhere

After cowboys Foster Crawford and Elmer (Kid) Lewis robbed the City National Bank and killed a popular teller, Texas Ranger Capt. Bill McDonald and some of his men tracked down the pair after a local posse had given up. When the rangers moved on to another assignment, assuming that the criminal justice process in Wichita County would proceed routinely, the captain soon received word that both suspects had been taken from the county jail on February 25,1896, and strung up in front of the bank they had robbed. A historical marker (800 Scott St.) tells the story.

The bank where the robbery occurred stood at the corner of 7th and Ohio Streets. As the outlaws had fled town, someone killed one of their horses. The owner of that horse, which had been stolen, had one of the animal's hooves converted by a taxidermist into a jewelry box for his wife. That unusual item is on display at the Museum of North Texas History.

INDEX

G

P

ABOUT THE AUTHOR

An elected member of the Texas Institute of Letters, **Mike Cox** is the author of more than thirty-five nonfiction books. Over an award-winning freelance career dating back to his high school days, he has written hundreds of newspaper articles and columns, magazine stories, and essays for a wide variety of regional and national publications. When not writing, he spends as much time as he can traveling, fishing, hunting, and looking for new stories to tell. He lives in the Hill Country village of Wimberley, Texas. Learn more about the author and his work at mikecoxauthor.com.